June's "Flour

by June Spencer

Old Fashioned, Great-Tasting Recipes

Many Updated for Today's Healthy Living

Oct 14, 98
CJ
Hope you enjoy
my book!
June Spencer

June's "Flour Power" Baking

First Printing 1997

Published by: Chuck Wagon Publishing
P.O. Box 1824
Silverdale, WA 98383-1824

Cover Photography by Steve Zugschewardt
Text by Terry Poe
Word Processing by Anne Jiles, Beyond Words, Poulsbo, WA
Illustrations by Steven Homman, Nordland, WA
Edited by June Spencer

Library of Congress Catalog Card Number: 97-92311

ISBN 0-96593-680-5

Printed in the USA by
Morris Publishing
3212 E. Hwy. 30
Kearney, Ne 68847
800-650-7888

Dedication

To my husband George for all his inspiration, patience, and support. To my parents George R. Sands and Anona G. Gray. To Daniel, Donald, Janice, and my grandchildren.

In loving memory of my grandparents: George C. and Viola G. Sands, and Charles A. Larson; my parents-in-law: George F. Spencer, Dorothy and Ervin Braun.

Acknowledgments

This book would never have been started or completed if not for the help and encouragement from some very special people.

Special thanks to my sister LuAnn and her husband Richard for all their assistance and computer skills in helping me get started and organized in the beginning.

Thank you to my sister Susie for contributing her raspberry-filled sugar cookie recipe.

Special thanks to my son Don for all his contributions, advice, and loving support.

Sincere thanks to my family, friends, and neighbors for all their help and support, and to Carol Ann for her creative assistance.

I am very fortunate to have been surrounded by such supportive friends and family. They played an important role, especially those who happily taste-tested my recipes. Thank you.

Table of Contents

About the Author

Friends joke that I was born to bake.

I was born in Clallam Bay in the home of Dr. Baker. (Years earlier he had delivered my father, as well.) I was so small that according to my mother I was kept on the open door of the oven to keep warm as the wind whistled through the walls.

As far back as I can remember, I've loved to bake. I remember standing on a chair, in front of the stove, stirring the lemon filling for my mother's delicious lemon meringue pies carefully so it wouldn't scorch. It rained a lot, so Mom kept me busy helping her in the kitchen.

As a young girl I loved to bake for our family of six, pies and cookies all from scratch. Whenever we had company, I was the one who did the baking. I could never make enough pies (especially the banana cream).

We lived in Sekiu, Washington. Every summer, about the middle of July, we'd go pick wild blackberries out where the trees had been logged or where there had been a fire years before. We would fill our buckets to overflowing with the best tasting wild blackberries (many times with black bears on the other side of the bushes getting their fill as well!). Mother would bake up the most delicious pies in the world. We would eat most all that we picked because we had no freezer and then we canned the rest.

Grandma did a lot of canning, also. Every time we visited her and Grandad, she would open a jar of her preserves. My grandparents grew their own fruits and vegetables to eat and can for the winter. Grandma loved to cook and bake. I remember cooking and baking on her old wood stove. Everything tasted and smelled so good! I learned a lot from her.

I never dreamed that I would have my own bakery one day.

It all started years later. My son Don took some brownies I had baked to his after-school job at Ralph's Grocery downtown Poulsbo. They were putting in a new deli and needed some baked goods. The next thing I knew, I was in the bakery business.

For the next ten years we would grow June's Home Bakery into a successful wholesale and retail operation serving the greater Puget Sound area, specializing in wholesome, homemade, fat free and sugar free baked goods. In 1992 we sold the wholesale bakery, in 1994 the retail bakery was sold and I started work on this book. It's been a lot of work but also a lot of fun. I hope you enjoy it.

Introduction

by Don Spencer

Baking has been an important part of people's lives since ancient times. Early civilizations were, in part, created and then nourished through the cultivation of grains and the application of fire. Baking is basic. It is a science and an art. In baking lies a human story—a story of all people, from all cultures and all regions of the world.

Baking is a family affair. Like most people I was introduced to baking by my mother. As a child, I remember helping her decorate cookies by the hundreds every holiday season. Several times a week she would bake bread, pies and cakes using the same skills and recipes handed down to her from my grandmother and great-grandmother.

The argument could be made that true baking, in the way that I've known it, is a dying art because of the fast-paced society we live in. It is sad that too often too little time and thought is spent in preparing the food we eat. It is taken frozen from the freezer, thrown in the microwave, then put onto a plate.

There seems little time for baking, eating right, or spending time together. Yet, these are the things we should be doing. I would argue that real "scratch" baking is needed and appreciated now more than ever *because* our lives are so stressful. It can be a fun, relaxing activity that can bring the whole family together and provide a healthy, wholesome alternative to mass market, high fat, fast foods.

All of these are good reasons that make "Flour Power" such a valuable and refreshing addition to your kitchen. It combines the best collection of original old-fashioned recipes *and* healthier alternative recipes in one book. It literally gives you *power*. It allows you to choose between several variations of the same recipe depending on the individual tastes and health concerns of anyone in your family. Love the oat bran bread recipe but would like to make it fat free? How about a sugar free batch for Uncle Joe who has diabetes? This book will show you how.

In 1994, after running our own bakery for several years in Poulsbo, Washington, my parents decided to retire. Called "June's Home Bakery," the business thrived on providing old-fashioned baked goods from scratch as well as healthier fat free, sugar free, low calorie, and wheat free baked items. Many of the healthier baked goods were revised old-fashioned recipes that tasted just as good as the originals.

"Flour Power" is partly a result of that experience.

Mom had accumulated such a collection of bakery recipes over the years and many of them had become family favorites. Recipes had been filed on scraps of paper and scribbled on napkins. Others were stored only in Mother's head. We yearned for a comprehensive, easy-to-follow collection of all her recipes.

I hope you enjoy this book. A lot of hard work and love has gone into it by my mother. Truly, it is the culmination of a lifetime spent baking for her family, her friends, and her community.

Ingredients

BAKING POWDER – I use baking powder free of aluminum sulfate. One teaspoon baking powder equals 1½ teaspoons cream of tartar and ¾ teaspoon baking soda. For corn-free baking powder use 1 teaspoon baking soda, 2 teaspoons arrowroot and 2 teaspoons cream of tartar. One teaspoon regular baking powder equals 1¾ teaspoons home made baking powder.

BAKING SODA – Used alone, baking soda has no leavening powder, but used in combination with some acid ingredient such as sour milk, buttermilk, or molasses it makes a very tender crumb. The proportion of baking soda to sour milk, buttermilk and molasses is usually ½ teaspoon soda to 1 cup.

CAROB is a chocolate substitute that comes in a powdered form similar to cocoa. In recipes calling for cocoa, substitute an equal amount of carob or 3 tablespoons of carob can replace 3 tablespoons flour. To replace one square of chocolate, dissolve 3 tablespoons of carob powder in 2 tablespoons water.

COCOA – Only unsweetened cocoa is used in my recipes. It has the taste of chocolate without the fat. So substitute 3 tablespoons cocoa plus 1 tablespoon liquid, water, buttermilk, or fruit sauce for 1 ounce of chocolate.

DAIRY –

BUTTERMILK: To make your own, mix 1 cup skim or 1% milk with 1 tablespoon lemon juice or vinegar. Let set 30 minutes. To make a large amount mix 4 cups skim milk, ½ cup cultured buttermilk and ⅛ teaspoon salt. Stir well and cover. Let stand at room temperature until thick. Also 1 cup fat free sour cream or yogurt can be used to replace ½ to ⅔ cup buttermilk in a recipe.

MILK: To cut down on fat use 2% or skim milk. One cup skim milk equals 1 cup water plus ⅓ cup nonfat dry milk powder. If you have a dairy product allergy, you will need to use soybean products, soy milk, goat milk, or rice milk. In bread-making recipes, you sometimes see the term "scalding" the milk. Unless you are using raw milk, scalding isn't necessary. Milk now days has been pasteurized which is what scalding the milk does, killing the enzymes that might destroy the yeast action.

WHIPPED CREAM: Substitute nonfat evaporated milk or skim milk. Place ⅓ cup skim milk in freezer until ice starts to form. Beat in ⅓ cup instant nonfat dry milk; continue beating for two minutes. Add 1 tablespoon honey or fruit juice concentrate. Beat two more minutes. Whip chilled evaporated skim milk the same as skim milk. Whipped skim milk does not hold up as well as evaporated canned milk but has a more cream like flavor. Be sure to chill before whipping and serve soon after as it doesn't hold up as well as whipped cream.

EGGS – To lower the fat in your favorite recipe use 2 egg whites in place of 1 egg or, if you want, substitute 1 egg white plus 1 teaspoon canola oil for every yolk not used, or use ¼ cup nonfat egg product for each egg called for in a recipe. Cooking without eggs or fat can be very difficult to replace. There really is no substitute for an egg in baking. Eggs are good food. They are a complete protein. Egg yolks contain lecithin, a B complex which naturally combats and breaks down cholesterol. To replace eggs in a recipe, substitute 3 tablespoons fruit sauce such as apple, plums, carrots, pumpkin or mashed banana. Experiment with this in your favorite recipes.

FATS – Fat makes cookies crisp, cakes tender and moist and pastries flaky. Decreasing fat can change the texture of these products. Typically, you can reduce the amount of fat by 25–30% in your favorite recipe without significantly affecting the texture.

When choosing a fat for baking you should know your priorities. Are you concerned about calories? Is cholesterol important? Do you simply want to treat yourself and your family to something rich and chewy? Would you like a combination of all these things?

Let's now look at the choices we have when selecting one of the most important parts of any recipe when we think about health, the fats.

BUTTER: In baking, butter gives a richness and flavor that cannot be matched by other fats. Butter is a highly saturated fat (saturated fats have been proven to raise cholesterol). All butter is made from cream and must, by law, contain 80% fat. The other 20% is mostly water. In baking, butter gives a richness and flavor that cannot be matched by other fats. You should not immediately discount butter in favor of margarine on the grounds of health. Both margarine and butter contain the same amount of calories from fat. It is my opinion that it is easier to cut back the amount of butter in a recipe and still maintain much of the texture and richness it provides.

CHOLESTEROL is a fat-like substance found in the bloodstream; some of it is manufactured by the body and some comes from the foods we eat. When my recipes call for oil, I use and recommend using soy, safflower, olive or canola oil as they are mildest in flavor and are healthiest for you. Be sure to check the label of ingredients to avoid chemical additives. A term used in my recipes "sprayed" or when greasing a pan, I spray or grease with a non-stick vegetable oil spray, sometimes called liquid lecithin.

MARGARINE: Margarine is a combination of vegetable oils and other ingredients. Many times the oils used, soy, corn and safflower, are hydrogenated. In this process the good unsaturated oils are turned into saturated fat. There are "soft" margarines which contain more oil, but often more chemicals as well. Check the ingredients. Producers of margarine have been making great improvements as of late, even some of the new lower fat margarine I find I can bake with and the results are good. Ironically, I have found that sometimes the cheaper brands appear to be better for you than the more expensive brands. Margarine and butter have the same amount of calories: 100 calories per tablespoon compared with 120 calories per tablespoon for oil. Oil is 100% fat, while butter is 80% fat and 20% water. If you wish to substitute oil for butter, use 20% less oil. For example, if the recipe calls for 1 cup butter, use 1 cup oil minus 3 tablespoons and add 3 tablespoons of liquid to the recipe. If the recipe doesn't call for any liquid, add 3 tablespoons of water or fruit juice with the oil.

OILS: There are three kinds of fat: saturated, polyunsaturated and monounsaturated.

1. Saturated fat is generally solid at room temperature, and is usually of animal origin, such as the fats in dairy products. Highest saturated fat is coconut, cotton seed and palm. They're even more highly saturated than butter and lard. Hydrogenated vegetable oils and cocoa butter (chocolate) are also classified as saturated fat. A

diet high in saturated fat tends to increase the amount of cholesterol in the blood.

2. Polyunsaturated fats are generally liquid at room temperature and are of vegetable origin. A diet with a high polyunsaturated fat content tends to lower cholesterol in the blood. These fats are sometimes substituted for saturated fats in a diet in an effort to lessen the hazard of fatty deposits in the blood vessels. Here's a list of polyunsaturated oils that are good for you: safflower, soy, sunflower, corn sesame, flax, peanut, primrose and walnut oil.

3. Monounsaturated fat has been found to lower cholesterol levels. The richest source of monounsaturated fats are olive and canola oils.

SHORTENING can be used instead of butter or margarine. In some cases you can use less. Deodorized shortening is a process where oils are refined, deodorized and hydrogenated. This process, which adds hydrogen, solidifies the polyunsaturated vegetable oils and converts them to saturated fats. Instead of adding water to the shortening process like butter and margarine, air is incorporated, which makes shortening great to use for baking. As did my mother, if I use shortening, I use Crisco.

FAT SUBSTITUTION – Fruit sauce or buttermilk can replace part of the fat in a recipe. Experiment on your favorite recipes.

FIBER – There are two basic classifications of dietary fiber: soluble and insoluble. Foods may contain both types of fiber, but some foods are better sources of one type than the other. Oats are an excellent source of cholesterol reducing soluble fiber. Whole wheat products are a primary source of insoluble fiber which helps to prevent constipation. Both types of fiber are important to a healthy diet, but generally only soluble fiber helps to reduce cholesterol.

For added fiber, nutrition or textured interest, you can substitute as much as half a cup of bran, wheat germ, cracked wheat, barley flour, buckwheat flour, cornmeal, oat flour, rice polish, spelt, or rye flour in a yeast bread recipe.

When eliminating all of the fat in a recipe, it is a good idea to substitute a whole grain flour for at least one-third to one-half of the refined flour used in the recipe. Oats, oat bran, and whole wheat bran are good examples. The fiber will help maintain pleasing texture in your baked goods.

FRUIT/JUICE – When a recipe calls for grated orange or lemon peel, grate the colored part of the fruit's skin, not the white part underneath which tends to be bitter. Substitute dried fruits in recipes to replace some of the sweeteners. For sugar-free baking use only unsweetened fruit juice concentrate. Be sure to check the ingredients on juices, canned fruit and dried fruits. They should either read *all natural, no sugar added* or sweetened with other fruit juices. Sometimes you will see *light* or *lite* on the label but when you read the ingredients you'll find that it's sweetened with corn syrup or sugar. When using frozen fruit juice concentrate, do not thaw; rather measure out what is needed, adding a little at a time and mixing well. The remaining concentrate can then be returned to the freezer in a plastic bag to be used later. When cooking with concentrate always combine all the ingredients well, then mix in baking soda and baking powder, mixing well, then bake.

GRAINS –

ALL PURPOSE BLEACHED AND/OR BROMATED ENRICHED WHITE FLOUR is bleached to make the flour whiter. This white flour is treated with chemicals and most of the nutrients removed. Be certain the flour you buy is not bromated (treated with bromine gas as a preservative), a process that destroys some of the flour's nutritional value. This process also increases the shelf life.

ALL PURPOSE UNBLEACHED WHEAT FLOUR is a blend of hard and soft wheat. Because it combines both, this flour can be used for virtually all kinds of baked goods. It contains all of the germ and part of the bran and is slightly less nutritious than whole wheat flour.

AMARANTH is not really a grain so can be tolerated by people who have grain allergies and celiac disease. It is high in protein, calcium, iron and fiber, as well as lysine and methionine (amino acids often lacking in other grains.) In baking with amaranth use it for about 25% of the flour, along with 75% wheat or other grain flour. To make a grain-free baked good as for grain allergies amaranth needs to be combined with some other non-grain such as soy flour, buckwheat flour or potato flour to provide the necessary starch. The most satisfactory proportions seem to be 75% amaranth with 25% arrowroot powder or tapioca starch flour.

BARLEY FLOUR is more commonly used in making alcoholic beverages than in bread, but it is sweet and the flour is very useful as a substitute for part of the flour in wheat-free recipes. Barley flour can be used to replace all the flour in breads, but the bread will be very heavy and moist like unleavened or sourdough bread. Let bread set overnight for easier slicing otherwise it tends to crumble. To substitute, use ½ cup barley flour for each cup of unbleached all purpose flour. Barley flakes are interchangeable with rolled oats. If you are allergic to one of them, just substitute one for the offending ingredient.

BUCKWHEAT FLOUR is not a cereal at all but belongs to the rhubarb family. Buckwheat contains a gluten analogue, which a lot of people with gluten allergies can tolerate. Buckwheat is not a wheat and can be tolerated by those with a wheat allergy, unless they are also allergic to buckwheat. Buckwheat is high in fiber and contains more high-quality protein than the other grains except rice and oats. It is a good source of B vitamins and is lower in calories than rice or corn. There are two kinds of buckwheat groats: raw (light) and roasted (dark). Both kinds can be ground into flour. Most people identify only the dark one as buckwheat flour. If its distinct flavor doesn't appeal to you, experiment with the light kind, best used in the proportion of ½ cup buckwheat to ¾ cup other flour.

CORNMEAL is tasty and nutritious. Yellow or white cornmeal can be milled into corn flour. Stone-ground cornmeal retains the germ and has a wonderful flavor. Yellow cornmeal has more vitamin A potential than white cornmeal, but there is little difference in its nutritional or baking qualities. Cornmeal can be used alone or mixed with other flours.

CORNSTARCH is a starch obtained from the endosperm of corn. Substitute 1 tablespoon cornstarch for 2 tablespoons flour.

CRACKED WHEAT is the wheat berry cracked into larger pieces, cut rather than ground. This gives up a little of its starch as a binder, therefore it must be mixed with either unbleached all purpose flour or whole wheat flour.

GRAHAM FLOUR or whole wheat flour for bread is made from "hard" wheat, which contains a high percentage of gluten. The gluten gives out an elasticity to the dough and allows it to expand and hold the gas.

MILLET MEAL/FLOUR has similar protein to wheat. Both the meal and finely ground flour may be used in small amounts in combination with other flours to make yeast and quick breads. Millet is very rich in minerals and is unusual in that unlike other grains it is alkaline, rather than acid.

OAT BRAN is derived from the outer layers of the hulled oat kernel. The process involves grinding and sieving the kernel to produce two fractions: the course fraction is the oat bran, and the fine fraction is the oat flour. Oat bran is the outer most part of the whole oat kernel. Approximately a third of the whole oat kernel is oat bran! Both oat bran and oatmeal have the inedible hull removed during processing. Oatmeal is the whole grain that has been flattened between rollers and oat bran is the outer portion of the grain. Oat bran and oat products have been found to reduce cholesterol when eaten along with a fat-modified diet. Quick breads and muffins can be made by replacing up to half the flour in the original recipe with oat bran, depending on the percentage of oat bran you wish to incorporate in your diet. Sprinkle oat bran on tops of breads, cookies or muffins also.

POTATO FLOUR is made from cooked potatoes that have been dried and ground. It can be used in combination with other flours or alone. To avoid lumping, blend it with sugar before mixing or cream with the fat in your recipe before adding a liquid. In bread recipes potato flour keeps bread and rolls moist while maintaining freshness and retarding mold growth.

QUINOA, like spelt, is an ancient grain that people who suffer from allergies find they can tolerate. Quinoa is called the "super grain" because it contains all the major nutrient groups needed by the body. This was the staple food for the Aztecs. Scientist have found it is the only grain that contains all eight essential amino acids, the building blocks of complete protein. This is one grain that you could easily survive on as did the Aztec Indians for thousands of years.

RICE FLOUR is made from brown rice and can be used measure to measure as a substitute for wheat flour for those who cannot tolerate wheat. It is a good source of iron, B vitamins, and protein and is very low in sodium. To use in wheat free recipes, replace 1 cup all purpose flour with 2 tablespoons cornstarch in a measuring cup and fill level with brown rice flour.

RICE POLISH, also known as rice bran, is ground from the outer coating of the rice grain. It contains fiber and all the other nutrients of rice flour.

ROLLED OATS are produced by rolling the whole grain into a flake like product. Old fashioned or quick oats with the germ intact are what I use in baking and recommend. Oats add moisture and a sweet flavor to breads. It has a natural preservative which helps bread to keep longer. Oats add a chewy texture to cookies plus nutrition. Substitute 1 1/3 cups rolled oats for 1 cup unbleached all purpose flour. To combine with whole wheat flour or unbleached flour in bread recipes, use 1/3 cup oats for each cup of flour.

RYE MEAL/FLOUR after wheat, this is the most popular of the bread grains. Rye flour is low in gluten so will need a lot of kneading to develop the gluten it does have. Rye flour makes a great sandwich bread. Rye meal is coarsely ground whole rye flour and may be substituted in breads. For example you can replace 1 cup rye flour for 1 cup wheat flour.

SPELT is a high gluten, high protein grain originating from Europe more than 9,000 years ago. Spelt is not a wheat but it can be used in place of wheat in almost any recipe. I have found it to be a nutritious and easily digestable alternative for some people with wheat allergies. Try it in place of wheat to create a wheat free bread, cookies and muffins.

Because spelt is a good source of both soluable and insoluable fiber you may wish to use this ancient grain in baking. Research suggests that diets containing spelt may help lower blood sugar levels in diabetics, lower cholesterol and remove toxins from the body.

SOY FLOUR is made from the best quality soybeans that have been dehulled and cracked before milling. Besides being gluten free it is very high in protein and potassium. Substitute only a little of it in yeast breads. For example place 2 tablespoons soy flour in the bottom of a cup and level off with wheat flour. Use as much as your taste dictates in quick breads.

TRITICALE is a cross between wheat and rye. It is a lot higher in protein than wheat and contains all the essential amino acids, thus making it a complete protein. It has a nutty flavor and is very high in fiber. You can use triticale flour in combination with wheat flours or other grain flours, or as a direct substitute in making bread and other baked goods. Since rye has very little gluten, triticale is low in gluten also, thus making bread with triticale flour is done the same as for rye flour. The dough needs to be kneaded longer to develop the gluten and is best if the bread rises only once.

WHOLE WHEAT FLOUR may be substituted for part of the unbleached all-purpose flour called for in any of my recipes or, if you prefer, used to replace all of the flour. For using coarsely ground whole grain flour, substitute ¾ cup for 1 cup of the unbleached all purpose flour. Yeast breads made from whole wheat flour do not have to rise twice, and can be mixed and allowed to rise just once in the pan. In this book I use unbleached all purpose flour for all the recipes unless specified otherwise. I do use "hard" flour or bread flour in my bread recipes if I have it on hand. But don't go out and buy it if you have enough of the all purpose flour.

WHOLE WHEAT PASTRY FLOUR is milled from soft wheat and is finely ground, though not as finely ground as cake flour. It is low in protein (gluten) and is best used in making pie crusts, cookies and pastry.

WHEAT GERM, either toasted or raw, can be used in these recipes to add more nutritional value. Raw wheat germ has slightly more nutritional value; toasted it keeps better and has more flavor. Store wheat germ in the freezer or refrigerator so it stays fresh longer.

WHEAT BRAN is the part richest in fiber and B vitamins and nearly 20% of the protein in the wheat seed.

SEEDS AND NUTS – Sometimes a recipe will give you the option of adding nuts. Nuts do contain fat, but they also provide vitamin E and important minerals. The fat in nuts is mostly unsaturated and does not raise blood cholesterol levels. Some studies, however, indicated that people who eat nuts along with a healthy diet have a lower risk of heart disease. Sunflower seeds, flaxseeds, sesame seeds, and pumpkin seeds are also very good for you. Like nuts, these crunchy ingredients provide a variety of minerals as well as vitamin E.

SUGAR – You can replace up to half the sugar and honey in your favorite recipes with fruit. One cup of granulated sugar is equal to ¾ cup honey. Reduce the liquid by ¼ cup. One cup brown sugar is granulated sugar to which some molasses has been added or ¾ cup molasses and reduce the liquid by ¼ cup, or add ¼ cup flour for each cup of honey or molasses. One tablespoon fruit juice concentrate is equal to 1 teaspoon sugar, ¾ cup fruit concentrate is equal to 1 cup sugar.

YEAST – Dry active yeast is used in my recipes only by preference, cake yeast can be used if desired. One tablespoon active dry yeast is equal to 1 package active dry yeast or 1³/₅-oz cake (compressed) yeast. Dissolve active dry yeast in very warm liquid (105–115 degrees). Dissolve cake yeast in warm water (80–90 degrees).

SUBSTITUTIONS

1 cup butter or margarine equals ¾ cups plus 1 tablespoon oil.

1 egg equals 2 egg whites or 1 egg white and 2 tablespoons nonfat milk or ¼ cup puréed apple, carrots, pumpkin, bananas or fruit of your choice.

1 cup sugar equals ¾ cup honey or fruit.

1 14-oz can of sweetened condensed milk equals 1 cup plus 1 tablespoon non fat milk or instant milk powder, ¾ cup sugar and ½ cup boiling water combined in a blender until creamy smooth.

EQUIVALENTS

1 lemon equals 3 tablespoons juice

1 orange equals ½ cup juice

2 tablespoons flour equals 1 tablespoon cornstarch

1½ cups corn syrup equals 1 cup sugar plus ½ cup water

EQUIVALENTS (cont.)

Sweet coconut equals ½ cup unsweetened coconut mixed with 1 tablespoon unsweetened fruit concentrate. Let set 10 minutes.

1 cup equals 8 to 10 egg whites

FLOUR EQUIVALENTS

1¾ cups all purpose flour equals 2 cups cake flour

In a recipe you can replace 1 cup all purpose flour with:

- ¾ cup coarsely ground whole wheat flour
- ⅞ cup whole wheat pastry flour
- ¾ to 1 cup finely ground general purpose whole wheat flour
- ¾ cup coarse corn meal
- ¾ to ⅞ cup rice flour
- ¾ cup rolled oats plus ¼ cup whole wheat flour
- 1 scant cup fine corn meal
- 1 cup rye flour
- 1 cup corn flour
- 1⅓ to 1½ cups rolled oat meal

FRUITS AND NUTS EQUIVALENTS

Almonds, Brazil or Pecan nuts: 1 pound = about 2 cups.

Apples (3): 1 pound = about 3 cups chopped or sliced.

Bananas (3): 1 pound = about 2 cups mashed.

Candied Fruits (cut up): 1 pound = about 3 cups.

Coconut (shredded or flaked): 1 pound = about 4 cups.

Dried Apples: 1 pound = about 5 cups.

Dried Apricots, Figs, Peaches, Pears, Prunes or Raisins: 1 pound = about 3¼ to 3½ cups.

Dates or Currants: 1 pound = about 2½ to 2⅔ cups.

FRUITS AND NUTS EQUIVALENTS (cont.)

Peaches (4 medium): 1 pound = about 2 cups.

Walnuts (chopped or whole): 1 pound = about 3 cups.

WEIGHTS

Butter or Margarine: 1 pound = 2 cups.

Chocolate Chips: 6 ounces = 1 cup.

Cocoa: 1 pound = 4 cups.

Flours –

All Purpose: 1 pound = 4 cups.
Cake: 1 pound = 4¾ cups.
Cornmeal: 1 pound = 3 cups.
Rye: 1 pound = 3¾ cups.
Whole Wheat: 1 pound = 3½ cups.

Marshmallows: ½ pound = 4½ cups.

Liquid: 1 pound = 2 cups.

Milk –

Evaporated: 5.33 oz. can = ¾ cup.
14½ oz. can = 1⅔ cup.
Sweetened condensed: 14 oz. can = 1¼ cup.
15 oz. can = 1⅓ cup.

Shortening: 1 pound = 2 cups.

Sugar –

Brown: 1 pound = 2¼ cups.
Granulated: 1 pound = 2 cups.
Powdered: 1 pound = 3½ cups.

Oatmeal: 1 pound = 2⅔ cups.

June's Helpful Hints

#1. Don't Count Calories. Choose calories. 1000 calories from complex carbohydrates is far better for you than 500 calories of fat or simple sugar.

#2. Know Your Oils. All oil is fat. Oils from animal products contain cholesterol. Vegetable oils don't. Avoid tropical oils and any oil that has been hydrogenated. Choose oils that are monounsaturated and polyunsaturated.

#3. Eliminate Fat. The largest source of fat in baking is the oil. Most times you can eliminate the fat from a recipe. If it turns out too dry, next time simply increase the liquid where the recipe calls for water, nonfat milk or juice.

#4. Eliminate the Eggs. Substitute eggs is an easy way to drop a fair amount of the cholesterol from a recipe. 1 egg = 2 egg whites. Avoid egg substitutes. Not only are they too expensive but many contain yellow dye #5, a known carcinogen.

#5. Limit Sugar. A general rule is that all sugars are the same. Even sugar substitutes can cause your body to behave in many of the same ways that sugar will. Check with your doctor. As a rule, however, raw unprocessed honey is better than plain white sugar for two reasons:

1. Honey is sweeter so less is needed in a recipe.

2. Raw, local honey contains a small amount of pollen. Research suggests that people with pollen allergies who eat raw, local honey regularly can build up their tolerance to the afflicting pollen.

Fruit is another substitute for sugar. Fresh fruit sauces, juices or concentrates can be used.

Homemade Biscuits, Scones & Shortcakes

These delicious little breads are a great substitute for more time-consuming yeast breads and rolls. Biscuit mix can be made ahead and ready at a moment's notice. I keep a bag of mix in the refrigerator. The freezer works great, too, to store the mix. When ready to use, pour out the amount you need, add the liquid to form a nice, moist dough that forms into a ball, then proceed to roll the dough out and cut into rounds. To make biscuits ahead of time simply mix, roll out and cut the dough, place onto a baking sheet, and put into the refrigerator for up to two hours before baking. Biscuits can also be frozen ahead of time and baked later. Store the cut-out biscuits in a freezer by placing on a baking sheet, then freeze and put into a plastic bag. Bake as needed in a 450-degree oven for 15 to 18 minutes.

Follow these directions and you'll have tender, flaky, light biscuits every time:

1. Combine dry ingredients together, mixing well.

2. Cut in shortening or margarine with electric mixer or pastry blender only until mixture resembles coarse cornmeal or crumbs. As in pie making, cold shortening and cold liquid ingredients make for a flakier product.

3. Make a well in the center. Pour in the liquid ingredients. Stir quickly around bowl with a fork until dough cleans the bowl and is nice and moist. If too dry, add a little more liquid.

4. Turn dough out onto a lightly floured surface. Gently form dough into a mass and knead lightly. Pick up dough from the side away from you, fold over toward you, press out lightly with the palm of your hand. Turn dough slightly, about a quarter turn, then repeat the process ten times.

5. Pat our lightly with hands or roll to even thickness, rolling out from the center of the dough. The thickness depends on how you like your biscuits. If you like them tall and flaky, cut them ½ to ¾ inch thick. If you prefer thin, crusty biscuits, roll them ½ inch thick.

6. With a floured 2½ inch biscuit cutter, cut straight down into the dough. For biscuits with soft sides, place the biscuits close together. For biscuits with crusty sides, arrange them 1 inch apart. Place biscuits on an ungreased baking sheet (unless recipe specifies "greased"). I like to brush the tops of my biscuits with buttermilk. This makes a rich brown crust.

Bake biscuits in a preheated, hot oven (400 to 425 degrees) for approximately 13 to 18 minutes, depending on the thickness. Serve hot.

To help keep them warm, transfer biscuits from the baking sheet to foil or napkin-lined basket or dish. Cover loosely. ENJOY!

Grandma's Biscuits

- 1 tablespoon active dry yeast
- ½ cup warm water
- 5 cups flour
- 4 teaspoons baking powder
- 2 teaspoons salt
- 3 tablespoons sugar
- ¾ cup shortening, or half shortening and half margarine
- 1 teaspoon baking soda
- 2 cups buttermilk

Combine yeast and water in a small bowl and let sit 5 minutes. Combine flour, baking powder, salt and sugar. Add shortening and mix until of a cornmeal-like consistency. In a separate bowl combine baking soda and buttermilk. Stir baking soda mixture into flour mixture along with the yeast mixture, mixing lightly until it forms a dough. Cover dough and chill at least 6 hours or overnight.

On a lightly floured surface knead dough lightly 10 times. Roll dough out until ½-inch thick. Cut out biscuits with a floured 2-inch round cutter or pan. Cover and let rise in a warm place for about 1 hour.

Preheat oven to 400 degrees. Bake until golden brown, about 15 minutes.

Raised Buttermilk Biscuits
(low fat)

- 1 tablespoon honey
- 1 tablespoon active dry yeast
- 2 tablespoons warm water
- 2 cups flour
- 1 teaspoon baking powder
- 1 teaspoon salt
- 2 tablespoons oil
- ⅔ cup buttermilk

Grease baking pan. Combine honey, yeast and water. Set aside for 5 minutes. Meanwhile, in a separate bowl combine flour, baking powder and salt. Cut in oil to make a crumbly mixture. Add yeast mixture and buttermilk to flour mixture. Stir to a moderately stiff dough. Roll out to ½-inch thickness. Place biscuits on pan so that they barely touch, prick top with fork, and brush with milk or spray with vegetable oil spray. Let biscuits rise until doubled in size. Preheat oven to 400 degrees. Bake for 20 minutes.

Variation: Replace 1 cup all-purpose flour with 1 cup whole wheat flour.

Old-fashioned Buttermilk Biscuits

2	cups flour	1	tablespoon sugar
2½	teaspoons baking powder	⅓	cup shortening, margarine, or half oil and half margarine
¼	teaspoon baking soda	⅔	to ¾ cup buttermilk
½	teaspoon salt		

Preheat oven to 400 degrees. Lightly grease cookie sheet. Combine flour, baking powder, baking soda, salt and sugar. Cut in shortening until mixture resembles cornmeal. Make a well in the center and pour in half the buttermilk. Mix lightly and quickly with a fork. Add more milk. Dough will be moist enough to leave sides of the bowl and cling to the fork.

Form dough into a ball. Turn dough onto a lightly floured surface and knead gently 8 times. Roll from center in all directions, lifting rolling pin at edges. Roll until ¼ to ½-inch thick. Cut with a biscuit cutter. Place biscuits on cookie sheet. Brush tops with buttermilk. Bake for 12–15 minutes.

Variations:

1. ***Shortcake:*** Add 3 tablespoons sugar or honey when adding buttermilk. ***Do not*** knead dough.

2. ***Whole Wheat Biscuits:*** Replace all-purpose flour with 2 cups whole wheat flour.

3. ***Sugar Free:*** Omit sugar.

4. ***Cholesterol Free:*** Substitute ⅓ cup oil for shortening when adding buttermilk.

425°

3 c flour
4 T sugar
½ tsp salt
4½ tsp Baking powder
⅓ tsp " soda
⅓ c shortening
1 egg mix w ¾ to 1 c buttermilk

Strawberry Shortcake

(low fat)

- 1¾ cups flour
- 2 tablespoons sugar
- 1 tablespoon baking powder
- ½ teaspoon orange peel, grated
- 3 tablespoons margarine or oil
- ¾ cup skim milk

Preheat oven to 400 degrees. Grease baking sheet. Combine flour, sugar, baking powder, orange peel and margarine. Stir until coarse crumbs form. Stir in milk until a soft dough forms. Roll dough out onto lightly floured surface to ½-inch thickness. Cut out biscuits with a 2 to 2½-inch cutter. Place on baking sheet. Brush tops with buttermilk and sprinkle lightly with sugar. Bake about 15 minutes.

Lite Buttermilk Shortcake

- 1½ cups flour
- 3 tablespoons sugar
- 1½ teaspoons baking powder
- ½ teaspoon baking soda
- ¼ teaspoon salt
- 1 tablespoon margarine
- ½ cup plus 2 tablespoons buttermilk
- 1 tablespoon oil
- 2 cups strawberries, raspberries, or peaches
- 1 tablespoon orange juice
- 1 tablespoon sugar

Preheat oven to 400 degrees. Grease baking sheet. Combine flour, sugar, baking powder, baking soda, salt and margarine. Stir until coarse crumbs form. Stir in ½ cup buttermilk and oil until a soft dough forms, adding additional buttermilk, if necessary. Roll out on lightly floured surface to a ½-inch thickness. Cut out biscuits with a 2 to 2½-inch cutter. Place on baking sheet. Brush tops with buttermilk and sprinkle lightly with sugar. Bake about 15 minutes.

Combine strawberries or other fruit, orange juice and sugar. Split biscuits in half, spoon fruit mixture between layers and over the top.

Variation: Use nonfat vanilla yogurt or a light whipped topping instead of whipped cream.

Brown Rice Biscuits

(gluten & wheat free)

- ¾ cup brown rice flour
- 1 tablespoon potato flour
- 3 tablespoons cornstarch
- ¼ teaspoon salt
- 2 teaspoons baking powder
- ¼ teaspoon baking soda
- ¼ cup margarine, cold
- 1 egg
- ½ cup buttermilk

Preheat oven to 400 degrees. Grease pan or muffin tins. Combine flours, cornstarch, salt, baking powder and baking soda. Cut in margarine and make a well in the center. In a separate bowl combine egg and buttermilk. Pour buttermilk mixture into the well and stir to make a soft dough. This dough is too soft to roll out but can be dropped onto baking pan. Bake until golden brown, about 12–15 minutes.

Variation: Substitute Spelt flour for rice and potato flour.

Soybean Flour Baking Powder Biscuits

These biscuits have a delightfully rich flavor.

- 1 cup all-purpose flour
- ¼ cup soybean flour
- 2 teaspoons baking powder
- ½ teaspoon salt
- 2 tablespoons shortening
- ½ cup milk

Preheat oven to 450 degrees. Grease cookie sheet. Sift flours well, then the baking powder and salt in a large bowl. Cut in shortening. Add milk and mix well. Roll out on a lightly floured board but do not handle too much as you knead. Roll out dough to ½-inch thick. Cut into biscuits. Place on cookie sheet. Bake for 15 minutes.

Buttermilk Scones

2 cups flour
⅓ cup margarine
2 teaspoons baking soda
¼ teaspoon baking powder
2 tablespoons honey
1 egg
½ cup buttermilk

Preheat oven to 400 degrees. Lightly grease cookie sheet. Combine flour, margarine, baking soda and baking powder. Add honey, egg and buttermilk and stir until moistened. Roll out dough and cut into 2-inch circles or scoop with an ice cream scoop. Spray tops with vegetable oil spray and flatten slightly. Bake 11–14 minutes.

Variations:

1. Biscuits can be sprinkled with a cinnamon and sugar mixture or just a little cinnamon before baking.
2. Add 1 teaspoon grated orange peel can be added to the flour mixture.
3. ½ to 1 cup whole wheat flour can replace an equivalent amount of all-purpose flour.
4. To reduce fat, substitute 2 egg whites or egg substitute for 1 egg. Reduce margarine to ¼ cup. If substituting oil for margarine, add with the buttermilk and honey.
5. ***Scotch Scones:*** Omit honey. Add ½ teaspoon salt to the flour mixture. Additional buttermilk may be needed. Stir until ingredients are moistened. Knead gently 6 to 8 times. Roll dough out into a 6-inch circle and cut into 6 wedges. Bake as above.

Scones

(fat & sugar free)

1½ cups all-purpose flour
½ cup whole wheat flour
1 tablespoon baking powder
¾ teaspoon baking soda
¼ teaspoon salt
¼ cup dates, chopped
¾ cup orange juice
¼ cup nuts, chopped, or oats

Preheat oven to 400 degrees. Spray cookie sheet with vegetable oil spray. Combine all ingredients. Roll out on a floured board and cut into 2½-inch circles. Bake for about 10–15 minutes.

Variation: Dough can be rolled into a 6-inch circle on the sheet and cut into 6 wedges. Separate wedges after baking.

Oatmeal Scones
(cholesterol free)

- 1 cup flour
- 1 cup oats
- 3 tablespoons brown sugar
- 1½ teaspoons baking powder
- 5 tablespoons oil
- 2 egg whites
- 2 tablespoons skim milk
- ½ cup raisins or dates, chopped

Preheat oven to 400 degrees. Grease cookie sheet. Combine flour, oats, brown sugar and baking powder. In a separate bowl blend oil, egg whites and milk. Add oil mixture to flour mixture. Fold in raisins. May need to add a little more flour if dough is too sticky. On a lightly floured surface roll or pat dough into a 7-inch circle. Cut dough into wedges, dipping knife into flour as needed. Place on sheet, separating wedges slightly. Brush wedges with skim milk. Bake for 10–12 minutes.

Oat Bran Apple Raisin Scones
(low fat)

- 1½ cups flour
- ¼ cup brown sugar
- 1 cup oat bran
- 1 tablespoon baking powder
- 1 teaspoon cinnamon
- ⅓ cup margarine, cold
- ¾ cup dried apples, chopped
- ½ cup raisins or dates, chopped
- 2 egg whites, beaten
- ⅓ cup water

Preheat oven to 400 degrees. Grease cookie sheet. Combine flour, brown sugar, oat bran, baking powder and cinnamon. Cut in margarine, mixing until crumbly. Fold in apple, raisins and dates. In a separate bowl combine egg whites and water. Add egg mixture to flour mixture, mixing until just moistened. Shape dough to form a ball. Roll out onto a lightly floured surface. Knead gently a few times. Place dough on cookie sheet and pat into a circle. Score into eight wedges. Do not separate wedges. Bake until lightly browned, about 18–20 minutes. Break wedges apart.

Barley Scones

(sugar & wheat free)

- ½ cup oil
- ¾ cup apple juice concentrate
- 2 eggs
- ¼ cup buttermilk
- 4½ cups barley flour
- 1½ teaspoons baking soda
- ½ teaspoon cinnamon
- ½ teaspoon nutmeg
- 1 teaspoon orange peel, grated
- 1 cup raisins or dried fruit, chopped

Preheat oven to 375 degrees. Grease or line cookie sheet with parchment or waxed paper. Combine oil, apple juice concentrate and buttermilk and stir for 1 minute. Add flour, baking soda, cinnamon, nutmeg and orange peel. Fold in raisins. Dough will be sticky. Use an ice cream scoop to drop batter into small mounds on cookie sheet. Press batter down to flatten to about ½-inch thick. Brush scones with buttermilk or water. Bake scones until golden brown, about 22–27 minutes.

Baked Cake Donuts

- 1 cup sugar
- 2 tablespoons oil
- 2 eggs
- ⅔ cup buttermilk
- 3½ cups flour
- 2 teaspoons baking powder
- 1 teaspoon baking soda
- ¼ teaspoon nutmeg
- ½ teaspoon cinnamon
- ½ teaspoon salt
- Butter, margarine, oil, or vegetable oil to brush doughnuts

Topping:

- ¼ cup sugar
- ¼ teaspoon nutmeg

Combine sugar, oil, eggs and buttermilk. Beat until smooth. Add flour, baking powder, baking soda, nutmeg, cinnamon and salt. Continue beating until smooth. Cover and chill 1 hour.

Preheat oven to 350 to 375 degrees. Grease baking sheet. On a lightly floured board, roll dough out ½-inch thick, adding additional flour if dough is too soft to handle. Cut dough with a 3-inch donut cutter. Place donuts 2 inches apart on baking sheet. Brush tops with melted butter, margarine, oil, or vegetable oil spray. Bake for about 20 minutes. Brush with melted butter, margarine, oil, or vegetable oil spray. Roll donuts in sugar and nutmeg mixture. Cool on wire racks. Store donuts in a tightly covered container.

Quick Breads

Quick breads refer to those breads in which the batter is leavened with baking powder or soda instead of yeast. Quick breads require no kneading or rising time. Non-wheat flours and grains can be used better in quick breads than in yeast breads as they do not rely on the gluten.

Quick breads are also faster to make. The batter can be mixed by hand or mixer. If the batter is mixed with a spoon, the dry ingredients should be blended together first, then add the liquid ingredients. If using a mixer, the reverse is preferred. Mix the liquid ingredients together, then add the dry ingredients. Blend in nuts, seeds, and dried fruits into the dry ingredients before adding liquid. This helps prevent them from sinking to the bottom of the loaf.

When bananas are plentiful, I freeze them with the peeling on and place them in freezer bags for later use. Quick breads made with natural ingredients are tastier and more nutritious.

The consistency of batters will vary depending on the variety of quick bread you are making.

When baking, it's best to check halfway through the specified time to see if it's browning too fast. (Your oven may run hotter than mine.) Also, a good way to see if bread is done is to insert a wooden toothpick gently into the center of the bread and if it comes out clean the bread should be done.

Cranberry Bread

(milk free)

- 2 cups flour
- ½ teaspoon salt
- 1½ teaspoons baking powder
- ½ teaspoon baking soda
- 1 cup sugar
- 1 egg, beaten
- 3 tablespoons oil
- ¾ cup orange juice
- ½ cup nuts
- 1 to 2 cups cranberries, cut in half, or frozen whole cranberries
- 1 teaspoon orange rind, grated

Preheat oven to 350 degrees. Grease loaf pan. Combine all ingredients. Pour batter into loaf pan. Bake for 1 hour.

Apple Walnut Bread

- 1½ cups all-purpose flour
- 2 teaspoons baking powder
- ½ teaspoon baking soda
- 1 teaspoon salt
- 1 teaspoon cinnamon
- ¼ teaspoon nutmeg
- ¼ teaspoon allspice
- ½ cup whole wheat flour
- 1 cup apple, chopped
- 1 egg, beaten
- ¾ cup brown sugar
- ½ cup buttermilk
- 4 tablespoons oil
- 1 cup nuts, chopped
- ¾ cup raisins, optional

Preheat oven to 350 degrees. Grease loaf pan. Combine all ingredients, mixing just enough to moisten the dry ingredients. Pour batter into pan. Bake for 1 hour.

Applesauce Nut Bread

- 2 cups flour
- ¾ cup sugar
- 1 tablespoon baking powder
- 1 teaspoon salt
- ½ teaspoon baking soda
- ½ teaspoon cinnamon
- 1 egg, lightly beaten
- 2 tablespoons oil
- 1 cup applesauce
- 1 cup nuts, chopped

Preheat oven to 350 degrees. Grease loaf pan. Combine all ingredients. Pour batter into pan. Bake for 1 hour.

Applesauce Raisin Bread

- 1 egg
- 1 cup applesauce
- ¼ cup margarine, melted
- ¼ cup granulated sugar
- ½ cup brown sugar
- 1½ cups all-purpose flour
- ½ cup whole wheat flour
- ½ cup oatmeal
- 2 teaspoons baking powder
- ½ teaspoon baking soda
- ¾ teaspoon salt
- 1 teaspoon cinnamon
- ½ teaspoon nutmeg
- ½ cup raisins
- 1 cup nuts, chopped

Preheat oven to 350 degrees. Grease loaf pan or tube pan. Combine egg, applesauce, margarine, and sugars, mixing well. In a separate bowl combine flours, oatmeal, baking powder, baking soda, salt, cinnamon, and nutmeg. Stir egg mixture into flour mixture, mixing until smooth. Fold in raisins and nuts. Turn batter into pan and bake for 50–60 minutes. Cool and, if desired, lightly frost.

Zucchini Walnut Bread

- 1½ cups flour
- 1½ teaspoons cinnamon
- ½ teaspoon salt
- 1 teaspoon baking powder
- ½ teaspoon baking soda
- 2 eggs, beaten
- 1 cup sugar
- 1½ teaspoons vanilla
- ½ cup vegetable oil
- 1½ cups zucchini, shredded
- ½ cup walnuts, chopped

Preheat oven to 350 degrees. Grease one 9½ by 5½-inch loaf pan or three 5 by 3½-inch loaf pans. In a medium bowl combine flour, cinnamon, salt, baking powder and baking soda. In a separate bowl beat eggs with sugar, vanilla and vegetable oil until thick. Fold flour mixture into egg mixture and stir until well blended. Fold in zucchini and walnuts. Pour batter into pan and bake until an inserted toothpick comes out clean, about 1 hour for a large loaf or 40–45 minutes for small loaves. Remove bread from pan and cool on a rack.

Zucchini/Carrot Bread

(low fat)

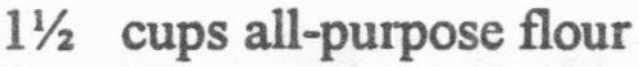

- 1½ cups all-purpose flour
- 1½ cups whole wheat flour
- 1 tablespoon cinnamon
- ½ teaspoon salt
- 1 teaspoon baking soda
- 1 teaspoon baking powder
- ¾ cup egg substitute
- ½ cup brown sugar
- ⅓ cup oil
- ⅔ cup buttermilk
- 2 teaspoons vanilla
- 2 cups zucchini, shredded, or 1 cup each carrot and zucchini, shredded
- ¼ cup nuts, chopped (optional)

Preheat oven to 350 degrees. Grease 2 loaf pans. Combine all ingredients, except zucchini or carrot and nuts. Mix lightly. Stir in zucchini or carrot and nuts. Pour batter into loaf pans. Bake for 50–60 minutes.

Notes:

Zucchini/Carrot Bread

(egg & milk free)

This recipe is cake-like, as it is baked in a cake pan, and has a chewy texture.

- 1½ cups hot water
- ¼ cup honey
- 1 cup carrot or zucchini, grated
- 1 cup raisins
- 1 teaspoon cinnamon
- ½ teaspoon allspice
- ½ teaspoon ground cloves
- 4 tablespoons margarine
- 1 cup all-purpose flour
- ½ cup whole wheat flour
- ½ cup wheat germ
- ¼ cup oatmeal
- 2 teaspoons baking soda
- 1 teaspoon baking powder
- ¼ teaspoon salt
- 1 cup nuts, chopped, or sunflower seeds

Grease a 9 x 13-inch baking pan. Combine hot water, honey, carrot or zucchini, raisins, cinnamon, allspice, ground cloves and margarine. Let cool to lukewarm.

Meanwhile, preheat oven to 350 degrees. In a separate bowl combine flours, wheat germ, oatmeal, baking soda, baking powder, and salt. Combine flour mixture with honey mixture. Stir in nuts. Pour batter into pan. Bake 50–60 minutes. Cool in pan for 5 minutes. Turn out of pan, cutting around edges if necessary. Cool on rack. Best when eaten the next day.

Banana Zucchini Bread

- 1 cup bananas, mashed
- 2 cups zucchini, grated
- ½ cup canola oil
- 3 eggs
- 1 teaspoon salt
- 1½ cups sugar
- 2 teaspoons vanilla
- 2 teaspoons cinnamon
- 1 teaspoon baking powder
- 1 teaspoon baking soda
- 3 cups all-purpose flour
- ½ to 1 cup whole wheat flour
- ½ cup buttermilk
- 1 cup nuts, chopped

Preheat oven to 350 degrees. Grease two 9 x 4 x 3-inch loaf pans. Combine all ingredients, mixing well. Bake for 45–55 minutes.

Dad's Banana Bran Bread

(low fat)

- ¼ cup margarine or oil
- 2 cups ripe bananas, mashed
- 1 egg
- 1 teaspoon vanilla
- ½ cup brown sugar
- 1 cup bran, oat or wheat
- 3 cups flour
- 2 teaspoons baking powder
- ½ teaspoon baking soda
- ½ teaspoon salt
- ½ cup nuts, chopped (optional)

Preheat oven to 350 degrees. Grease loaf pan. Combine margarine, bananas, egg, vanilla, brown sugar, and bran. In a separate bowl combine flour, baking powder, baking soda, and salt. Combine margarine mixture with flour mixture, mixing well. Stir in nuts. Pour batter into loaf pan. Bake for about 45 minutes.

Banana Bread

(gluten & wheat free)

- 1/3 cup shortening
- 1/3 cup sugar
- 1 egg
- 1 cup soy flour
- 1 cup brown rice flour
- ¼ cup potato flour
- 1 tablespoon tapioca or cornstarch
- 2½ teaspoons baking powder
- ½ teaspoon baking soda
- ½ teaspoon salt
- 1 cup banana, mashed
- ¼ cup buttermilk
- 1 teaspoon orange rind, grated
- ½ cup nuts, chopped (optional)

Preheat oven to 350 degrees. Grease one 8 x 4-inch loaf pan or two 5 x 3-inch loaf pans. Cream together shortening and sugar until light and fluffy. Add egg and beat well. In a separate bowl combine flours, tapioca, baking powder, baking soda and salt. Add flour mixture alternately with the mashed banana and buttermilk. Stir in orange rind and nuts, mixing until just combined. Pour into loaf pan(s). Bake large loaf pan for 50–60 minutes or small loaf pans for 30–40 minutes. Cool in pans 10 minutes. Remove from pans. Best when eaten next day.

Variation: Replace combination of soy, rice and potato flours with 1¾ cups brown rice flour, 1 tablespoon tapioca, 1 tablespoon potato flour, and 1 tablespoon cornstarch.

Banana Bread
(wheat free)

- ¼ cup butter or margarine
- ½ cup molasses
- 3 eggs
- 2 cups ripe bananas, mashed
- ½ cup buttermilk
- 1 teaspoon vanilla
- 1 teaspoon salt
- 2 teaspoons baking powder
- 1 teaspoon baking soda
- 2½ cups rye flour

Preheat oven to 325 degrees. Grease loaf pan. Combine butter and molasses. Add eggs and beat thoroughly. Stir in bananas, buttermilk, vanilla, salt, baking powder and baking soda. Beat in flour. Turn batter into loaf pan and bake for 1 hour. Leave bread in pan for 5 minutes before removing from pan to cool on rack.

Variation: Spelt flour can replace rye flour.

Banana Bread
(fat free)

- 4 medium bananas, mashed
- 4 egg whites
- ½ cup applesauce
- ½ cup brown sugar
- ½ teaspoon salt
- 2 cups all-purpose flour, *–or–* combine 1 cup all-purpose flour with 1 cup whole wheat flour
- 1 teaspoon baking soda
- 1 teaspoon vanilla

Preheat oven to 375 degrees. Grease a bread pan. Combine bananas, egg whites, applesauce and brown sugar. Add flour, baking soda and salt, mixing well. Stir in vanilla. Pour batter into a greased bread pan. Bake for 10 minutes. Reduce oven temperature to 350 degrees and bake for an additional 30–35 minutes. Cool in pan 5 minutes before removing bread to finish cooling on rack.

Lite Banana Bread

(low fat)

- ¾ cup sugar
- ⅓ cup unsweetened applesauce
- 1 tablespoon margarine
- 1 cup (3 small or 3 medium) bananas, mashed
- 1 egg
- 1 egg white
- 1 teaspoon vanilla
- 1½ cup all-purpose flour, or combine ¾ cup all-purpose flour with ¼ cup whole wheat flour
- 1 teaspoon baking soda
- ¼ teaspoon salt

Preheat oven to 350 degrees. Grease a 9 x 5-inch loaf pan. Combine sugar, applesauce and margarine. Blend in bananas, egg, egg white, and vanilla. In a separate bowl combine flour, baking soda and salt. Stir flour mixture into banana mixture and mix until just combined. Pour batter into loaf pan. Bake for about 1 hour.

'Delicious' Banana Bread

(egg & milk free)

- ½ cup shortening
- ⅔ cup brown sugar
- 1¾ cup all-purpose flour
- ¼ cup whole wheat flour
- 2 teaspoons baking powder
- ½ teaspoon baking soda
- ⅓ teaspoon salt
- 1 cup (2 medium or 3 small) bananas, mashed
- 1 tablespoon lemon juice

Preheat oven to 350 degrees. Grease 1 large or 2 small loaf pans. In a large bowl combine shortening and brown sugar. In a separate bowl combine flours, baking powder, baking soda and salt. In a small bowl combine bananas and lemon juice. Add flour mixture alternately with banana mixture to shortening mixture. Mix until smooth, about 1 minute. Fill loaf pan three-quarters full. Bake large loaf pan for 50–60 or small loaf pans for 35–40 minutes. Cool 5 minutes in pans. Remove to a rack to finish cooling. Best if eaten next day.

Variation: Pumpkin, applesauce, or other fruit or vegetable can replace the banana.

Old-fashioned Banana Bread

- ½ cup brown sugar
- ½ cup granulated sugar
- ½ cup margarine or oil
- 2 eggs
- 1 cup banana, mashed
- ¼ cup plain yogurt or buttermilk
- 1 teaspoon vanilla
- ½ teaspoon salt
- 1 teaspoon baking soda
- 1 teaspoon baking powder
- 2 cups all-purpose flour
- ½ cup whole wheat flour
- ½ cup walnuts, chopped

Preheat oven to 350 degrees. Grease loaf pan. Combine sugars and margarine. Beat until light and fluffy. Stir in remaining ingredients, mixing until well combined. Bake 40–45 minutes.

Old-fashioned Banana Bread

(low fat)

This recipe makes a larger batch.

- 1 cup low fat margarine (50% less fat) or ½ cup regular margarine or oil
- ¾ cup brown sugar
- ¾ cup granulated sugar
- 4 cups all-purpose flour
- 1 cup whole wheat flour
- 1 teaspoon salt
- 2 teaspoons baking powder
- 2 teaspoons baking soda
- 4 eggs, or 2 eggs plus 4 egg whites
- 2 cups (6 small or 4 medium) bananas, mashed
- ¼ cup buttermilk
- 1 teaspoon vanilla
- 1½ cups nuts, chopped

Preheat oven to 350 degrees. Grease 4 small loaf pans. Combine margarine and sugars. In a separate bowl combine flours, salt, baking powder and baking soda. Stir flour mixture into margarine mixture along with eggs, bananas, buttermilk, vanilla and nuts. Mix well. Pour batter into pans and bake for 40 minutes.

Fruit Nut Loaf

- ½ cup brown sugar
- 4 tablespoons oil
- 2 eggs, egg substitute, or 4 egg whites
- 1 cup apple, grated
- ½ cup buttermilk
- 1½ cups all-purpose flour
- ½ cup whole wheat flour
- 1 teaspoon baking powder
- ½ teaspoon baking soda
- ½ teaspoon salt
- ½ teaspoon nuts, chopped, or oats

Preheat oven to 350 degrees. Grease a 9 x 5-inch loaf pan. Combine sugar, oil and eggs. Beat until smooth and light. Stir in apple and buttermilk, set aside. In a separate bowl combine flours, baking powder, baking soda and salt. Combine flour mixture with egg mixture and stir just until blended. Do not over mix. Fold in nuts or oats. Bake for 40–45 minutes.

Variations:

1. ***Banana Nut Bread:*** Substitute 1 cup mashed banana for the grated apple.

2. ***Date Nut Bread:*** Reduce eggs to one. Omit buttermilk and apple. Pour 1 cup boiling water over 1 cup chopped dates and let cool. Substitute chopped dates and water for apple.

3. ***Orange Date Loaf:*** Omit buttermilk and grated apple. Add grated peel of 1 orange. Measure juice from the orange and add water to equal 1 cup. Add orange juice and water mixture to batter in place of apple. Add 1 cup chopped dates.

Date and Apricot Bread

- 1 cup whole wheat flour
- 1 cup all purpose flour
- 2 teaspoons baking powder
- ¾ teaspoon salt
- ½ cup granulated sugar or brown sugar
- 2 eggs or egg substitute
- 4 tablespoons oil
- 1 cup dates, chopped
- 1 cup apricots, chopped

Preheat oven to 350 degrees. Grease one 9 x 5 x 3-inch loaf pan. Combine flours, baking powder and salt. In a separate bowl combine sugar, eggs, oil, dates and apricots. Pour sugar mixture into flour mixture. Stir until thoroughly moistened. Pour batter into pan. Bake for 1 hour.

Honey Date Bread

(milk free)

- 2 cups dates, chopped
- 3 tablespoons oil
- ½ cup brown sugar
- ½ cup honey
- 1 teaspoon vanilla
- ¾ teaspoon orange peel, grated
- ¾ cup hot water
- ¼ cup orange juice
- 1 egg, beaten
- 2 cups flour
- 1 teaspoon baking soda
- 1 teaspoon salt
- 1 cup nuts, coarsely chopped

Grease loaf pan. Combine dates, oil, brown sugar, honey, vanilla, orange peel, hot water, and orange juice. Set aside for 20 minutes.

Preheat oven to 325 degrees. Beat egg into date mixture. Add flour, baking soda, salt and nuts, mixing just enough to moisten. Turn batter into loaf pan. Bake for 1 hour. Let stand in pan for 10 minutes. Turn out on a rack to cool.

Honey & Nut Loaf

- 1 cup whole wheat flour
- 1 cup all-purpose flour
- 2 tablespoons baking powder
- ¾ teaspoon salt
- ½ cup brown sugar
- 2 eggs
- 4 tablespoons oil
- 2 tablespoons honey
- ½ cup nuts, chopped

Preheat oven to 350 degrees. Grease a 9 x 5 x 3-inch loaf pan. Combine flours, baking powder and salt. In a separate bowl combine sugar, eggs, oil and honey. Pour sugar mixture into flour mixture. Mix until thoroughly moistened. Stir in nuts. Pour into pan and bake for 1 hour.

Variation: ***Maple Nut Loaf***: Add 2 tablespoons maple syrup to the sugar mixture.

Pumpkin Bread

- 1 cup whole wheat flour
- 1 cup all-purpose flour
- 2 teaspoons baking powder
- ¾ teaspoon salt
- 1 teaspoon cinnamon
- ½ teaspoon ground cloves
- ½ cup brown sugar
- 2 eggs
- 4 tablespoons oil
- 1 cup pumpkin
- ⅓ cup skim milk

Preheat oven to 350 degrees. Grease a 9 x 5 x 3-inch loaf pan. Combine flours, baking powder, salt, cinnamon and ground cloves. In a separate bowl combine sugar, eggs, oil, pumpkin and milk. Stir sugar mixture into flour mixture, mixing until thoroughly moistened. Pour into pan and bake for 1 hour.

Variation: Cinnamon and ground cloves can be replaced by 1½ teaspoon pumpkin spice.

Whole Wheat Pumpkin Bread

(egg & milk free)

- 1 cup pumpkin
- 1/3 cup oil
- ½ cup honey
- ½ cup raisins
- 1½ to 1 2/3 cups whole wheat flour
- ¼ teaspoon salt
- ½ teaspoon cinnamon
- 1/8 teaspoon nutmeg
- 1½ teaspoons baking soda

Preheat oven to 350 degrees. Grease a loaf pan. Combine all ingredients and blend well. Pour batter into pan. Bake 50–60 minutes.

Pumpkin Bread

(egg & milk free)

- 2 cups flour
- 1 cup sugar
- ½ cup oil
- 1 cup pumpkin
- 1½ teaspoons baking soda
- ¾ teaspoon cinnamon
- ¼ teaspoon ground cloves
- ¼ teaspoon nutmeg
- ½ cup dates, chopped
- ½ cup nuts, chopped

Preheat oven to 350 degrees. Grease a loaf pan. Combine all ingredients and mix well. Pour batter into pan. Bake for 1 hour.

Pumpkin Bread

(gluten, milk & wheat free)

- 1 cup pumpkin
- 1 tablespoon minute tapioca
- 2 eggs
- 2 tablespoons potato flour
- 3 tablespoons cornstarch
- 1 cup brown rice flour
- ¾ cup rice flour
- 1 tablespoon baking powder
- ¾ teaspoon baking soda
- 1 teaspoon cinnamon
- ½ teaspoon salt
- ½ teaspoon nutmeg
- ⅓ cup shortening
- ⅓ cup sugar
- ½ cup nuts, chopped (optional)

Grease a 9 x 5 x 3-inch loaf pan or three 5 x 3-inch pans. Combine pumpkin, tapioca and eggs. Set mixture aside until tapioca softens, about 15 minutes.

Meanwhile, place potato flour and cornstarch in a 1-cup measure. Add brown rice flour to fill measuring cup level. In a separate bowl combine potato flour mixture with rice flour, baking powder, baking soda, cinnamon, salt and nutmeg. In a separate bowl cream shortening and sugar.

Preheat oven to 350 degrees. Add pumpkin-tapioca mixture to shortening mixture, beating well. Stir flour mixture into shortening mixture. Fold in nuts. Pour batter into pan. Bake small loaves 40–45 minutes or large loaf for 1 hour. Let cool 20 minutes in pan. Remove and cool on rack. Cool completely before cutting.

Pineapple Bread

(wheat free)

- 2 cups unsweetened coconut, shredded
- 1 cup crushed pineapple with juice
- 4 large eggs
- 1½ cups brown sugar
- 4 cups millet flour, finely ground
- 2 teaspoons baking soda
- 1 teaspoon salt

Grease two 9 x 5-inch loaf pans. Combine coconut and pineapple. Stir in eggs, beating until light. Add sugar, flour, baking soda and salt. Mix until all lumps are removed. Let sit 15–30 minutes.

Preheat oven to 325 degrees. Stir batter and pour into pans. Bake for 1 hour. Cool slightly before removing from pans.

Oatmeal Bread

(yeast free)

- 1½ tablespoons baking powder
- 1½ cups oats
- 3 cups flour
- 1½ teaspoons salt
- ¼ cup honey
- 1 cup milk
- 1 egg
- 1 tablespoon oil

Preheat oven to 350 degrees. Grease loaf pan. Combine baking powder, oats, flour and salt. In a separate bowl combine honey, milk, egg and oil. Pour honey mixture into flour mixture and stir until moist. Spoon batter into pan. Bake until top is crusty brown, about 60 minutes. Remove from bread pan and brush top with butter. Let cool.

Raisin Oatmeal Bread

(egg, fat & yeast free)

- 1⅓ cups buttermilk
- ¼ cup molasses
- ¼ cup sugar
- 1 cup oats
- 1 cup rye or whole wheat flour
- 1 cup all-purpose flour
- 1 teaspoon salt
- 1 teaspoon baking powder
- 1 teaspoon baking soda
- 1 cup raisins
- ½ cup walnuts, chopped (optional)

Grease 9 x 5-inch loaf pan. Combine all ingredients and beat until smooth. Pour into pan. Let stand at room temperature for 20 minutes.

Preheat oven to 350 degrees. Bake for 1 hour. Cool and turn bread out of pan.

Buttermilk Soybean Bread

(wheat & yeast free)

- 1 egg, beaten
- 1 tablespoon oil
- 1 cup buttermilk
- ½ teaspoon baking soda
- ¼ teaspoon salt
- 1 cup soybean flour

Preheat oven to 350 degrees. Grease loaf pan well. Combine egg, oil and buttermilk. Stir in baking soda, salt and flour. Mix well. Spoon into pan. Bake for about 1 hour. Serve while hot.

Brown Bread

(fat & yeast free)

- 2 cups all-purpose flour
- 1 cup whole wheat flour
- 1 cup unprocessed bran
- 1 cup oats
- 2 tablespoons sesame seeds
- 2 tablespoons poppy seeds
- 1 tablespoon baking powder
- 1½ teaspoons baking soda
- ¼ cup honey
- 2 cups nonfat plain yogurt

Preheat oven to 375 degrees. Spray 9 x 5-inch loaf pan with vegetable oil spray. In a large bowl combine flours, bran, oats, sesame seeds, poppy seeds, baking powder and baking soda. Stir in honey. Add enough yogurt to make a sticky dough. Knead lightly in bowl until dough is well blended. Place dough in pan. Bake for 40 minutes.

Buttermilk Brown Bread

(fat & yeast free)

- 1½ cups all-purpose flour
- 1½ cups rye flour
- 1 cup yellow cornmeal
- 1 teaspoon baking soda
- 1 teaspoon baking powder
- 1 teaspoon salt
- ½ cup raisins
- ½ cup molasses
- 2 cups buttermilk
- ½ cup nuts, chopped (optional)

Preheat oven to 375 degrees. Spray a 9 x 5-inch loaf pan with vegetable oil spray. In a large bowl combine flours, corn meal, baking soda, baking powder and salt. Stir in molasses. Add enough buttermilk to make a sticky dough. Knead lightly in bowl until dough is well blended. Place dough in prepared pan. Bake for 40 minutes.

Sandwich Bread

(gluten, wheat & yeast free)

- 2 teaspoons gelatin
- 2/3 cup warm water
- 2½ cups rice flour, brown or white
- 4 tablespoons potato flour
- 2 tablespoons baking powder
- ½ cup cornstarch
- ¾ teaspoon salt
- 1 tablespoon sugar
- 3 tablespoons margarine, melted
- 1 cup milk
- 2 eggs, well beaten

Grease three 5 x 3-inch loaf pans or 1 large loaf pan. Combine gelatin and warm water. Let stand five minutes.

Preheat oven to 375 degrees. In a separate bowl combine flours, baking powder, cornstarch, salt and sugar. Make a well in the center. In a separate bowl combine margarine, milk, gelatin mixture and eggs. Pour margarine mixture into the well and mix well. Bake for 10 minutes. Reduce oven temperature to 350 degrees and bake small loaves about 30 minutes or a large loaf about 40 minutes. Let bread sit in pan for 5 minutes to cool, then remove to rack to finish cooling.

Variations:

1. Vary bread by using soya, oats, oat bran, or a flour of your choice. Use them sparingly until you are familiar with the strong flavor and slightly heavier texture. Start by substituting ¼ cup soya or other grains for ¼ cup brown rice flour.

2. Chopped fruits or nuts may be added.

Oatmeal & Rye Bread

(yeast free)

- 2 cups oats
- 3 cups buttermilk
- ⅔ cups brown sugar
- 2¼ cups rye flour
- 1 teaspoon salt
- 2 teaspoons baking soda
- 1 teaspoon baking powder

Grease 9 x 5-inch loaf pan. Combine oats and buttermilk. Let stand 15 minutes.

Preheat oven to 325 degrees. Stir brown sugar into oat mixture. In a separate bowl combine flour, salt, baking soda and baking powder. Combine flour mixture with buttermilk mixture, mixing well. Spoon batter into pan. Bake for 30 minutes. Reduce oven temperature to 300 degrees and continue baking until bread tests done with a toothpick, about 1 hour. Cool in pan 10 minutes. Turn out on rack to finish cooling. Cool before slicing bread.

Buttermilk Rye Bread

(egg, wheat & yeast free)

- 1 teaspoon baking soda
- 1½ cups buttermilk
- ¼ cup molasses
- 3 cups rye flour
- 2 teaspoons baking powder
- 1 teaspoon salt
- ½ cup raisins or dates, chopped
- ¼ teaspoon anise or caraway seeds, or both
- 2 tablespoons margarine, melted, or oil

Preheat oven to 350 degrees. Grease loaf pan. Combine baking soda, buttermilk and molasses. Add flour, baking powder, salt and raisins; mix well. Add margarine, stirring until smooth. Pour into pan, smoothing the batter. Bake 45–55 minutes. Cut sides of bread away from pan and cool on rack.

Soybean Buttermilk Cornbread

- 2 cups cornmeal
- ¼ cup soybean flour
- 1 cup all-purpose flour
- ½ teaspoon salt
- ¼ cup sugar
- 1 egg
- 3 tablespoons oil
- ½ teaspoon baking soda
- 1 teaspoon baking powder
- 1¼ cups buttermilk

Preheat oven to 400 degrees. Grease a 9 x 13 x 2-inch baking dish or pan. Combine cornmeal, flours, salt and sugar. In a separate bowl combine egg, oil, baking soda, baking powder and buttermilk. Add egg mixture to cornmeal mixture, stirring just enough to moisten. Pour into pan. Bake for 30 minutes.

June's Buttermilk Cornbread

- 1 cup unbleached flour
- 1 cup cornmeal
- ¼ cup sugar
- 2½ teaspoons baking powder
- ½ teaspoon baking soda
- ½ teaspoon salt
- 1 cup buttermilk
- 1 egg
- ¼ cup oil or corn margarine, melted

Preheat oven to 400 degrees. Grease 8-inch square baking pan. Combine flour, cornmeal, sugar, baking powder, baking soda and salt. In a separate bowl combine buttermilk, egg and oil. Stir buttermilk mixture into flour mixture, mixing just enough to moisten. Pour into pan. Bake 20–25 minutes.

Variations:

1. Low fat: Omit oil.
2. Fat free: Omit oil and replace egg with 2 egg whites.
3. Substitute unbleached flour with whole wheat flour.
4. Substitute 3 tablespoons honey for sugar.
5. Egg substitute can replace the egg or egg whites.

Blueberry Rice Bread

(wheat free)

- 2 large eggs
- ¾ cup vanilla or plain yogurt
- ½ cup honey
- 2½ cups brown rice flour
- 2 teaspoons baking soda
- 1 cup blueberries

Grease 2 small loaf pans. Combine eggs, yogurt and honey, blending until smooth. Stir in flour and baking soda. Fold in blueberries. Pour batter into loaf pans and place in cold oven. Set oven temperature to 350 degrees. Bake for 40–45 minutes. Let bread sit in pans for 5 minutes. Then turn out on rack to finish cooling.

Notes:

Muffins

Hot muffins can turn the simplest meal into a delight; the wonderful aroma of muffins can pick up even the dullest of appetites.

Muffins made with whole wheat flour or whole grains and sweetened and flavored with fruit and honey are not only nutritious, but quick to make.

The perfect muffin is moist, light and tender. You can accomplish this by combining the dry ingredients together then adding the mixed liquid to the dry. Most important is not to overmix, which makes the muffins tough, causes tunnels to form throughout the dough, and decreases the volume as the muffin bakes.

When mixing, mix gently and quickly for no more than 15 seconds. Don't worry about the lumps. Fold in chopped fruits, seeds or nuts to the batter during the last few strokes.

Spray muffin tins with a no-cholesterol pan coating or line with paper baking cups; fill two-thirds full. Bake in a hot oven (400 degrees) about 20 minutes. If oven is not hot enough, muffins will not rise properly.

After baking, let muffins set for about 5 minutes before removing from the tins. Best eaten warm.

Buttermilk Muffins with Raspberry Filling

- 3½ cups flour
- ¼ cup sugar
- 2 teaspoons baking powder
- ½ teaspoon baking soda
- 1½ teaspoons salt, optional
- 1½ cups buttermilk
- 2 eggs, beaten
- ½ cup oil
- Raspberry jam or jelly

Topping:

- ¼ cup sugar
- 1 teaspoon cinnamon

Preheat oven to 375 to 400 degrees. Grease muffin tins. Combine flour, sugar, baking powder, baking soda and salt. In separate bowl combine buttermilk, eggs and oil; add all at once to flour mixture. Stir until just moistened. Fill muffin tins three-quarters full. Top each with 1 teaspoon of raspberry jam, pushing down toward center of batter slightly. Combine sugar and cinnamon for topping and sprinkle over muffins before baking. Bake for 20 minutes.

Variation: Can also fill muffin tins less then half full, drop a teaspoon of jam into center, and spoon remaining batter on top.

Buttermilk Bran Muffins

(low fat)

- 1½ cups buttermilk
- ⅓ cup honey
- 2 tablespoons oil
- 1 egg or 2 egg whites
- 1½ cups whole wheat flour
- 2½ cups bran
- 2 teaspoons baking powder
- ½ teaspoon baking soda
- ½ cup nuts, chopped, raisins, sunflower seeds, or sesame seeds, optional

Preheat oven to 375 degrees. Grease muffin tins. Combine buttermilk, honey, oil and egg. In a separate bowl combine whole wheat flour, bran, baking powder, baking soda, and nuts. Stir all ingredients together until just moistened. Bake for 20 minutes.

Variation: A combination of wheat bran, wheat germ or oat bran can be used for bran.

Buttermilk Whole Wheat Muffins

(low fat)

- 1 cup all-purpose flour
- 1 cup whole wheat flour
- 2 teaspoons baking powder
- ½ teaspoon baking soda
- ½ teaspoon salt
- 1 cup buttermilk
- 2 tablespoons oil
- 4 tablespoons honey or brown sugar
- ¼ cup egg substitute

Preheat oven to 375 degrees. Grease muffin tins. Combine flours, baking powder, baking soda and salt; set aside. In a separate bowl combine buttermilk, oil, honey, and egg substitute. Add to flour mixture, stirring until just combined. Fill muffin tins three-quarters full. Bake for 20 minutes.

Poppy Seed Muffins

- ½ cup margarine, softened
- ¾ cup sugar
- 2 eggs
- ¾ cup sour cream
- 1½ teaspoons vanilla
- 2 cups flour
- ¼ cup poppy seeds
- ½ teaspoon salt
- ¼ teaspoon baking soda
- 1 teaspoon baking powder

Preheat oven to 375 degrees. Grease muffin tins. Cream butter and sugar until thick and light. Beat in eggs one at a time. Blend in sour cream and vanilla. In a separate bowl combine flour, poppy seeds, salt, baking soda and baking powder. Gradually combine flour mixture with sour cream mixture. Lightly spoon batter into muffin tins. Bake for 20 minutes.

Variation: To reduce fat, replace sour cream with ½ cup buttermilk.

Poppy Seed Muffins
(fat free)

- 1 cup whole wheat flour
- ½ cup oat flour
- 1/3 cup brown sugar
- 1 teaspoon baking soda
- ¼ teaspoon salt
- ¾ cup fat free yogurt, sour cream, or buttermilk
- 1 teaspoon vanilla or lemon extract
- 2 egg whites
- 2 tablespoons poppy seeds

Preheat oven to 375 degrees. Grease muffin tins. Combine flours, brown sugar, salt and baking soda. Add yogurt, sour cream or buttermilk, vanilla or lemon extract, and egg whites. Stir until just moistened. Stir in poppy seeds. Fill muffin tins three-quarters full. Bake for about 15 minutes. Let muffins sit for 5 minutes before removing from pan.

Lemon Poppy Seed Muffins
(no cholesterol)

- ¾ cup oil
- 1 1/3 cups brown sugar
- ¼ cup lemon juice
- ½ tablespoon vanilla
- 2 to 2½ cups buttermilk
- ½ cup egg whites
- 1½ to 2 cups whole wheat flour
- ¾ cup oatmeal
- ¾ cup oat bran
- 3 tablespoons poppy seeds
- ¾ teaspoon baking soda
- ¾ teaspoon baking powder
- ¾ teaspoon salt

Frosting, optional:

- 1 cup powdered sugar
- 1 tablespoon lemon juice

Cream oil, brown sugar, lemon juice, and vanilla, mixing well until thick. Add buttermilk, egg whites, whole wheat flour, oatmeal, oat bran, poppy seeds, baking soda and baking powder, mixing well. Let sit for 30 minutes or put into refrigerator (will last up to 4 days).

Preheat oven to 350 degrees. Line muffin tins with cupcake papers or grease well. Scoop batter into muffin tins. Bake for 20 minutes.

To make frosting, combine powdered sugar and lemon juice, adding enough water for desired consistency. Brush or drizzle on top of warm muffins.

Cocoa Apple Muffins

(fat free)

- 2 cups applesauce
- 1 cup honey
- ¾ cup warm water
- 3 tablespoons nonfat powdered milk
- 1 teaspoon vanilla
- 1 cup cocoa
- ½ cup egg whites
- 2 cups whole wheat flour
- 1 cup all-purpose flour
- 1⅓ cups oats
- 3 tablespoons oat bran
- ¾ tablespoon baking soda
- ½ tablespoon baking powder
- ½ tablespoon cinnamon
- ½ cup nuts, chopped (optional)

Topping:

- 1 cup brown sugar
- ¼ cup cocoa
- ¼ cup oatmeal
- ¾ teaspoon cinnamon
- ¼ cup nuts, chopped (optional)

Preheat oven to 350 degrees. Combine applesauce, honey, water, milk, vanilla, and cocoa. Mix in egg whites. Add flours, oats, oat bran, baking soda, baking powder, cinnamon and nuts; mix until well combined. Batter will last up to 4 days in refrigerator.

To make topping, combine brown sugar, cocoa, oatmeal, cinnamon, and chopped nuts. Spread over muffins before baking. Bake for 25 minutes.

Black Bottom Muffins

(low fat)

2 cups all-purpose flour
1/3 cup whole wheat flour
1½ cups sugar
1½ teaspoons baking soda
¾ teaspoon salt
1/3 cup cocoa
1½ cups water
½ cup oil
2 tablespoons vinegar
1½ teaspoons vanilla

Topping:

8 ounces cream cheese, softened
1/3 cup sugar
1 egg
¾ cup chocolate chips

Preheat oven to 350 degrees. Combine flours, sugar, baking soda, salt and cocoa. In a separate bowl combine water, oil, vinegar and vanilla. Add oil mixture to flour mixture, stirring to mix well. Batter will last up to 4 days in refrigerator.

To make topping, combine cream cheese, sugar, egg, and chocolate chips until fluffy. Scoop muffin mix into cupcake paper lined or greased muffin tins, filling three-quarters full. Add a tablespoon of topping to each muffin, pressing down into batter slightly. Bake for 25 minutes.

Variation: For lower fat, combine 8 ounces nonfat sour cream or 8 ounces nonfat cream cheese, 1/3 cup sugar, ¼ cup egg substitute, and ¾ cup lower fat chocolate chips.

Notes:

Old fashioned Cranberry Muffins

¼ cup margarine, softened or oil
⅓ cup sugar
¾ cup buttermilk
1 egg
¾ teaspoon vanilla
¾ teaspoon nutmeg
⅓ teaspoon baking soda
1½ teaspoons baking powder
1½ cups flour
1 cup cranberries

Preheat oven to 350 degrees. Grease or line muffin tins with cupcake papers. Cream margarine, sugar, butter milk, egg and vanilla. Add nutmeg, baking powder, baking soda, flour, and cranberries, stirring just to moisten. Do not over mix. Bake for 20–25 minutes. Let muffins sit in tins for 10 minutes before removing to cool on racks.

Variations:

1. ***Blueberry Muffins:*** Decrease sugar to ¼ cup. Substitute 1 cup blueberries for cranberries.
2. After baking, brush tops of muffins with ¾ tablespoon orange juice combined with ¾ cup sugar.

Blueberry & Cranberry Bran Muffins

1 cup flour
⅓ cup oatmeal
⅓ cup oat bran
⅓ cup wheat germ
1 teaspoon baking soda
2 teaspoons baking powder
¾ cup brown sugar
¼ teaspoon salt
1 cup buttermilk
1 egg
¼ cup oil
1 cup blueberries
½ cup cranberries

Preheat oven to 350 degrees. Grease muffin tins. Combine flour, oatmeal, oat bran, wheat germ, baking soda, baking powder, brown sugar, and salt. In a separate bowl combine buttermilk, egg and oil. Add buttermilk mixture to flour mixture and stir until just moistened. Fold in blueberries and cranberries. Do not over mix. Bake for 20–25 minutes.

Blueberry, Cranberry & Yogurt Muffins
(fat free)

- ¾ cup oat bran
- 1¼ cups whole wheat flour
- 1 teaspoon baking soda
- 2 teaspoons baking powder
- ¼ cup honey
- ¾ cup fat free yogurt
- ½ teaspoon lemon peel, grated
- 1 teaspoon vanilla
- ¾ cup blueberries, fresh or frozen

Glaze:

- 1 tablespoon orange juice
- 1 tablespoon lemon juice
- ½ cup powdered sugar
- Couple drops of water, Optional

Preheat oven to 350 degrees. Grease muffin tins. Combine oat bran, whole wheat flour, baking soda, and baking powder. In a separate bowl combine honey, yogurt, lemon peel, vanilla and blueberries. Add honey mixture to oat bran mixture, stirring until just moistened. Do not over mix. Bake for 20–25 minutes. Allow to sit for 5 minutes before removing from pan.

For glaze, combine orange juice, lemon juice, and powdered sugar. Brush on top of warm muffins.

100% Oat Bran Blueberry Muffins
(fat & sugar free)

These muffins are not only healthy for you but delicious too, although they tend to be on the crumbly side.

- 2¼ cup oat bran
- ¼ teaspoon nutmeg or cinnamon
- 1 tablespoon baking powder
- 1 cup unsweetened banana or applesauce
- ⅓ cup skim milk
- 2 egg whites
- ¾ cups blueberries

Preheat oven to 375 degrees. Spray muffin tins with vegetable oil spray. Combine oat bran, nutmeg or cinnamon, and baking powder. Add banana or applesauce, skim milk and egg whites, and mix well. Stir in blueberries. Fill muffin tins three-quarters full. Bake for 20 minutes. Yield: 10–12 medium-sized muffins.

Variation: Chopped dates, dry fruits or raisins can be added to blueberries to make ¾ cup.

Blueberry Muffins
(fat & sugar free)

- 1 cup whole wheat flour
- 1½ cups all-purpose flour
- 2 cups oatmeal
- 1 teaspoon baking soda
- 1 tablespoon baking powder
- 1 teaspoon orange peel, grated
- ¼ teaspoon nutmeg
- ½ cup unsweetened applesauce
- 1 cup apple juice concentrate
- ½ cup egg whites
- 1 cup buttermilk
- 1 teaspoon vanilla
- 1½ cups blueberries
- ½ cup nuts, chopped
- ½ teaspoon cinnamon

Preheat oven to 375 degrees. Grease muffin tins. Combine flours, oatmeal, baking soda, baking powder, orange peel, and nutmeg. In a separate bowl combine applesauce, egg whites, buttermilk and vanilla. Stir applesauce mixture into flour mixture. Fold in blueberries and stir just to moisten. Do not over mix. Fill muffin tins three-quarters full. Sprinkle chopped nuts and cinnamon on top before baking. Bake for about 20 minutes.

Blueberry Muffins
(sugar free)

- ¼ cup oil
- 1 cup apple juice
- ½ cup apple juice concentrate
- ⅔ cup egg whites
- 1⅓ cups oatmeal
- ⅓ cup oat bran
- 1⅓ cups whole wheat flour
- 1¾ tablespoons baking powder
- ½ teaspoon cinnamon
- ⅛ teaspoon nutmeg
- 1 cup blueberries

Preheat oven to 350 degrees. Grease muffin tins. Combine oil, apple juice and apple juice concentrate, mixing well. Stir in egg whites and mix lightly. Add oatmeal, oat bran, whole wheat flour, baking powder, cinnamon, nutmeg and blueberries, mixing lightly. Sprinkle oat bran or oatmeal on top of muffins before baking. Bake for 20 minutes.

Original Blueberry Muffins

- 2 cups flour
- ¼ cup sugar
- 2 tablespoons baking powder
- ½ teaspoon baking soda
- ½ teaspoon salt
- ¼ cup melted margarine, shortening or oil
- 1 egg, beaten
- 1 cup buttermilk
- 1 cup blueberries

Preheat oven to 400 degrees. Grease or line muffin tins with cupcake liners. Combine flour, sugar, baking powder, baking soda, and salt. In a separate bowl combine margarine, egg and buttermilk. Stir margarine mixture into flour mixture, stirring just to moisten. Fold in blueberries. Bake for 25 minutes.

Page 52 – Blueberry Muffins

2 teaspoons baking powder, not 2 tablespoons

Page 55 – Berry Bran Muffins

Add 1 tablespoon baking powder

Blueberry Muffins

(fat free)

- 2 cups flour
- ½ cup sugar
- 1 tablespoon baking powder
- ½ teaspoon salt
- ½ teaspoon cinnamon
- ½ cup egg substitute or 4 egg whites
- 1¼ cups fat free sour cream or yogurt
- ¼ cup honey
- ½ cup blueberries
- 1 cup Grape Nuts cereal

Preheat oven to 375 degrees. Grease muffin tins. Combine flour, sugar, baking powder, salt and cinnamon. Beat together in a separate bowl egg substitute, sour cream and honey, mixing until blended. Stir into flour mixture, stirring just to moisten. Fold in blueberries and cereal. Bake for about 25 minutes.

'Good Morning' Muffins

(low fat & no cholesterol)

- 1 cup crushed pineapple in juice (undrained)
- ½ cup carrots or apples, shredded
- ½ cup buttermilk
- ⅓ cup oil
- 2 egg whites or 1 egg
- 1 cup oatmeal
- 1 cup all-purpose flour
- ½ cup whole wheat flour
- ½ cup brown sugar
- 1 tablespoon baking powder
- ½ teaspoon baking soda
- ½ teaspoon salt, optional
- 1 teaspoon cinnamon
- ⅓ cup raisins, dates, or currants

Glaze:

- 2 tablespoons buttermilk
- ½ cup powdered sugar

Preheat oven to 375 to 400 degrees. Grease or line muffin tins with cupcake papers. Combine pineapple with juice, shredded carrots, buttermilk, oil, and egg whites. In a separate bowl combine oatmeal, flours, brown sugar, baking powder, baking soda, salt, cinnamon, raisins. Add pineapple mixture with oatmeal mixture all at once and stir until just moistened. Fill muffin tins three-quarters full. Bake for 20–25 minutes. Let muffins cool for 5 minutes in tins before removing to finish cooling. To make glaze, combine buttermilk and powdered sugar. Drizzle glaze over muffins.

Nature's Complete Muffin

(no cholesterol & low fat)

- 1 banana, mashed
- 1/3 cup honey
- 1/3 cup oil
- ½ cup applesauce or apples, finely diced
- ¾ cup chopped carrots
- 2½ tablespoons buttermilk
- ¾ teaspoon vanilla
- 1½ tablespoons nonfat powdered milk
- ¼ cup egg whites or 2 eggs
- ½ teaspoon orange peel or lemon peel, grated
- 1½ to 1¾ cup whole wheat flour
- 1/3 cup oat bran
- 2 teaspoons baking powder
- 1½ teaspoons baking soda
- 1 teaspoon cinnamon, optional

Combine banana, honey, oil, carrots, buttermilk, vanilla, powdered milk, egg whites, and orange peel, mixing well. Add flour, oat bran, baking powder, baking soda, and cinnamon, mixing lightly. Let batter sit for at least 1 hour or overnight.

Preheat oven to 350 degrees. Grease muffin tins. Bake for about 20–25 minutes.

Dried Fruit Bran Muffins

- 1 cup whole wheat flour
- ½ cup all-purpose flour
- ½ cup bran flakes
- 1 teaspoon baking soda
- ½ teaspoon baking powder
- ¼ teaspoon salt
- ½ to ¾ cup chopped dried apples apricots, bananas, cherries, dates, prunes, pineapple, or raisins
- ⅓ cup nuts, chopped
- 1 egg, beaten
- 1¼ cup buttermilk
- ½ cup honey
- ¼ cup margarine, melted

Preheat oven to 350 degrees. Grease muffin tins or line with cupcake papers. Combine flours and bran flakes. Stir in baking soda, baking powder, and salt. Fold in dried fruit and nuts. Mix to coat well with flour mixture. Set aside. In a separate bowl mix or combine egg, buttermilk, honey and margarine. Stir egg mixture into flour mixture, stirring until moistened. Fill muffin tins three-quarters full. Bake for 20–25 minutes.

Berry Bran Muffins

- 1 cup flour
- 1 cup unprocessed wheat bran
- ¼ cup sugar
- 1 teaspoon salt
- 1 egg, beaten
- ¼ cup oil
- 1 cup 2% milk
- 1 cup raspberries, fresh or frozen (partially thaw berries)

Preheat oven to 400 degrees. Spray muffin tins with vegetable oil spray or line with cupcake papers. Combine flour, wheat bran, sugar, baking powder and salt; make a well in center. In a separate bowl combine egg, oil and milk. Pour egg mixture into well and stir until just moistened. Fold in raspberries. Fill muffin tins two-thirds full. Bake for about 20 minutes. Remove and cool on rack.

Oat Bran Muffins

(no cholesterol & low fat)

This recipe contains 100% oat bran making it really high in soluble fiber. Soluble fiber is the substance that appears to reduce cholesterol.

- 2¼ cups oat bran
- ½ cup dried fruit, diced
- 1 teaspoon cinnamon
- ½ teaspoon baking soda
- ½ teaspoon baking powder
- ¼ teaspoon salt
- 2 egg whites
- 1 cup unsweetened applesauce
- ½ cup brown sugar
- ½ cup buttermilk
- 2 tablespoons oil

Preheat oven to 350 degrees. Spray muffin tins with vegetable oil spray. Combine oat bran, dried fruit, cinnamon, baking soda, baking powder and salt. In a separate bowl mix egg whites, applesauce, brown sugar, buttermilk, and oil. Add egg mixture to oat bran mixture, stirring until just combined. Fill muffin tins half full. Bake for 30–35 minutes. Cool on wire rack.

Note: Because oat bran does not contain gluten, these muffins won't have the same texture as regular muffins.

Apple Pumpkin Muffins

2 cups flour
2 teaspoons baking powder
1 teaspoon baking soda
1 teaspoon cinnamon
1 teaspoon allspice
¼ teaspoon nutmeg
¼ teaspoon ground cloves
¾ cup brown sugar
2 eggs
¼ cup margarine or oil
1 cup pumpkin
½ cup buttermilk
½ cup raisins
¾ cup apples, chopped

Streusel Topping:

2 tablespoons flour
¼ cup brown sugar
½ teaspoon cinnamon

Preheat oven to 400 degrees. Grease muffin pans. Sift together flour, baking powder, baking soda, cinnamon, allspice, nutmeg and ground cloves. In a large bowl beat together brown sugar, eggs and margarine until light and fluffy. Add flour mixture, raisins and apples, stirring just enough to moisten flour mixture. Spoon into muffin pans.

To make Streusel Topping, combine flour, brown sugar and cinnamon. Sprinkle on top of muffins before baking. Bake for about 18 minutes.

Pumpkin Bran Muffins

(fat & milk free)

- 2 cups pumpkin
- ¾ cup water
- ¾ cup honey
- ½ teaspoon salt
- 2 teaspoons cinnamon
- ½ teaspoon nutmeg
- ½ cup egg whites
- 2 cups all-purpose flour
- 1 cup whole wheat flour
- ¼ to 2 tablespoons oat bran or meal
- 2 teaspoons baking soda
- ½ cup raisins, optional

Topping:

- ½ cup nuts, finely chopped
- ½ teaspoon cinnamon

Combine pumpkin, water, honey, salt, cinnamon, nutmeg and egg whites, mixing well. In a separate bowl combine flours, oat bran, baking soda and raisins. Combine flour mixture with pumpkin mixture, mixing lightly. Do not over mix. Place mixture in a cool place for at least 1 hour.

Preheat oven to 350 degrees. Combine nuts and cinnamon to make topping; sprinkle on top of muffins. Bake for 20 minutes.

Variations:

1. Honey can be replaced by 1 cup sugar.

2. For sugar free muffins, substitute 1½ cups apple concentrate for honey and water.

3. Use spelt flour for wheat free muffins.

Pumpkin Muffins

(original)

- ¾ cup brown sugar
- 2 cups flour
- 1 tablespoon baking powder
- ½ teaspoon baking soda
- 3 teaspoons pumpkin pie spice
- 1 teaspoon cinnamon
- ½ cup nuts, chopped
- ½ cup raisins, optional
- ¼ cup oil or margarine, melted
- 2 eggs
- ½ cup buttermilk
- 1 cup pumpkin

Streusel Topping:

- 1 tablespoon margarine, melted
- 2 tablespoons brown sugar
- ½ cup oatmeal
- ¼ teaspoon cinnamon
- ¼ cup nuts, chopped (optional)

Preheat oven to 375 degrees. Grease muffin tins. Combine sugar, flour, baking powder, baking soda, pumpkin pie spice, cinnamon, nuts and raisins. In a separate bowl, combine oil, eggs, buttermilk and pumpkin. Add oil mixture to sugar mixture, stirring until just combined. Fill muffin tins three-quarters full.

For Streusel Topping, combine margarine, brown sugar, oatmeal, cinnamon, and nuts. Sprinkle on topping before baking. Bake for about 25 minutes.

Variations:

1. For less fat, omit margarine in the Streusel Topping.
2. Cooled muffins may be lightly frosted.

Pumpkin Muffins

(fat & sugar free)

- 1 cup pumpkin
- ¾ cup apple juice concentrate
- ½ teaspoon vanilla
- ⅓ cup buttermilk (or liquid of your choice)
- 2 egg whites
- ¾ cup whole wheat flour
- 1 cup all-purpose flour
- 1½ teaspoons baking powder
- ½ teaspoon baking soda
- 1 teaspoon cinnamon
- ½ teaspoon nutmeg
- 1 cup raisins, optional

Preheat oven to 375 degrees. Grease muffin tins. Combine pumpkin, apple juice concentrate, vanilla, buttermilk and egg whites. In a separate bowl combine flours, baking powder, baking soda, cinnamon, nutmeg and raisins. Add flour mixture to pumpkin mixture, stirring just until combined. Bake for 20 minutes.

Pumpkin Muffins

(low fat)

- ½ cup brown sugar
- ¼ cup granulated sugar
- 1½ cups flour
- 1 teaspoon baking powder
- ½ teaspoon baking soda
- 1 teaspoon pumpkin pie spice
- 1 teaspoon cinnamon
- ⅓ cup nuts, optional
- ¾ cup pumpkin
- 2 tablespoons oil
- 2 tablespoons buttermilk
- 1 egg plus two egg whites
- 1 teaspoon vanilla

Preheat oven to 375 degrees. Grease muffin tins. Combine brown sugar, granulated sugar, flour, baking powder, baking soda, pumpkin pie spice, cinnamon and nuts. In a separate bowl combine pumpkin, oil, buttermilk, egg whites and vanilla. Add pumpkin mixture to sugar mixture, stirring until just combined. Fill muffin tins three-quarters full. Bake for about 15 minutes.

Pumpkin Muffins

(fat free)

- 1¾ cups whole wheat flour
- ½ cup oat bran
- ½ cup brown sugar
- 1 tablespoon baking powder
- 1 teaspoon pumpkin pie spice
- ⅔ cup pumpkin
- 1 cup skim milk
- 2 egg whites
- 1 teaspoon vanilla

Preheat oven to 350 degrees. Grease muffin tins. Combine flour, oat bran, brown sugar, baking powder and pumpkin pie spice. In a separate bowl combine pumpkin, skim milk, egg whites, and vanilla. Add pumpkin mixture to flour mixture, stirring until just combined. Spoon batter into muffin tins. Bake for about 25 minutes. Allow to sit in tins for 5 minutes before removing.

Pumpkin Muffins

(egg, milk & wheat free)

- 1 cup pumpkin
- ⅓ cup oil
- ⅓ cup honey
- ½ cup raisins
- 1 cup all-purpose flour
- 1½ cups whole wheat flour
- 3 tablespoons oatmeal or oat bran
- ¼ teaspoon salt
- ¾ teaspoon cinnamon
- 1½ teaspoons baking soda

Topping, optional:

- ½ teaspoon cinnamon
- ½ cup nuts, chopped

Preheat oven to 350 degrees. Grease muffin tins. Combine pumpkin, oil, honey and raisins. Add flours, oatmeal, salt, cinnamon and baking soda, mixing until just combined. Spoon batter into muffin tins. To make topping, combine cinnamon and nuts. Sprinkle topping over muffins in tins. Bake for 20–25 minutes.

Variations:

1. ***Fat free:*** Substitute water for oil.
2. ***Sugar free:*** Substitute apple juice concentrate for honey.
3. ***Wheat free:*** Substitute spelt flour for all-purpose and whole wheat flours.

Apple Muffins
(low fat)

- 2 cups flour
- 1/3 cup brown sugar
- 1 teaspoon baking powder
- ½ teaspoon baking soda
- ½ teaspoon cinnamon
- ¼ teaspoon salt
- ¾ cups plus 2 tablespoons buttermilk
- 2 tablespoons oil
- 1 teaspoon vanilla
- 1 egg
- 1½ cups apple, peeled and shredded

Preheat oven to 375 degrees. Spray muffin pans with cooking spray. Combine flour, brown sugar, baking powder, baking soda, cinnamon, and salt. Make a well in the center of mixture. In a separate bowl combine buttermilk, oil, vanilla and egg. Pour buttermilk mixture into well in flour mixture. Stir until ingredients just moistened. Fold in shredded apple. Spoon batter into muffin tins. Bake for 25 minutes.

Fresh Fruit Oat Muffins

- 2 cups whole wheat flour
- 1 cup rolled oats
- ½ cup wheat bran
- 1/3 cup brown sugar
- 1½ teaspoons baking soda
- 1 teaspoon salt
- 2 eggs
- 1½ cup buttermilk
- ¼ cup oil
- 2 cups peaches, finely chopped, or 2 cups pears, plums or apples
- 1 tablespoon orange juice

Preheat oven to 375 degrees. Grease muffin tins. Combine all ingredients, blending but not over mixing. Spoon batter into muffin tins. Bake for 20 minutes.

Applesauce Oatmeal Muffins

(no cholesterol, low fat)

- 1½ cups oats
- 1¼ cups flour
- ¾ teaspoon cinnamon
- 1 tablespoon baking powder
- ¾ teaspoon baking soda
- ½ cup brown sugar
- 1 cup applesauce
- ½ cup buttermilk
- 3 tablespoons oil
- 1 egg white

Preheat oven to 375 degrees. Spray muffin tins with vegetable oil spray or line with cupcake papers. Combine oats, flour, cinnamon, baking powder, baking soda and brown sugar. Mix together in a separate bowl applesauce, buttermilk, oil and egg white. Stir into dry ingredients, mixing only until ingredients are moistened. Fill muffin cups almost full. Bake for about 20 minutes.

Whole Wheat Apple Muffins

(egg & fat free)

- 2¼ cups whole wheat flour
- 1½ teaspoons baking soda
- ⅓ cup brown sugar or ¼ cup molasses
- ¾ cup buttermilk
- 1 teaspoon vanilla
- 1½ cups apples, chopped
- ½ cup dates, apricots or raisins, chopped

Preheat oven to 350 degrees. Grease muffin tins. Combine whole wheat flour, baking soda and brown sugar. Add buttermilk, vanilla, apples and dates. Stir to mix well. Spoon batter into muffin tins. Bake for 15–20 minutes.

Whole Wheat Apple Bran Muffins

(egg, fat and sugar free)

- 1½ cups buttermilk, or 1½ cups nonfat milk plus 1 tablespoon vinegar
- 1 cup wheat bran
- 1 cup oatmeal
- 1 cup whole wheat flour
- 1 teaspoon baking soda
- 1 teaspoon baking powder
- 1½ cups apple, chopped
- 1 teaspoon cinnamon
- 1 teaspoon orange peel grated

Combine buttermilk, wheat bran and oatmeal. Soak for 1 hour.

Preheat oven to 400 degrees. Grease muffin tins. Stir whole wheat flour, baking soda, baking powder, apple, cinnamon and orange peel into buttermilk mixture, mixing lightly. Fill muffin tins full. Bake for 25–30 minutes. Let muffins sit in tins for 5 minutes before removing.

Fruit and Bran Muffins

(fat free)

- 1 cup fruit (banana, apricot, applesauce, zucchini, carrots or any combination)
- 4 egg whites or egg substitute equal to 2 eggs
- 1½ cups apple juice
- 2 tablespoons lemon juice
- ¼ cup honey
- ¼ cup molasses
- 1½ cups whole wheat flour
- 1½ cups bran
- ½ teaspoon salt
- 1½ teaspoons baking soda
- 1 teaspoon cinnamon
- ½ teaspoon nutmeg

Preheat oven to 375 degrees. Grease muffin tins. Combine fruit, egg whites, apple juice, honey and molasses. In a separate bowl combine whole wheat flour, bran, salt, baking soda, cinnamon and nutmeg. Add fruit mixture to dry ingredients. Mix until just moistened. Pour into muffin tins. Bake for 20–25 minutes.

Banana Bran Muffins

- ½ cup bran
- 1½ cups flour
- 1 teaspoon baking soda
- 1 teaspoon baking powder
- ¼ teaspoon salt
- 1 cup nuts, chopped
- ½ cups brown sugar
- ½ cup margarine, softened
- ¼ cup buttermilk
- 2 eggs
- 1 teaspoon vanilla
- 3 bananas (1½ cups mashed)

Preheat oven to 375 degrees. Grease muffin tins. Combine bran, flour, baking soda, baking powder and salt. In a separate bowl cream margarine and sugar until fluffy. Add buttermilk, eggs, vanilla and bananas. Mix well. Stir in dry ingredients until just moistened. Stir in nuts. Spoon batter into muffin tins. Bake for 20–25 minutes.

Notes:

Banana Bran Muffins

(low fat)

- 1/3 cup margarine or oil
- ½ cup brown sugar or 1/3 cup honey
- 1½ cups (3 or 4 medium) mashed bananas
- 2 eggs, or 4 egg whites, or egg substitute
- ¼ cup buttermilk
- 1 teaspoon vanilla
- ¾ cup all-purpose flour
- ¾ cup whole wheat flour
- ¼ teaspoon salt, optional
- ½ cup bran (oat, wheat or wheat germ)
- 1 teaspoon baking powder
- 1 teaspoon baking soda
- ½ cup nuts, chopped (optional)

Preheat oven to 350 to 375 degrees. Grease muffin tins. Cream margarine or oil and brown sugar until fluffy. Add bananas, eggs, buttermilk and vanilla, mixing well. In a separate bowl combine flours, salt, bran, baking powder, and baking soda. Combine banana mixture with flour mixture, mixing lightly just until moistened. Fill muffin tins three-quarters full. Bake for 20–25 minutes. Cool in tins 5 minutes, then remove to cool.

Variation: Sprinkle chopped nuts and/or a little brown sugar over muffins before baking.

Banana Bran Muffins

(fat free)

- 2 mashed bananas
- ¾ cup honey
- ¾ cup water
- 3 tablespoons nonfat powdered milk
- 1 teaspoon vanilla
- 1 teaspoon salt
- ¼ teaspoon cinnamon
- ⅓ cup egg whites
- 1⅓ cups whole wheat flour
- 1 cup all-purpose flour
- ½ cup oat bran
- ½ cup oatmeal
- 4 teaspoons baking powder
- 1 teaspoon baking soda
- ½ cup walnuts, chopped (optional)
- Oat or wheat bran to sprinkle on top

Combine bananas, honey, water, powdered milk, vanilla, salt and cinnamon, mixing well. Stir in egg whites, mixing well. Add flours, oat bran, oatmeal, baking powder, baking soda, and walnuts. Mix lightly after all dry ingredients are added. Store in a cool place for at least an hour.

Preheat oven to 350 degrees. Spoon batter into muffin tins. Sprinkle tops with oat bran or wheat bran. Bake for 20 minutes.

Variations:

1. Sugar free: Substitute 1½ cups apple juice concentrate for honey and water.

2. Egg free: Omit egg whites, increase water to 1 cup, or add 3 tablespoons oil.

Oatmeal Bran Muffins

(fat free)

- 1½ cups oatmeal
- ½ cup wheat bran
- 1½ cups buttermilk, or 1 tablespoon lemon juice in skim milk
- 1 cup whole wheat flour
- 1 teaspoon baking soda
- 2 egg whites, beaten
- 4 tablespoons brown sugar

Soak oatmeal and bran in milk for about 1 hour. Preheat oven to 375 degrees. Grease muffin tins. Combine whole wheat flour and baking soda. In a separate bowl combine egg whites and brown sugar. Stir egg mixture into flour mixture. Add oatmeal and bran mixture, mixing lightly just until moistened. Pour into muffin tins. Bake for 20 minutes.

Oatmeal Muffins

- 1 cup oatmeal
- 1 cup buttermilk
- 1 egg
- ½ cup brown sugar
- 1 cup flour
- 1 teaspoon baking powder
- 1 teaspoon salt
- ½ teaspoon baking soda
- ⅓ cup oil

Soak oatmeal in buttermilk for 1 hour. Preheat oven to 350 degrees. Grease or line muffin tins with cupcake papers. Stir egg into oatmeal mixture and beat. Stir in brown sugar. In a separate bowl combine flour, baking powder, salt and baking soda. Add flour mixture to oatmeal mixture. Stir in oil. Mix until well combined. Pour into muffin tins, filling three-quarters full. Bake for about 20 minutes.

Variation: Add ¾ teaspoon cinnamon to flour mixture. Stir 1 cup grated apple into batter before pouring into muffin tins.

Honey Oatmeal Muffins

- 1 cup buttermilk
- 3 tablespoons honey
- 1 egg
- ¼ cup oil
- 1 cup flour
- 1 cup oatmeal
- ¼ teaspoon salt
- 2 teaspoons baking powder
- ½ teaspoon baking soda
- Granola, optional

Preheat oven to 400 degrees. Grease muffin tins or line with cupcake papers. Combine buttermilk, honey, egg and oil. In a separate bowl combine flour, oatmeal, salt, baking powder and baking soda. Make a well in the center of the flour mixture. Pour buttermilk mixture into the well. Blend until just moistened. Fill muffin tins three-quarters full and sprinkle granola on top. Bake for 15–20 minutes.

Soybean Muffins

(wheat free)

- 1 cup soy bean flour
- ½ teaspoon salt
- 1 teaspoon baking powder
- 1 teaspoon sugar, optional
- ⅓ cup nonfat milk
- 1 tablespoon oil
- 1 egg, beaten

Preheat oven to 400 degrees. Grease muffin tins. Combine flour, salt, baking powder and sugar. In a separate bowl blend milk, oil and egg together. Stir milk mixture into flour mixture and blend lightly, but well. Spoon into muffin tins. Bake for 15–20 minutes.

Yeast Breads

More and more people are making their own bread. They are finding out it's not as difficult as they thought and the extra work and time involved is well worth it. Nothing beats the wonderful smell and taste of fresh baked bread. If using a bread machine is your preferred method of making bread, go to it, but I personally think the new bread machines are a great waste of money. The recipes in my book are very easy to make. If you haven't tried to make bread, thinking it's too difficult, I'll try to show you some steps that might help you.

1. First step is to dissolve the yeast in warm liquid, then mix the other ingredients in, adding the flour last. Sprinkle over the yeast mixture, 1 cup at a time, stirring or mixing in half of the flour. Beat the batter with a wooden spoon for about 5 minutes or with a heavy-duty mixer for about 3 minutes. You can see the gluten developing and as you add more of the flour, the dough will slowly become glassy and elastic. Add remaining flour to make the dough stiff enough to pull away from the sides of the bowl.

2. Next is the kneading of the dough. Kneading helps to develop the gluten even more and make a tender loaf of bread. To knead by hand, sprinkle flour on a flat surface. Turn the dough out onto this area. As you knead, make sure the dough is evenly coated with a small amount of flour to prevent the dough from sticking to the board. To knead the dough, begin by pulling the dough toward you in a rolling motion, then push it away with the heels of you hands and fold the dough almost in half over itself. Stretch and pull the dough slowly with both hands, then fold it over itself, giving the dough a turn and repeating the process. Dough has been kneaded enough when it no longer sticks to your hands or the work surface. This usually takes about 10 minutes. If you knead longer, your finished loaf will be higher and very tender. The dough should be smooth and no longer sticky. If you have a mixer with a dough hook, knead dough the same way as you would by hand, kneading about 5 minutes until dough is smooth and elastic.

The rising of the dough is next. Roll the dough into a ball and place into a greased bowl turning once to grease the top. Cover and let rise in a warm place, or if in hurry or recipe calls for only one rising, you can place the dough directly into a greased loaf pan. Cover and let rise, if in a hurry you can heat up the oven slightly for 3 or 4 minutes, turn it off, and place the pan or bowl into the oven. Dough rises best in temperatures of 75 to 80 degrees. Dough has risen enough when it is almost double in size. After dough has risen once in the bowl, turn it out on a floured board and knead briefly to release air bubbles. Again, if in a hurry, just punch dough down in the bowl and form into a loaf and let rise. I like to make little slashes in the top of the rising loaf or prick the dough with a knife, not too deeply. This releases gas in the dough and does the same thing as the additional kneading after the first rising. Also, if you have lots of time or it's inconvenient to shape the loaves after the first rising, just punch dough down and let it rise again. You can punch dough down two or three times and still make an excellent loaf of bread. This process is called *proofing the dough*.

Time Saving Tips

Mix up bread dough the night before you want it. Place dough in a greased loaf pan. Cover and put into refrigerator. The next morning the dough should have doubled so you can bake it right away. You can do the same thing if you have time in the morning. Mix up dough in the morning, put into refrigerator, and bake in the evening for supper. If in a hurry for a loaf of bread, mix up dough, place it in a greased glass loaf pan and place in a microwave on very low for 5–15 minutes, checking often. Take out and let finish rising and bake or place bread in a cold oven and turn to the temperature you want to bake at (350 degrees) and let it finish rising as the oven gets hotter. The bread will rise and bake just like the new bread machines do. Also, if after mixing the dough you find you haven't the time to wait for the dough to rise and bake, just place it in refrigerator until you do have time or freeze the dough in plastic wrap until needed.

Baking Wheat-Free and Gluten-Free Breads

Baking breads without wheat makes a bread that has a different flavor and texture from those containing gluten. The action of yeast on the moistened gluten gives an elastic quality that we associate with bread. Without gluten, breads tend to be very dense, soggy, or crumbly. All rye and cornmeal breads are good examples. Most recipes for gluten-free breads use baking powder and/or baking soda for leavening. The addition of eggs, milk, potato flour, cornstarch, gelatin, or tapioca improves the texture.

Grains containing gluten are wheat, rye, barley, buckwheat, and oatmeal. Wheat has the highest percentage of gluten. For those individuals who are allergic to wheat or gluten, flours made from rice, corn, soybeans, potato flour, and millet are best. If you have a wheat allergy alone, oats, rye, and barley are usually acceptable.

Non-wheat breads taste different. The stronger flavors can be unpleasant. Combining grains can help; adding spices, fruits, peels, and juices can also add interest and pleasing flavors. Wheat-free breads do best baked as muffins or in small pans.

Baked Bagels

(fat free)

2 tablespoons active dry yeast
3 tablespoons honey or sugar
2 cups warm water
1 teaspoon salt
5½ to 6 cups flour

Egg Wash:

1 egg or egg white
3 tablespoons water

Dissolve yeast and honey in warm water. Add salt and half the flour. Mix 3 minutes. Slowly add remaining flour, kneading to make a moderately stiff dough that is smooth and elastic. Let dough rest for 15 minutes. Knead briefly and form into balls, flat rounds, or rings. Glaze bagels with egg wash. Let bagels rise. Preheat oven to 375 degrees. Place bagels on a greased baking sheet. Bake until crusty and golden, or 20–25 minutes.

Variations:

1. ***Whole Wheat Bagels:*** Replace up to 2 cups all-purpose flour with whole wheat flour.

2. ***Jalapeño Bagels:*** Add 1 cup chopped Jalapeño.

3. ***Onion Bagels:*** Add ¾ to 1 cup chopped onion.

4. ***Cheese Bagels:*** Add ½ cup parmesan cheese and ½ cup sharp cheddar cheese.

5. ***Garlic Bagels:*** Add 4 tablespoons garlic and ¼ cup chopped parsley.

6. ***Sugar Free Bagels:*** Omit honey or sugar.

7. ***Original Bagels:*** Omit glazing after bagels rise. Boil in 2 quarts rapidly boiling water and add 1 tablespoon sugar. As they rise, turn bagels over and boil for another 3 minutes. Drain and glaze. Bake as directed.

Pitas

(fat free)

- 2 cups warm water
- 1 tablespoon active dry yeast
- 2 tablespoons honey
- 1 teaspoon salt
- 5 to 6 cups flour

Combine water, yeast, honey and salt with 2½ to 3 cups flour. Beat 3 minutes. Beat in rest of flour ½ cup at a time. Knead in as much of an additional ½ cup of flour as required to make a dough that is not too dry. Place dough in greased bowl, turning once to grease top. Let rise until doubled.

Preheat oven to 450–500 degrees. Grease a cookie sheet. Turn dough out onto a floured board and cut into 12 equal pieces. Roll each piece into a ball, flatten until dough is about 5 inches across and ¼-inch thick. Place on cookie sheet and flatten a bit more. Repeat for each, leaving a little space between each pita. Bake until bottom turn brown and pitas puff up, about 5 minutes.

Whole Wheat Pitas

(sugar free)

- 2 cups warm water
- 1 tablespoon active dry yeast
- 1 teaspoon salt
- 5 to 6 cups whole wheat flour
- 2 tablespoons oil, optional

Combine water, yeast and salt with 2½ to 3 cups flour. Beat 3 minutes. Beat in rest of flour ½ cup at a time. Knead in as much of an additional ½ cup of flour as required to make a dough that is not too dry. Knead another 3 minutes by hand, dust hands with flour as necessary. Place dough in greased bowl, turning once to grease top. Let rise until doubled.

Preheat oven to 450 to 500 degrees. Grease a cookie sheet. Turn the dough out onto a floured board and cut into 12 equal pieces. Roll into balls, flatten until dough is approximately 5 inches across and ¼ inch thick. Place on cookie sheet and flatten a bit more. Repeat for each, leaving a little space between each pita. Bake or until bottom turns brown and pitas puff up, about 5 minutes.

Crisp Pizza Crust

(fat & sugar free)

- 1 tablespoons active dry yeast
- 1¼ cups warm (110 to 115-degree) water
- 3½ to 4 cups flour
- ½ teaspoon salt

Dissolve yeast in the warm water. Add 2 cups flour and salt. Beat thoroughly. Stir in remaining flour. If using a heavy duty mixer, use the dough hook and knead dough, adding a little flour as needed until dough is smooth and elastic. If kneading by hand, turn dough out onto lightly floured board and knead until smooth and elastic, about 10 minutes. Place in a lightly greased bowl and turn dough over. Cover and let rise until doubled.

Preheat oven to 425 degrees. Grease two 12-inch pizza pans. Knead dough again, just long enough to remove air bubbles. Divide dough in half. Press each ball of dough out with rolling pin to make an 11-inch circle and stretch each circle to fit a 12-inch pizza pan. Add pizza fillings. Bake for 15–20 minutes.

Variation: Whole wheat flour can be substituted for all-purpose flour.

Cornmeal Pizza Crust

- 1 tablespoon sugar
- 1 tablespoon active dry yeast
- ¾ cup warm water
- 1⅔ cups flour
- ½ cup cornmeal
- ¼ teaspoon salt
- ½ teaspoon olive oil

In a large bowl dissolve sugar and yeast in warm water. Let stand 5 minutes. Stir in 1⅓ cups flour, cornmeal, salt and olive oil. Knead dough until smooth and elastic, about 5 minutes. Add enough of the remaining flour, 1 tablespoon at a time, to prevent dough from sticking to hands. Place dough in a bowl coated with vegetable oil spray, turning to grease top. Let rise until doubled, about 45 minutes.

Punch dough down and roll into a 12-inch circle on a floured surface. Cover and let rise in a warm place, about 30 minutes.

Preheat oven to 450 degrees. Spray a 12-inch pizza pan or baking sheet with pan spray and sprinkle with cornmeal. Crimp down edges to form a rim. Put your favorite pizza fillings on top of dough. Bake for 10 minutes on bottom rack of oven. Let stand 5 minutes. Remove pizza to a cutting board.

Pizza Crust

(original recipe)

- 1 tablespoon active dry yeast
- 1 teaspoon sugar or honey
- 1⅓ cups warm water (110 to 115 degrees)
- 3½ to 4 cups flour
- ¾ teaspoon salt
- 2 tablespoons oil
- ¾ teaspoon garlic powder, optional

Dissolve yeast and sugar in warm water. Add 2 cups flour, salt, oil and garlic powder. Beat thoroughly. Stir in remaining flour. If using a heavy duty mixer, use the dough hook and knead dough, adding a little flour as needed until dough is smooth and elastic. If kneading by hand, turn out onto lightly floured bard and knead until smooth and elastic, about 10 minutes. Place in a lightly greased bowl. Turn dough over. Cover and let rise until doubled.

Preheat oven to 425 degrees. Knead dough again, just long enough to remove air bubbles. Divide dough in half. Press each ball of dough out with rolling pin to make an 11-inch circle, stretch each circle to fit a 12-inch pan. Add fillings. Bake for 15–20 minutes.

Variation: All-purpose flour may be replaced by 1½ cups whole wheat flour or oat bran.

Hurry Up Pizzas

- 1 tablespoon (1 package) active dry yeast
- 1 cup warm water
- 2¼ to 2½ cups flour
- 1 teaspoon sugar
- ½ teaspoon salt
- 2 tablespoons oil

Dissolve yeast in the warm water. Mix in half of the flour. Add sugar, salt and oil, mixing thoroughly. Add remaining flour. Dough will be soft and sticky. Allow the dough to rest 10 minutes. Spray two 10-inch pizza pans or a cookie sheet with non-stick spray. Divide dough in half. Spread dough on greased sheets with floured fingers. For a crisp crust, prebake 5 minutes in a 425 degree oven. Spread with your favorite sauce and sprinkle with mozzarella cheese evenly over crust. Bake for 12 minutes.

Whole Wheat Pizzas

- 1 tablespoon (1 package) quick rise dry yeast
- 1 cup warm water
- 2½ cups whole wheat flour
- ½ teaspoon salt
- 2 tablespoons oil
- 1 teaspoon honey
- ½ teaspoon garlic powder, optional
- ½ teaspoon onion powder, optional

Dissolve yeast in warm water. Stir in half of the flour. Add salt, oil, honey, garlic and onion powders, mixing thoroughly. Allow dough to rest 10 minutes. Spray two 12-inch pizza pans or a cookie sheet with nonstick vegetable spray. Divide dough in half. Dough will be soft and sticky. Spread dough on pan with floured fingers. For a crisp crust, prebake 5 minutes in a 425-degree oven. Spread with your favorite sauce and sprinkle with mozzarella cheese evenly over crust. Bake for 12 minutes.

Pizza Dough
(wheat free)

- 1 tablespoon (1 package) active dry yeast
- 1 cup warm (105 to 115-degree) water
- 1½ teaspoons sugar
- ⅔ to 1 cup rice flour
- ⅓ cup potato starch flour
- ¾ teaspoon salt
- 2 teaspoons oil

Preheat oven to 400 degrees. Grease a 10 x 15-inch jelly roll pan or baking pan. Dissolve yeast in water. Let sit 5 minutes. Stir in sugar, flours, salt and oil, adding enough rice flour to make a stiff dough that holds together but is spreadable, like a cake. Pour batter into pan. Spread evenly. Raise edges slightly to hold the sauce and toppings. Spread with sauce and toppings. Bake for 25–30 minutes.

Fallacia—Italian Flat Bread

- 1 cup warm (110 degrees) water
- 1 tablespoon active dry yeast
- 1 tablespoon sugar
- 2½ cups flour
- ½ teaspoon vinegar
- ¾ teaspoon salt
- 1 tablespoon olive oil or vegetable oil spray
- 1 teaspoon dried rosemary or basil leaves, crushed

Combine water, yeast, and sugar. Let sit 5 minutes. Add half the flour and beat 2 minutes. Gradually add remaining flour, vinegar and salt. Knead dough for 5 minutes. Let dough rest 20 minutes. Place dough on greased cookie sheet. Roll and press to a 12-inch circle. Cover loosely with greased plastic wrap and a towel. Let rise until double in size, about 30 minutes.

Preheat oven to 400 degrees. With fingers or wooden spoon handle, poke holes in dough at 1-inch intervals. Drizzle 3 or 4 tablespoons of olive oil on top of dough. Sprinkle evenly with rosemary or basil leaves. Bake until golden brown, about 20–25 minutes.

Notes:

No-knead Herb Breadsticks

(low fat, cholesterol & egg free)

- 1 package active dry yeast
- 1⅓ cups warm (105 to 115-degree) water
- 3 tablespoons vegetable oil
- 1 tablespoon honey
- 1 teaspoon instant minced onion
- 1 teaspoon dill seed or dill weed
- 1 teaspoon salt
- 3 to 3½ cups bread flour
- 1 egg white, slightly beaten
- 2 tablespoons water or buttermilk

In a large bowl dissolve yeast in warm water. Stir in oil, honey, onion, dill seed, salt, and 1 cup flour. Beat until smooth. Stir in remaining flour, scraping dough from side of bowl, until soft dough forms. Cover and let rise in warm place until double, about 45 minutes.

Preheat oven to 400 degrees. Grease cookie sheet. Stir down dough by beating about 25 strokes. Turn dough onto well-floured surface and gently roll dough in flour to coat. Divide into 24 equal parts. Roll and shape each part into rope about 9 inches long, sprinkling with flour if dough is too sticky. Place on cookie sheet. Brush with egg white. Bake until crust is deep golden brown and crisp, about 15 minutes. Immediately remove from cookie sheet. Store loosely covered. Yield: 24 breadsticks.

Taco or Tortilla Shells

(fat free)

I cook these up as we need them as they are best that way and are quick to fix. I use half all-purpose flour and half whole wheat flour.

- 1¼ cups flour
- ¼ teaspoon salt, optional
- ⅓ to ½ cup warm water

Combine ingredients and mix well with a fork until mixture can be shaped into a ball. Allow to sit for 5–10 minutes. Additional flour may need to be added at that time.

Divide into 6 balls. Flour wax paper or counter and roll each ball into a thin, flat round. Pan fry in a medium-hot Teflon pan until lightly browned on each side, less than a minute on each side.

Corn Flour Taco Shells

(fat free)

½	cup boiling water	¼	teaspoon salt, optional
½	cup cornmeal	1¼	cup flour

Combine water, cornmeal and salt. Let stand for 15–20 minutes. Stir flour into cornmeal mixture to make a stiff dough. Turn dough out onto a floured surface and knead for 5 minutes. Cover and let rest for 5 minutes. Divide dough into 6 parts and shape into balls. Roll out each ball into a 6-inch crust circle. Place into an ungreased Teflon pan heated to medium-high. Cook for about 1 minute on each side.

Corn Flat Bread Chips

2	cups water	2	tablespoons unsaturated oil
½	teaspoon salt, optional	2	cups yellow cornmeal

Lightly grease 2 cookie sheets. In a saucepan combine water, salt and oil. Bring to a boil. Pour water mixture over cornmeal in a mixing bowl. Mix quickly until all water is absorbed and mixture is smooth. Divide into 14–16 balls. Flatten each ball between fingers until about 6 inches across and more or less round to about ⅙ inch or thicker, or chips will become too hard to chew. If dough sticks to fingers, wash and dry hands and then continue. Preheat oven to 400 degrees. Place rounds onto cookie sheet, almost touching. Bake until just brown around the edges and crisp, about 20–25 minutes.

Buttermilk Oat Rolls

(egg free)

2 cups rolled oats
2 cups buttermilk
1½ tablespoons active dry yeast
¼ cup warm (105 to 115-degree) water
3½ cups flour, approx.
¼ cup oil
2 teaspoons salt
½ cup sesame seeds

Combine oats and buttermilk in a medium-sized bowl. Cover with plastic and refrigerate at least 2 hours or overnight.

Dissolve yeast in warm water. Let stand 5 minutes.

Meanwhile, combine oat mixture, 1 cup flour, oil and salt in a heavy duty mixer's bowl or dough can also be mixed by hand. Using mixer paddle attachment, mix on medium speed for 2 minutes. Add yeast mixture. Using dough hook, mix in enough flour, ½ cup at a time, to form a soft, sticky dough. Knead dough on a lightly floured surface until smooth, elastic and slightly sticky, about 5 minutes, adding more flour if necessary. Grease large bowl. Add dough, turning to coat entire surface. Cover bowl with plastic. Let dough rise in warm area until double in size.

Gently punch dough down. Knead on a lightly floured surface until smooth. Form into balls. Roll each ball in sesame seeds to coat. Transfer rolls to baking sheet, spacing them 2 inches apart. Cover loosely with plastic and let rise in a warm, draft-free area until almost doubled in volume, about 30 minutes.

Preheat oven to 400 degrees. Place on greased baking sheet. Bake rolls until golden brown, about 30 minutes. Cool slightly on rack before serving. Yield: 16 rolls.

Tender & Moist Crescent Rolls

(egg free)

- 2 tablespoons active dry yeast
- ½ cup warm water
- 6 tablespoons shortening, margarine, or oil
- 2 tablespoons sugar
- 1 teaspoon salt
- 1 cup warm milk
- 2½ to 3 cups flour

Dissolve yeast in water. In a separate bowl cream shortening, sugar and salt. Add milk and bubbly yeast to shortening mixture. If using shortening, don't worry if it doesn't all dissolve. Beat in flour with a spoon. Dough should be too soft to handle. Mound into a greased bowl and cover with plastic wrap. Let rise until doubled.

Grease a baking sheet. Roll dough out on a floured board into a large circle about ¼-inch thick. Cut as a pie into pieces 1½ inches at outer rim. Roll each piece up beginning at the large end. Place rolls on baking sheet. Cover and let rise until double or almost double in size.

Preheat oven to 400 degrees. Bake for 15 minutes.

Notes:

Whole Wheat Honey Crescents

(cholesterol & egg free)

- 1 tablespoon active dry yeast
- 1 cup warm water
- 1½ teaspoons salt
- 2½ tablespoons honey
- ¼ cup instant nonfat milk powder
- 3 cups whole wheat pastry flour
- 3 tablespoons plus 1 tablespoon canola oil

Glaze, optional:

- 1 egg white
- 1 tablespoon water or buttermilk
- 1 teaspoon poppy seeds, optional

Dissolve yeast in water and let stand 5 minutes. Add salt, honey, powdered milk, pastry flour, and 3 tablespoons oil. Knead 5–8 minutes. Let dough rest 10 minutes.

Grease a baking sheet. Roll dough out onto a lightly floured board. Roll into a 14 to 15-inch circle about ¼-inch thick. Brush with 1 tablespoon oil. Cut into 16 pie-shaped wedges. Beginning with the wide end, roll each wedge into a crescent. Curve, placing pointed end underneath. Place crescents on baking sheet. Let rise until nearly doubled, about 1 hour.

Preheat oven to 375 degrees. Combine egg white and water or buttermilk to make a glaze. Glaze tops of crescents and sprinkle with poppy seeds. Bake for 15–20 minutes. Serve warm.

Cheddar Rolls

- 2 tablespoons active dry yeast
- 1¼ cups warm (105 to 115-degree) water
- ¾ to 1 cup extra sharp cheddar cheese, grated (low fat can be used)
- 2 tablespoons honey
- 2 eggs, egg substitute, or 4 egg whites
- ¼ cup oil or margarine, melted
- 1½ teaspoons salt
- 4 to 4½ cups flour

Grease muffin tins. Dissolve yeast in water, let stand 5 minutes. Mix in cheese, honey, egg, oil, salt, and half the flour. Mix for 2 minutes. Gradually stir in remaining flour. Mix well. Fill muffin tins half full. Cover and let rise until doubled. Preheat oven to 375 degrees. Bake until golden brown, about 15 minutes.

Buttermilk Honey Rolls

- 2 tablespoons active dry yeast
- 1 cup warm buttermilk
- 1 cup warm water
- ¼ cup honey
- 2 eggs
- ⅓ cup oil
- 1½ teaspoons salt
- 5¼ cups flour
- Vegetable oil spray

Grease a baking pan. Dissolve yeast in buttermilk and water. Add honey and let stand 5 minutes. Add eggs, oil , salt, and half the flour. Mix for 3 minutes. Gradually stir in remaining flour. Knead for 2 or 3 minutes to make a nice, soft, elastic dough. Place in a greased bowl, turning dough over to grease top. Let rise. Punch dough down and form into balls or desired shapes. Place rolls on baking pan to rise. Preheat oven to 375 degrees. Spray tops of rolls with vegetable oil spray and bake for about 20 minutes. **Variation: *Buttermilk Potato Rolls:*** Add ¾ cup warmed mashed potatoes.

Delicious Potato Rolls

Adding potatoes to rolls makes them light and tender.

- 1 package active dry yeast
- ½ cup lukewarm water
- ½ cup hot potatoes, smoothly mashed
- 1 cup potato water, reserved from cooking potatoes
- 1 cup margarine or butter
- ⅔ cup sugar
- 1 tablespoon salt
- 2 eggs, beaten
- 8 cups flour

Soften yeast in lukewarm water and set aside. Combine mashed potatoes with potato water, margarine, sugar and salt. Stir until margarine is melted. Add yeast to warm potato mixture. Work in 4 cups of flour. Knead dough on floured board and work in ½ cup flour as while kneading. When dough is smooth and satiny, shape into a ball and place in a greased bowl, cover with cloth, and set aside to rise in warm spot until doubled in bulk. Punch dough down. Work with a quarter of the dough at a time. Roll to thickness of ¼ inch on a well-floured pastry cloth or board. Cut into 2-inch rounds, brush with melted margarine and then fold over, overlapping the top over the lower portion, and pinch edges together. Place rolls on a baking sheet and cover with cloth. Let rise in warm place until doubled in bulk. Preheat oven to 400 degrees. Bake until golden brown, about 10–15 minutes. Serve hot.

Potato Rolls

- 2 tablespoons active dry yeast
- 1⅓ cups warm water
- 1 cup potatoes, mashed
- ¾ cup margarine or oil
- ⅔ cup sugar
- 2½ teaspoons salt
- 2 eggs
- 6 to 7 cups flour

Soften yeast in lukewarm water and set aside. Combine mashed potatoes with potato water, margarine, sugar and salt. Stir until margarine is melted. Add yeast to warm potato mixture. Work in flour. Shape dough into a ball and place in a greased bowl. Turn dough over cone to grease the top. Cover bowl with cloth and set aside to rise in warm spot until doubled in bulk.

Grease three 9-inch round baking pans. Punch dough down. Shape dough into small 2 to 3-inch balls. Arrange balls in baking pans, leaving enough space between balls to rise until they are doubled in size.

Preheat oven to 375 degrees. Bake for 20–25 minutes. Remove rolls from pans and cool on racks.

Potato Rolls

(low fat & cholesterol free)

- 2 cups hot water or buttermilk
- ⅓ cup sugar or honey
- 2½ teaspoons salt
- ⅓ cup oil
- 5½ to 6 cups flour
- 1 cup potatoes, mashed
- 2 tablespoons active dry yeast
- 1 cup oatmeal
- Vegetable oil spray

Combine water, sugar, salt and oil. Mix in 2 cups flour and beat for 2 minutes. Add 1 cup flour, mashed potatoes and yeast. Beat 1 more minute. Stir in oats and add enough additional flour to make a soft dough. Knead on a floured board, adding flour as needed, until dough is smooth and satiny. Roll out dough and cut with a 2½-inch cutter to ¼-inch thickness. Spray tops of rolls with vegetable oil spray. Let rise until doubled in size.

Preheat oven to 400 degrees. Bake for about 15 minutes.

Whole Wheat Yeast Muffins

(fat free)

¼ cup warm water
1 tablespoon active dry yeast
1 cup buttermilk
½ cup all-purpose flour
½ cup molasses
¼ teaspoon salt
1 plus ½ cup whole wheat flour
½ cup raisins, optional

Grease muffin tins. Combine water and yeast; let sit for 5 minutes. Combine buttermilk, all-purpose flour, molasses, salt, and 1 cup whole wheat flour, mixing for 2 minutes. Add additional ½ cup whole wheat flour and raisins, mixing for another minute. Fill muffin tins two-thirds full. Let muffins rise.

Preheat oven to 350 degrees. Bake for 20 minutes.

Notes:

Sun-dried Tomato Rolls

These are not low fat, but are very delicious rolls. Whole wheat or grains of your choice can replace part of the flour.

- 2 tablespoons active dry yeast
- 1¼ cups warm (105 to 115-degree) water
- ¾ cup tomato juice
- ⅓ cup sugar
- ⅔ cup olive oil
- 4 eggs
- 2 teaspoons salt
- 6 to 7 cups flour
- ⅓ cup fresh basil, thinly sliced
- ½ cup sun-dried tomatoes, chopped
- Garlic oil to brush on rolls

Dissolve yeast in water and set aside for 5 minutes. Combine yeast mixture, tomato juice, sugar, oil, eggs, salt, and 3 cups flour. Beat 3 minutes. Stir in basil, tomatoes, and enough flour to form a soft dough. Knead dough on a lightly floured surface, adding flour as needed. Knead until smooth and elastic, about 5 minutes. Dough will be slightly sticky. Place dough in greased bowl, turning to coat entire surface. Cover, let rise until doubled.

Grease muffin tins. Punch dough down. Knead dough on a lightly floured surface until smooth. Shape dough into 20–24 balls, pulling edges under to create a smooth top. Place rolls round side up in muffin tins. Using floured scissors, snip a ½-inch-deep X into the top of each roll. Cover and let rise for 30 minutes.

Preheat oven to 375 degrees. Gently brush rolls with garlic oil. Bake until golden brown, about 20 minutes. Brush warm rolls with garlic oil. Best when served warm.

Crust Brown Rolls

This recipe makes hard, chewy, delicious rolls.

2 packages active dry yeast
1¾ cups warm (110 to 115-degree) water
4 teaspoons sugar or honey
2 teaspoons salt
3 tablespoons margarine, melted
6½ to 7 cups flour, sifted
3 egg whites, beaten stiff
Cornmeal

Egg Wash:

1 egg white
2 tablespoons water

Dissolve yeast in warm water. Add sugar, salt, margarine, and 2 cups flour. Beat well. Fold in egg whites. Add remaining flour, mixing until dough leaves the sides of the bowl. Turn dough out on a lightly floured surface. Knead until dough is smooth and elastic, and tiny blisters show on the surface, about 15 minutes. Place dough in a lightly greased bowl, turning dough over to grease the top. Cover with a damp cloth. Let rise in a warm place until doubled.

Grease baking sheets and sprinkle lightly with cornmeal. Punch dough down. Dough may be shaped at this point. Follow directions for shaping given with each type of roll (see Variations, below). Place rolls on baking sheets. Make egg wash by slightly beating egg white and water. Brush rolls with egg wash or water. Cover and let rise until doubled, about 20 minutes.

Preheat oven to 400 degrees. Place a large shallow pan of boiling water on the bottom of oven to provide steam while the rolls bake. This makes the rolls crusty. Brush rolls again with egg wash or water. Bake until brown and crusty, about 20 minutes.

Variations:

1. ***French Rolls:*** Shape raised dough into 3-inch balls. Flatten under hands to make 4-inch circles or 6-inch tapered oblongs ¾-inch thick. Using a very sharp knife or razor, make shallow cuts about ¼-inch deep on top of each roll. Place rolls on baking sheet, brush with egg wash, and sprinkle with poppy or sesame seeds. Let rise until doubled. Brush again with egg wash and bake.

2. ***Italian Bread Sticks:*** Divide raised dough into 4 portions;. Roll out each portion to a 4 x 4-inch rectangle. Cut lengthwise in ½-inch strips. Roll under hands to make strips 8 inches long. Place strips 1 inch apart on baking sheet. Brush strips with water and let rise. Brush again with water before baking.

Rolls or Bread

(fat free)

- 2 tablespoons active dry yeast
- 1 cup warm water
- 2 cups nonfat milk or 4 tablespoons nonfat powdered milk plus 2 cups water
- ¼ cup honey
- 4 teaspoons salt or to taste, optional
- 8 to 10 cups flour

Mix yeast with warm water. Add nonfat milk, honey, salt, and half the flour. Mix in mixer for 3 minutes. Gradually add remaining flour (use little less flour for rolls or more flour for bread). Knead dough until smooth and elastic. Place in greased pans. Let rise once.

Preheat oven to 350 degrees. Bake rolls for 20 minutes or bread for 35 minutes.

Sourdough Starter

A starter is the "Mother" of all sourdough breads. Refrigerate starter between uses.

- 1 tablespoons active dry yeast
- ½ cup plus 2 cups warm (105 to 115 degrees) water
- 2 cups flour
- 1 tablespoons honey

In a large nonmetal container or bowl, dissolve yeast in ½ cup warm water. Stir in 2 cups warm water, flour and honey, beating until smooth. Cover bowl with cheesecloth or a towel. Let stand at room temperature, stirring 2–3 times a day, until mixture has a sour aroma, about 5–10 days. A warm room will hasten fermentation.

Starter may be refrigerated indefinitely, as long as it is replenished every 2 weeks. To replenish starter, stir in equal amounts of flour and water. For instance, replenish 1 cup of starter by adding 1 cup flour and 1 cup water. Cover and let stand in a warm place overnight. Cover and store in the refrigerator. If refrigerated starter is not used for 2–3 weeks, remove ½ cup of starter and either discard or give it to a friend. Replace as directed above.

Variation: ***Rye or Whole Wheat Sourdough Starter:*** Prepare as above using whole grain rye or wheat flour.

Sourdough Starter

(sugar free)

Always stir starter with a wooden spoon—never a metal spoon. Excess starter, unless reactivated, may become rancid.

- 1 tablespoon active dry yeast
- 2 cups warm water
- 2 cups whole grain wheat or rye flour

Using a wooden spoon, combine yeast and warm water. Let starter stand uncovered at 80–90 degrees, stirring with a wooden spoon once a day, until it bubbles and emits a good sour odor, about 4–7 days. Use starter at once or refrigerate for later use. To replenish starter, discard all but 1 cup. Stir 1 cup flour and 1 cup warm water into the reserved starter. Let stand overnight until fermented and bubbling. Use immediately or refrigerate.

Sourdough Fennel Biscuits

- 1 cup sourdough starter, at room temperature
- ½ cup warm (90-degree) water
- 2¾ cups flour
- ¼ cup olive oil
- 1½ teaspoons fennel seed
- 2 teaspoons baking powder
- ¾ teaspoon salt
- ½ teaspoon baking soda
- 1 egg white, lightly beaten

Preheat oven to 400 degrees. Grease a 12 x 15-inch baking sheet. Combine starter, water and 1 cup flour. If time allows, for the sourest flavor, cover and let starter mixture stand in a warm place until bubbly and sour smelling, 12–24 hours.

Stir in oil. Crush ½ teaspoon of the fennel seed, reserving remaining seed. In a separate bowl stir crushed fennel, baking powder, salt, baking soda, and 1¾ cups flour. Add starter mixture, stirring until dough cleans sides of bowl. Turn dough out onto a lightly floured board and knead for about 30 seconds. Add flour as needed to prevent sticking. Flour board, then roll out dough into a 6 x 14-inch rectangle. Brush dough with egg white and sprinkle with reserved fennel seed. Cut into 2 x 3-inch rectangles. Place biscuits about ½ inch apart on prepared baking sheet. Bake until deep gold, about 15 minutes. Transfer to a rack. Serve warm or cool.

Sourdough Biscuits

(fat free)

Serve biscuits while still warm. They become very firm when cold.

- ½ cup sourdough starter
- 1 cup skim
- 2½ cups flour
- ¾ teaspoon salt
- 1 tablespoon sugar
- 1 teaspoon baking powder
- ½ teaspoon baking soda
- Vegetable oil spray

At least 8 hours before serving, combine starter, milk, and 1 cup flour in a large bowl. Cover bowl and let stand at room temperature to rise.

Grease a 9-inch square pan. Place 1 cup flour on a breadboard. Turn starter mixture onto the breadboard. In a separate bowl using hands, combine salt, sugar, baking powder, and baking soda with remaining ½ cup flour. Mix flour mixture into starter mixture, kneading lightly to get the right consistency. Roll dough out to a ½-inch thickness. Cut out biscuits with a cutter. Place biscuits close together on pan. Spray tops of biscuits with vegetable oil spray. Set in a warm place to rise for about ½ hour.

Preheat oven to 375 degrees. Bake for 30–35 minutes. Yield: about 12 biscuits.

Sourdough Biscuits

(original)

- 1½ cups flour
- 2 teaspoons baking powder
- ¼ teaspoon baking soda (increase to ½ teaspoon if starter is very sour)
- ½ teaspoon salt
- ½ teaspoon sugar
- ¼ cup butter, margarine, or shortening
- 1 cup sourdough starter, at room temperature
- Butter, melted

Grease a 9-inch square baking pan well. Combine flour, baking powder, baking soda, salt, and sugar. Cut in margarine. Stir in starter. Turn dough out on a lightly floured board. Knead lightly. Roll out to ⅛-inch thickness. Cut biscuits with a floured 2½-inch cutter. Place biscuits in pan. Brush with melted butter. Let rise about an hour in a warm place.

Preheat oven to 400 degrees. Bake for 20 minutes.

Sourdough Bread with Honey and Oil

1 cup starter, at room temperature
1¾ cups warm (105 to 115-degree) water
1 tablespoon salt
1 tablespoon honey
4 tablespoons oil
3¾ to 4¼ cups flour

Combine starter, water, salt, honey, and oil with 2¾ cups flour. Mix until dough pulls cleanly away from bowl. Knead for 5 minutes, adding 1–1½ cups more flour as needed. Place dough in greased bowl, covering loosely. Let rise in warm place overnight.

Punch dough down several times to remove air bubbles. Divide dough into 3 parts. Shape dough into rounded loaves. Place loaves on cookie sheets. Cover and let rise in warm place until doubled in size.

Preheat oven to 375 degrees. Bake until loaves sound hollow when tapped and are golden brown, about 20–25 minutes.

For a crispy crust, either brush or spray water on top of bread while baking. Also, a mixture of 1 egg white and 2 tablespoons of water can be brushed onto the loaves. Sprinkle with seeds of your choice.

Sourdough French Bread

(fat free)

- 1 tablespoon active dry yeast
- 1 cup warm water
- 3½ to 4 cups flour
- 1 tablespoon sugar
- 1½ cups sourdough starter, at room temperature
- 2 teaspoons salt
- Cornmeal

Dissolve yeast in warm water and let stand 5 minutes. Stir in 2 cups flour, sugar, starter and salt, mixing for 2 minutes. Gradually stir in enough of the remaining flour to make a firm dough. Knead until smooth and elastic, about 5 minutes. Place dough in a greased bowl, turning dough to grease the top. Cover and let rise until light and doubled.

Grease and sprinkle a cookie sheet with cornmeal. Punch dough down and divide into 2 parts. Form dough into rounds or oval shapes. Place on cookie sheet. Cover and let rise at room temperature until doubled. Preheat oven to 375 degrees. With a very sharp knife make 2–3 diagonal slashes across top of each loaf. Spray or brush loaves with water. Bake until golden brown, about 30–35 minutes. Spray or brush loaves with water several times during baking for a crisper crust. Remove loaves from sheet and cool.

Sourdough Rye Bread

- 1 tablespoon active dry yeast
- 1 cup warm water
- 2¼ to 2¾ cups bread flour
- 1½ cups sourdough starter, at room temperature
- 2 tablespoons oil or shortening
- 1 tablespoon sugar
- 2 teaspoons salt
- 2 teaspoons caraway seeds
- 2 cups medium rye flour

Dissolve yeast in warm water and let stand 5 minutes. Stir in 2 cups flour, starter, oil, sugar, salt and caraway seeds, mixing for 2 minutes. Gradually stir in rye flour and enough remaining flour to make a firm dough. Knead about 5 minutes. Place in a greased bowl, turning to grease the top. Cover and let rise until doubled. Grease a cookie sheet. Punch dough down and divide into 2 parts. Shape dough into round loaves. Place loaves on cookie sheet. Cover and let rise until doubled.

Preheat oven to 375 degrees. With a very sharp knife make an 'X' on top of each loaf. Bake until loaves sound hollow when tapped, about 35–40 minutes.

Sourdough Whole Grain Loaves

- 1 cup sourdough starter, at room temperature
- 1½ cups warm milk or water
- 3¼ to 3¾ cups bread flour
- 1 tablespoon active dry yeast
- ¼ cup warm (110-degree) water
- ⅓ cup honey or brown sugar, firmly packed
- 1½ teaspoons salt
- 1 large egg
- 2 tablespoons margarine, melted, or oil
- ½ cup rolled oats
- ½ cup bulgur
- ½ cup cornmeal
- ½ rye flour
- 1 cup unprocessed bran
- 1½ cups whole wheat flour

In large bowl combine starter, milk and 1½ cups bread flour. If time allows, at this point for the sourest flavor, cover and let mixture stand in a warm place until bubbly and sour smelling, 12–24 hours.

In a separate bowl soften yeast in water. Stir yeast mixture into starter mixture. Stir in honey, salt, egg, margarine or oil, oats, bulgur, cornmeal, rye flour, and bran. Mix for 3 minutes. Add whole wheat flour and more bread flour and knead 5 minutes. Cover with plastic wrap and let rise in a warm place until doubled.

Grease a 12 x 15-inch baking sheet or two 5 x 9-inch loaf pans. Punch dough down and briefly knead. Divide dough in half. Shape each half into a smooth round about 2 inches thick and 6 inches across and place on baking sheet to rise, or shape into 3 x 8-inch logs. Place logs into pans. Cover loosely with plastic wrap and let rise in a warm place, about 1 hour.

Preheat oven to 375 degrees. For round loaves, make slashes about ¾-inch deep. Bake until well browned, about 35 minutes. Switch positions of pans halfway through baking. Remove from pans to racks and cool completely.

Whole Wheat Sourdough Bread

- ½ cup sourdough starter, at room temperature
- 2 tablespoons water
- 2 tablespoons plus 3 cups all-purpose flour
- 2 tablespoons sugar
- 1 tablespoon active dry yeast
- 2 cups warm (105 to 115-degree) water
- 2 teaspoons salt
- ¼ cup boiling water
- ¼ cup honey
- 2 tablespoons oil
- ¼ cup rolled oats
- ¼ cup wheat germ
- ¼ cup unprocessed bran flakes
- ¼ cup wheat flakes
- 2 tablespoons soy flour
- 1½ teaspoons sunflower seeds
- 3 to 4 cups whole wheat flour

Combine starter, 2 tablespoons water and 2 tablespoons all-purpose flour. Let stand overnight at room temperature.

In a heavy-duty mixer bowl, dissolve sugar and yeast in ½ cup water. Stir to blend. Let stand about 10 minutes. Add starter mixture, 1½ cups water, 3 cups all-purpose flour, and salt, beating until smooth. Cover and let stand in a warm, draft-free area until light and foamy, about 1 hour.

In a separate bowl whisk ¼ cup boiling water, honey and oil. Cool mixture completely. Meanwhile, combine oats, wheat germ, bran flakes, wheat flakes, soy flour, and sunflower seeds. Beat oatmeal mixture and cooled honey mixture into sugar and starter mixture. Turn dough out onto a floured surface. Knead 10 minutes, adding enough whole wheat flour to create a slightly sticky dough. Place dough in a greased bowl, turning to coat entire surface. Cover and let rise in warm, draft-free area until doubled.

Grease baking sheets. Punch dough down. Shape dough into 2 rounds. Set dough on baking sheets. Slash tops. Cover and let rise.

Preheat oven to 350 degrees. Bake bread until golden brown, about 45 minutes. Cool bread completely. Yield: 2 loaves.

Sourdough Vinland Raisin Bread

(low fat)

- 2 cups warm water
- 2 tablespoons active dry yeast
- ¼ cup nonfat powdered milk
- 2½ tablespoons honey
- 3 tablespoons brown sugar
- 4 to 5 cups bread flour, combined with ¾ to 1 cup whole wheat flour
- ¾ teaspoon cinnamon
- ½ teaspoon allspice
- ¼ teaspoon cardamom
- 1¼ cups raisins or currants
- 1 egg or 2 egg whites
- 1 teaspoon salt
- ¾ cup sourdough starter, at room temperature
- ½ cup nuts, optional
- ½ teaspoon baking soda

Grease loaf pans. Combine water, yeast, milk, honey, and brown sugar. Stir in half the flour. Add cinnamon, allspice, cardamom, and raisins. Beat with an electric mixer on low speed for 30 seconds. Add egg and salt, beating on high speed for 3 minutes. Add all but the last ½ cup flour, stirring with a spoon.

Turn dough out onto a floured surface. Knead in enough remaining flour to make a moderately stiff dough, about 6–8 minutes. Place in loaf pans. Make a slash on top of each loaf. Let rise until doubled.

Before baking, brush tops with skim milk or water. Combine 2 tablespoons sugar and ¼ teaspoon cinnamon. Sprinkle on top.

Preheat oven to 350 degrees. Bake for about 30 minutes.

Yield: 2 loaves.

Variation: For sugar free bread, substitute 4 tablespoons of all natural apple concentrate for honey and brown sugar.

Sourdough Lite

(fat & sugar free)

- 2¼ cups warm water
- 4 cups sourdough starter, at room temperature
- 2 tablespoons active dry yeast
- ½ cup oatmeal
- ¾ cup whole wheat flour
- ½ tablespoon salt
- 6 cups all-purpose flour

Combine water, starter and yeast. Stir in oatmeal, whole wheat flour, salt, and half the all-purpose flour. Mix for 3 minutes. Let dough rest for 10 minutes.

Knead in remaining all-purpose flour until dough pulls away from bowl, about 4 minutes. Make 2 rounds or loaves. Slash tops. Let rise until doubled.

Preheat oven to 350 degrees. Grease 2 pans. Punch dough down. Place dough in pans. Bake for 40 minutes. For crisp crusts, spray inside oven with a fine mist off and on during baking.

French Bread

(fat free)

- 3 cups warm water
- 2 tablespoons active dry yeast
- 2 tablespoons sugar or honey, optional
- 7 to 8 cups flour
- 2½ teaspoons salt
- Cornmeal

Egg Wash, optional:

- 1 egg white
- 2 tablespoons water

Combine water, yeast and sugar. Add 4 cups flour and mix for 3 minutes. Gradually add salt and additional flour. Place dough in bowl and knead until dough cleans bowl. Let dough rise until doubled in size.

Punch dough down and let rest for 15 minutes. Meanwhile, grease a cookie sheet and sprinkle it with cornmeal. Divide dough in half and form into oblong or round loaves. Place loaves on cookie sheet. Brush with water and let rise until almost double in size.

Preheat oven to 375 degrees. With a sharp knife slash 3–4 cuts ¼-inch deep across the top of each loaf. For a crispy, chewy crust brush or spray water on loaves as they bake, or combine egg white and water to make a wash to brush on loaves. Bake for about 40 minutes.

Variation: ***Sugar free:*** Omit sugar or honey and increase yeast to 3 tablespoons.

Rye Bread

(low fat, wheat free)

This bread is a dense, heavy bread.

2½	cups warm milk	6	cups rye flour
2	tablespoons active dry yeast	1	egg, beaten
1	tablespoon honey or sugar	2	tablespoons caraway seeds
2	tablespoons oil	2	tablespoons sesame seeds
2	teaspoons salt		Vegetable oil spray

Combine milk, yeast and honey. Let stand for 5 minutes. Stir in oil, salt and 2 cups rye flour. Let stand for 1 hour.

Slowly stir in 3 cups rye flour, egg, caraway seeds, and sesame seeds. Let rise for 2 hours.

Grease baking sheet. Sprinkle board with 1 cup rye flour. Place dough on floured board and knead about 10 minutes. Divide dough in half and form into rounds. Place rounds onto baking sheet. Spray rounds with vegetable oil and allow to rise again for about 2 hours.

Preheat oven to 350 degrees. Bake loaves for 45–60 minutes.

Finn Hill Rye

- 2½ tablespoons active dry yeast
- 3 cups warm (105 to 115-degree) water
- ⅓ cup brown sugar
- 3 tablespoons honey or molasses
- ¾ tablespoon caraway seeds
- ½ tablespoon fennel seeds, optional
- ½ tablespoon cocoa
- ½ tablespoon orange peel, grated
- 4 tablespoons oil
- ½ tablespoon salt
- 3 cups rye flour
- ¾ cup whole wheat flour
- 4½ to cups 5 cups bread flour
- Vegetable oil spray, optional

Dissolve yeast in water. Mix in brown sugar, honey, molasses, caraway and fennel seeds, cocoa, orange peel, oil, salt, rye flour, whole wheat flour, and half the bread flour. Mix for 3 minutes. Knead in remaining bread flour until dough is smooth and elastic and comes away from bowl, about 5–10 minutes. Divide dough in half and roll out as for French bread. Slash tops of loaves. Spray or brush on water for a crusty bread or spray tops with vegetable oil spray before and after baking. Sprinkle tops with caraway seeds and let loaves rise.

Preheat oven to 350 degrees. Bake for 40 minutes. Yield: 2 loaves.

Spelt Bread

(wheat & fat free)

- 2 tablespoons active dry yeast
- 2 cups warm water
- 3 tablespoons honey
- 2½ teaspoons salt
- 6½ to 7½ cups spelt flour

Dissolve yeast in water. Add honey, salt and half flour, mixing for 3 minutes. Gradually stir in remaining flour to form a stiff dough. Knead 5–8 minutes until dough is smooth and elastic. Place dough in a greased bowl and let rise until doubled.

Grease two 9 x 5-inch bread pans. Punch dough down and knead. Shape into loaves and place into pans. Cover and let rise until almost doubled.

Preheat oven to 350 degrees. Bake for 35–45 minutes.

Many Grains Bread

This recipe makes a dense, dark bread.

- 2 tablespoons active dry yeast
- 3 cups warm (105 to 115-degree) water
- 2¾ to 3¼ cups bread flour
- 2 cups graham flour
- ½ cup molasses
- ¼ cup oil
- 3 to 4 teaspoons salt
- 1 cup oats
- ½ cup rye flour
- ½ cup buckwheat flour
- ½ cup soy flour
- ½ cup cornmeal
- 1 cup whole wheat flour

Combine yeast and water. Let stand 5 minutes. Stir in 1½ cups bread flour and graham flour, mixing well. Add molasses, oil and salt, and mix 3 minutes. Gradually stir in oats and remaining flours to make a firm dough. Knead dough about 5 minutes. Place dough in a greased bowl, turning to grease the top, and let rise until doubled.

Grease a cookie sheet. Punch dough down and divide into 2 parts. Shape each half into a round loaf and place on cookie sheet. Cover and let rise about 30 minutes.

Preheat oven to 350 degrees. With a very sharp knife make a cross slash across top of each loaf. Bake for 35–40 minutes.

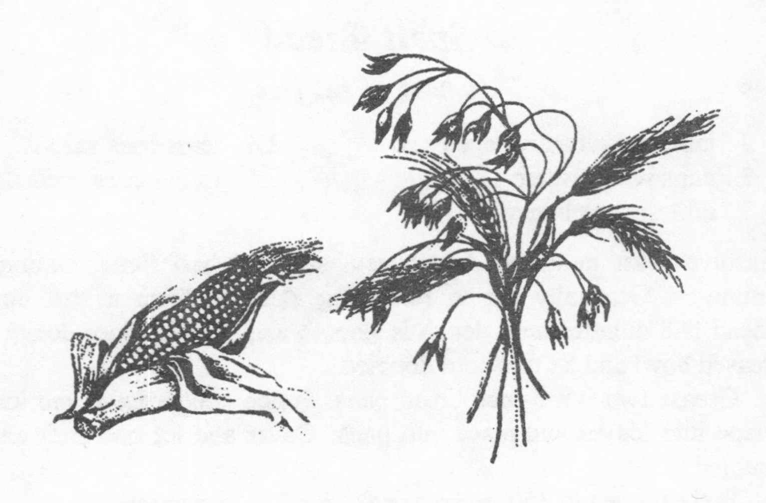

Quinoa Bread

This recipe makes a dense bread. Make rolls from this dough by using a little less flour.

- 3 cups warm (105 to 115-degree) water
- ⅓ cup Quinoa grain, or 1 cup Quinoa flour
- ⅓ cup oil
- ⅓ cup honey
- 2 cups seven grain
- 2¼ tablespoons active dry yeast
- ½ cup oat bran
- 1 cup whole wheat flour
- 2 tablespoons nonfat powdered milk
- ⅓ tablespoon salt
- 4½ to 5 cups bread flour
- Vegetable oil spray
- Quinoa grain or flour plus wheat bran to brush tops of loaves

Grease pans. Combine water, Quinoa, oil, honey, seven grain, yeast, oat bran, whole wheat flour, nonfat powdered milk, salt, and half the bread flour. Mix for about 3 minutes. Stir in remaining bread flour, mixing until dough cleans bowl but is still soft. Form dough into 2 loaves. Roll loaf tops in a mixture of Quinoa and wheat bran. Place loaves in pans, then spray with vegetable oil. Let rise.

Preheat oven to 350 degrees. Bake for about 40 minutes. Spray warm loaf tops with vegetable oil spray. Yield: 2 loaves.

Earth Bread

(fat & sugar free)

This is a heavy, dense bread.

3	cups warm water or skim milk	2	tablespoons active dry yeas
½	cup rice bran	¾	cup oat bran
1	cup plus 2 tablespoons oatmeal	1½	cups whole wheat flour
¾	cups multi grain (7 grain)	1	teaspoon salt
¼	cup egg whites	4½	cups bread flour
			Vegetable oil spray

Combine water, rice bran, oatmeal, multi grain, egg whites and yeast. Set aside for 10 minutes.

Meanwhile, in a separate bowl combine oat bran, whole wheat flour and salt. Combine oat bran mixture with yeast mixture and mix for about 3 minutes. Knead in remaining bread flour. Kneading until dough cleans bowl. Grease 2 loaf pans. Form dough into 2 loaves, cover, and let rise until doubled in size. Spray loaf tops with vegetable oil spray.

Preheat oven to 350 degrees. Bake for 35 minutes. Cool bread in pans for 5 minutes, then remove loaves to finish cooling on a rack.

Cracked Wheat Bread

Before shaping dough into loaves, weigh each dough half so that they weigh the same.

- 2¼ cups warm (105 to 115-degree) water
- 2 tablespoons active dry yeast
- ¼ cup molasses
- ¼ cup oil
- 1 cup rye flour
- 1 cup cracked wheat
- 1½ teaspoons salt
- 4 to 4½ cups bread flour

Combine water, yeast, molasses, oil, rye flour, cracked wheat, salt, and 2 cups bread flour, beating for 3 minutes. Stir in remaining bread flour, a little at a time, to make a dough that leaves the sides of the bowl. Knead dough until satiny and elastic. Place dough in a greased bowl, turning dough over to grease the top. Cover and let rise in a warm place until doubled.

Grease 2 loaf pans. Punch dough down. Divide dough into 2 balls. Let rest 10 minutes. Shape balls into loaves and place in pans. Let rise until doubled.

Preheat oven to 350 degrees. Bake for about 45 minutes.

Variations:

1. ***Fat free:*** Omit oil and increase water to 2½ cups.
2. ***Sugar free:*** Omit molasses and increase water to 2½ cups.

Whole Wheat Bread

- 2 tablespoons active dry yeast
- 2¾ cups warm (105 to 115-degree) water
- ½ cup brown sugar, or a combination of honey and molasses
- 2 teaspoons salt
- ⅓ cup margarine or oil
- ½ cup wheat germ
- 4 cups all-purpose flour
- 3 cups whole wheat flour

Dissolve yeast in water and set aside for 5 minutes. Meanwhile, combine brown sugar, salt, margarine, wheat germ, 2 cups all-purpose flour, and 1 cup whole wheat flour. Beat for 3 minutes. Stir in remaining all-purpose and whole wheat flours. Knead dough until smooth and elastic and dough pulls away from the bowl, about 10–15 minutes. Place dough in a greased bowl, turning once to grease top. Let rise until doubled.

Grease two 9 x 5 x 3-inch loaf pans. Punch dough down. Divide dough in half. Roll each half into a ball and let rest 10 minutes. Shape balls into loaves and place in pans. Let rise until doubled.

Preheat oven to 375 degrees. Bake for 40 minutes. Cool bread in pans for 5 minutes before removing to rack to finish cooling.

Raisin Pumpernickel Bread

- 2 tablespoons active dry yeast
- 1¼ cups warm water
- 1 cup rye flour
- 1 cup whole wheat flour
- ¼ cup molasses
- 1 tablespoon oil
- 2 tablespoons cocoa
- 1 tablespoon instant coffee powder
- ½ teaspoon salt
- ½ cup raisins
- ¾ to 1 cup all-purpose flour
- Cornmeal

Egg Wash:

- 1 egg white combined with 1 tablespoon water

Dissolve yeast in water and set aside for 5 minutes. Add rye flour, whole wheat flour molasses, oil, cocoa, instant coffee powder and salt. Beat with electric mixer for 1 minute, adding raisins. Then using a dough hook mix in all-purpose flour. Beat until dough is smooth and elastic and cleans bowl. Add more flour if needed. Knead for 3 minutes. If mixing by hand, stir in the flour and knead, adding as little flour as possible until dough is smooth and elastic, about 5 minutes.

Place dough in a greased bowl, turning to grease the top. Cover bowl and keep warm. Let dough rise until doubled.

Sprinkle cornmeal onto a lightly greased cookie sheet. Punch dough down and knead briefly. Form dough into a ball and place on cookie sheet. Flatten dough down to make a round loaf. Cover, let rise until almost doubled.

Preheat oven to 350 degrees. Brush loaf with egg wash. Bake for 30 minutes.

Old-fashioned Potato Bread

- 2 tablespoons active dry yeast
- ½ cup warm water
- 2 medium potatoes, cooked, reserving water, and mashed
- 1½ cups reserved potato water, warm
- 1½ cups skim milk, warm
- ½ cup honey or sugar
- 1½ tablespoons salt
- ½ cup margarine or oil
- 12 cups all-purpose flour, or a mixture of 8 cups all-purpose flour plus 4 cups whole wheat or other grain
- Cornmeal

Topping for Breakfast Bread:

- ¼ cup brown sugar
- 2 teaspoons cinnamon

Dissolve yeast in water and set aside for 5 minutes. Combine with mashed potatoes, reserved potato water, milk, honey, salt, margarine, and half the flour. Beat for 3 minutes, gradually adding more flour as needed. Knead dough until smooth and elastic. Place dough in a greased bowl. Let rise until doubled in size.

Grease a cookie sheet and sprinkle it with cornmeal. Grease 2 loaf pans. Divide dough into 3 equal pieces. Shape one piece into an oval or round loaf. Shape the second piece to fit into a loaf pan.

The third piece can be rolled out into a breakfast bread: Roll dough into a rectangle and brush with water. Sprinkle a topping of brown sugar and cinnamon over the top. Roll like a jelly roll, pressing ends under, and place in a greased loaf pan. Let loaves rise until doubled.

Preheat oven to 375 degrees. Bake until crust is golden brown, about 40 minutes.

Barley Bread

(wheat free)

Sliced thinly, it is a deliciously different sort of bread.

- 2 tablespoons active dry yeast
- ¼ cup honey
- 2 cups skim milk, warm
- 1 tablespoon salt
- 3 tablespoons oil
- 5 to 5½ cups barley flour

Grease a cookie sheet. Dissolve yeast in milk and honey. Set aside for 5 minutes. Combine with salt, oil and half the flour. Beat for 3 minutes to develop air bubbles and gluten. Add remaining flour and knead until smooth and elastic. Shape dough into 2 loaves and place on cookie sheet. Cover with a damp cloth and let rise for 1 hour. Dough will rise slightly but will not double in bulk.

Preheat oven to 325 degrees. Bake for 1 hour.

Rice Soy Bread

(wheat free)

- 1½ tablespoons active dry yeast
- ¼ cup molasses
- 3 cups warm water
- 1 tablespoon oil
- ½ teaspoon salt, optional
- 2 to 2½ cups rice flour
- 1 cup soy flour
- Vegetable oil spray

Combine yeast, molasses and water. Let stand for 5 minutes. Add oil, salt and flours. Mix for 2 minutes to form a sticky dough. Pat dough into a large bread pan. Spray top of dough with vegetable oil spray. Cover with a wet towel. Let rise until almost double.

Preheat oven to 350 degrees. Bake for about 30 minutes. Leave bread in pan for 30 minutes, then remove to finish cooling on a rack. Wrap bread. Do not slice bread for 12 hours, as it tends to crumble.

Christmas Bread
Cardamom Raisin Swirl
(low fat)

- 3 tablespoons honey
- 2 cups warm (110 to 115-degree) water
- 1 tablespoon active dry yeast
- 4 tablespoons nonfat powdered milk
- ¾ teaspoon cinnamon
- 1 teaspoon cardamom
- ½ teaspoon lemon peel, grated
- 1 egg or 2 egg whites
- 2 tablespoons oil or pumpkin
- ½ teaspoon salt
- ¾ to 1 cup raisins
- ½ cup whole wheat flour
- 4½ to 5 cups bread flour
- Maraschino cherries
- Almond slices

Filling:

- ¼ cup honey
- 1 teaspoon cinnamon
- ¼ cup nuts, chopped

Glaze:

- 1 cup powdered sugar
- 1 teaspoon vanilla
- 2 teaspoons water

Grease a loaf pan. Combine honey, water, yeast, milk, cinnamon, cardamom, and lemon peel. Stir in egg, oil, salt, raisins, whole wheat flour, and 2½ cups bread flour. Beat for 3 minutes. Add remaining bread flour until dough cleans bowl. Roll dough out like cinnamon rolls. Spread with honey, cinnamon and nuts. Place in loaf pan seam down. Slash and grease top. Let rise until doubled.

Preheat oven to 350 degrees. Bake for 35–40 minutes. Let bread sit in pan for 10 minutes. Meanwhile, make a glaze by combining powdered sugar, vanilla and water, beating until smooth. Remove bread from pan. Spread glaze over bread and arrange maraschino cherries and/or almond slices on top. Cool bread before slicing.

Cinnamon Swirl Raisin Bread

- 2 tablespoons active dry yeast
- 1¾ cups warm water
- 4 tablespoons nonfat powdered milk
- ⅓ cup honey or sugar
- 2 teaspoons salt
- ¼ cup margarine, melted, or oil
- 1 cup oatmeal
- 1 cup raisins
- 6 to 6½ cups bread flour, or a mixture of 4 to 4½ cups bread flour plus 2 cups whole wheat flour
- Water of butter, melted, to brush onto dough

Filling:

- ½ cup brown sugar
- 1 tablespoon cinnamon

Dissolve yeast in water and set aside for 5 minutes. Stir in powdered milk, honey, salt, margarine, oatmeal, raisins, and half the flour. Mix for 3 minutes. Gradually add remaining flour. Knead dough until smooth and elastic, about 10 minutes. Place dough in a greased bowl, turning over to grease top. Cover and let rest in warm place until doubled in size.

Grease 2 loaf pans. Punch dough down. Divide dough in half. Roll each half into a rectangle. Brush with melted butter or water. Sprinkle half the filling over the top and roll up as for cinnamon rolls. Tuck ends under. Place rolls in loaf pans. Cover and let rise until nearly double in size.

Preheat oven to 375 degrees. Bake for 40 minutes. Leave bread in pans for 5 minutes, then remove to a rack to finish cooling.

Old-fashioned Buttermilk Honey Bread

- 2 tablespoons active dry yeast
- ½ cup warm water
- 1½ cups buttermilk
- ⅓ cup margarine or oil
- ½ teaspoon baking soda
- 2 teaspoons salt, optional
- ⅓ cup honey
- 5 to 6 cups flour
- Margarine, melted, to brush tops of baked loaves

Dissolve yeast in water and set aside for 5 minutes. Combine with buttermilk, margarine, baking soda, salt, honey and half the flour. Mix for 3 minutes. Gradually add more flour, kneading until dough is smooth and elastic, about 10 minutes. Place dough in a greased bowl, turning to grease top of the dough. Let rise until doubled.

Grease 2 loaf pans. Punch dough down and knead to release air bubbles. Divide dough into 2 parts. Form into 2 loaves and place in loaf pans. Let rise until nearly doubled.

Preheat oven to 375 degrees. Bake for 35–40 minutes. Let bread rest in pans for 5 minutes. Brush tops with margarine. Cool loaves on a rack.

Variations:

1. ***Fat free:*** Substitute an equivalent amount of water for margarine or oil.

2. ***Sugar free:*** Substitute an equivalent amount of water for honey.

Honey White Bread

3 cups warm water
2 tablespoons active dry yeast
⅓ cup honey
7 to 9 cups bread flour
1 tablespoon salt
⅓ cup oil
Vegetable oil or spray

Combine water and yeast. Set aside for 5 minutes. Add honey and 3 cups flour, mixing for 3 minutes. Add salt and oil. Stir in 2 additional cups of flour if using dough hook, adding a little flour slowly for 5–8 minutes until dough is smooth and cleans bowl. If in a hurry, let bread rest 20 minutes.

If time permits, let dough rise until it doubles. Punch down dough and knead out air bubbles. Let rise 20 additional minutes.

Preheat oven to 350 degrees. Grease 2 loaf pans. Punch dough down. Form dough into 2 loaves. Lightly slash top of bread to release remaining air bubbles. Brush top with vegetable oil or spray with vegetable oil spray. Bake for about 30 minutes. Let bread sit in pans for 5 minutes, then remove to a rack to cool.

Note: Rolling dough out with a rolling pin all the way to the edges helps remove big air bubbles that might otherwise leave holes in the bread.

Variations:

1. ***Fat free:*** Omit oil and increase water to 3⅓ cups.
2. ***Sugar free:*** Omit honey and increase water to 3⅓ cups.
3. ***Salt free:*** Omit salt.
4. ***Potato Bread:*** Add 1½ cups warm mashed potatoes and reduce oil and honey to ¼ cup each. Sprinkle loaf pans with cornmeal. Proceed as for above, sprinkle flour over tops.

Old-fashioned Oatmeal Bread

2 tablespoons active dry yeast
3 cups warm (105 to 115-degree) water or skim milk
⅓ cup honey, molasses, or brown sugar
⅓ cup oil
2½ teaspoons salt
3 cups oatmeal
7 to 7½ cups flour
Vegetable oil spray
Oats for top of loaves

Dissolve yeast in water and set aside for 5 minutes. Add honey, oil, salt, oatmeal and half the flour, mixing for 3 minutes. Stir in enough flour to make a soft dough. Knead for 6–8 minutes, adding flour as needed, until dough is smooth and elastic. Place dough in a greased bowl, turning once to grease top. Let rise 30 minutes. Punch dough down. Knead out air bubbles. Let rest 15 minutes. Grease 2 large or 3 small loaf pans. Punch dough down. Form dough into 2 large or 3 small loaves. Spray loaf tops with vegetable oil spray and sprinkle oats on top, pressing down firmly on tops of loaves. Place into pans and let dough rise until almost doubled. Spray tops with vegetable oil spray. Preheat oven to 350 degrees. Bake for about 40 minutes. Let loaves sit in pans for 5 minutes, then remove to cool on a rack.

Variations:

1. ***Rolls:*** Follow same recipe for bread, only use less flour. Dough for rolls is softer. Shape dough into balls, place in a greased pan, and spray tops with vegetable oil spray. Let rise until doubled and bake in a 375-degree oven for 15–20 minutes.
2. ***Fat free:*** Omit oil and increase water to 3⅓ cups.
3. ***Sugar free:*** Omit honey and increase water to 3⅓ cups.
4. ***Salt free:*** Omit salt.
5. ***Oat Bran Bread:*** Substitute 1 cup oat bran and 2 cups oatmeal for 3 cups oatmeal.
6. ***Wheat Bran Bread:*** Substitute 2 cups wheat bran and 1 cup wheat germ for oatmeal.
7. ***Buckwheat Bread:*** Substitute 2 cups whole wheat and 1 cup buck wheat for oatmeal.
8. ***Triticale Bread:*** Substitute 2 cups Triticale and 1 cup whole wheat for oatmeal.
9. ***Honey Raisin Bread:*** Add 1 cup raisins. As an option, add ½ cup chopped nuts and ½ teaspoon cinnamon.

Honey Oatmeal Raisin Swirl Bread

2 tablespoons active dry yeast
3 cups warm (105 to 115-degree) water or skim milk
⅓ cup honey, molasses or brown sugar
⅓ cup oil
2½ teaspoons salt
3 cups oatmeal
½ cup raisins
7 to 7½ cups flour

Filling:

½ cup brown sugar
1 tablespoon cinnamon

Dissolve yeast in water and set aside for 5 minutes. Add honey, oil, salt, oatmeal, raisins, and half the flour, mixing for 3 minutes. Stir in enough flour to make a soft dough. Knead dough, adding flour as needed, until smooth and elastic, about 6–8 minutes. Place dough in a greased bowl, turning once to grease top. Let rise 30 minutes.

Punch dough down. Knead out air bubbles. Let rest 15 minutes. Grease two 8½ x 4½-inch loaf pans. Divide dough in half and roll out to form a 5 x 8-inch rectangle. Brush top with water. Combine brown sugar and cinnamon to make a filling. Spread half the filling on top of the dough. Roll up as for jelly roll, tuck ends under. Place roll in loaf pan. Repeat with other half of dough. Let rise until nearly double in size.

Preheat oven to 375 degrees. Bake for 40–45 minutes. Let sit in pans 5 minutes, then remove to finish cooling.

Honey Oat Bran Bread

- 2 tablespoons (2 packages) active dry yeast
- 3 cups warm (105 to 115 degree) water
- 1½ cups oatmeal
- ⅓ cup honey
- ⅓ cup canola or soy oil
- 4 tablespoons nonfat powdered milk
- 2 egg whites, optional
- 5 to 6 cups all-purpose flour
- 1½ cups oat bran
- 1½ teaspoons salt, optional
- Vegetable oil spray

Dissolve yeast in water. Add oatmeal, honey, oil, nonfat powdered milk, egg whites, and half the flour. Mix for 3 minutes. Let batter rest for 15 minutes. Meanwhile, grease 2 bread pans.

Stir remaining flour, oat bran and salt into yeast mixture. Knead dough for 5 minutes, adding more flour as needed to make a soft dough. Add just enough flour so dough becomes soft and elastic and cleans the bowl. Place dough into bread pans, spray tops of loaves with vegetable oil spray, and let rise until doubled in size.

Preheat oven to 350–375 degrees. Bake for 30–35 minutes. Leave in pans to cool for 5 minutes. Remove bread from pans to finish cooling on wire rack.

Variations:

1. ***Rolls:*** Follow same recipe for bread, only use less flour. Dough for rolls is softer. Shape dough into balls, place in a greased pan, and spray tops with vegetable oil spray. Let rise until doubled and bake in a 375-degree oven for 15–20 minutes.

2. ***Fat free:*** Substitute water for oil.

3. ***Sugar free:*** Substitute water for honey.

Honey Squaw Bread

- ½ cup oatmeal
- ½ cup cornmeal
- ½ cup wheat bran or bran] cereal
- ¼ cup wheat germ
- 2 cups boiling water
- 2 tablespoons active dry yeast
- ½ cup warm water
- ⅓ cup honey
- 2 tablespoons margarine or oil
- 2 cups whole wheat flour
- 3 cups all-purpose flour

In a large bowl combine oatmeal, cornmeal, wheat bran and wheat germ. Add boiling water and stir thoroughly. Set aside to cool.

Meanwhile, dissolve yeast in water. Add honey and margarine, mixing thoroughly. Add cooled oatmeal mixture, mixing until smooth. Stir in whole wheat flour. Gradually add 2–2¼ cups all-purpose flour, reserving remaining ½ to ¾ cup for kneading. Mix until stiff enough to knead. Sprinkle remaining flour on a flat surface.

Knead dough for 10 minutes. If using a mixer with a dough hook, knead dough until smooth, adding more flour as necessary to keep dough from sticking. Shape dough into a ball. Place in a greased bowl, turning over to grease the top. Cover and let rise in a warm place until doubled.

Grease a cookie sheet. Punch dough down to remove air bubbles. Divide dough in half. Shape each half into a round loaf. Place loaves on cookie sheet. Cover and let rise until almost doubled in size.

Preheat oven to 350 degrees. Bake for 45 minutes. Cool.

Molasses Beer Bread

- 1 cup cornmeal
- 3 tablespoons oil
- ½ cup molasses
- 1 tablespoon salt
- 2 cups beer or water, hot
- 2 tablespoons active dry yeast
- ½ cup warm water
- 7 to 8 cups all-purpose flour, or a mixture 6 to 7 cups all-purpose flour plus 1 cup wheat germ
- Cornmeal
- Vegetable oil spray

Combine cornmeal, oil, molasses and salt with boiling beer or water. Cool to lukewarm.

Meanwhile, in a separate bowl dissolve yeast in warm water and set aside for 5 minutes. Combine yeast mixture with cornmeal mixture. Add 3 cups flour and mix for 3 minutes. Knead in additional flour as needed to make a stiff, smooth and elastic dough. Place dough in a greased bowl, turning to grease top. Cover and let rise until doubled.

Grease 2 loaf pans and if desired sprinkle with cornmeal. Punch dough down and knead for 5 minutes to release air bubbles. Divide dough into two pieces and shape each piece into a loaf. Place loaves into loaf pans. Spray loaf tops with vegetable oil spray and sprinkle cornmeal on top. Let rise until almost doubled.

Preheat oven to 375 degrees. Bake for 40–50 minutes. Brush or spray loaves with vegetable oil spray. Cool loaves on a wire rack.

Variation: Substitute 3 cups of Triticale plus 3 cups whole wheat flour for the all-purpose flour.

Baked Donuts

- 2 tablespoons active dry yeast
- ¼ cup warm water
- 1½ cups warm milk or buttermilk
- ½ cup sugar
- 1 teaspoon salt
- 1 teaspoon nutmeg, optional
- 1 teaspoon cinnamon, optional
- 2 eggs
- ⅓ cup shortening or margarine
- 4½ cups all-purpose flour
- Vegetable oil, margarine, or butter for spreading over unbaked donuts

Topping:

- ½ teaspoon cinnamon
- ¼ cup sugar

Glaze:

- 2 cups powdered sugar
- ½ cup buttermilk
- 2 teaspoons vanilla

Dissolve yeast in water. Add milk, sugar, salt, nutmeg, cinnamon, eggs, shortening, and half the flour. Mix for 2 minutes. Stir in remaining flour until smooth. Cover and let rise in warm place until doubled.

Grease baking sheet. Turn dough out onto a floured tablecloth. Roll soft dough around lightly to coat. Gently roll dough out to ½-inch thick. Cut with a floured donut cutter. Lift donuts carefully with a spatula and place 2 inches apart on baking sheet. Spray tops with vegetable oil or brush with melted butter or margarine. Cover and let rise until doubled.

Preheat oven to 425 degrees. Bake for 20 minutes. Spray donuts with vegetable oil or brush with melted butter or margarine. Shake cinnamon and sugar mixture over warm donuts or glaze donuts after baking. To make glaze, combine powdered sugar, buttermilk, and vanilla until of spreadable consistency.

Variations:

1. For maple bars, a corned beef or spam can works great as a cutter.

2. ***Chocolate Donuts:*** Omit spices. Reduce flour to 4¼ cups total. Mix in ½ cup cocoa with first addition of flour. After baking, sprinkle donuts with powdered sugar or spread with Chocolate Glaze. Add 3–4 tablespoons unsweetened cocoa to recipe above to make a Chocolate Glaze.

3. ***Applesauce Donuts:*** Substitute 1½ cups warm applesauce for the milk. Substitute 1 teaspoon cinnamon, ½ teaspoon nutmeg, and ½ teaspoon ground cloves for 1 teaspoon nutmeg and ¼ teaspoon cinnamon. Reduce all-purpose flour to 4 cups and add ¼ cup whole wheat flour.

Old-fashioned Hot Cross Buns

- 1 tablespoon active dry yeast
- ¼ cup warm (110 to 115-degree) water
- ½ cup sugar
- 1 cup milk
- 3 tablespoons butter or margarine
- ¾ teaspoon salt
- 1 teaspoon cinnamon
- ½ teaspoon nutmeg
- ¼ teaspoon cardamom or cloves
- 3½ to 4 cups flour
- 2 eggs, beaten
- 1 tablespoon oil
- ¾ cup dried currants
- ¼ cup candied orange peel, citron, or pineapple, finely diced
- 1 egg yolk
- 3 tablespoons water

Lemon Glaze:

- 1 cup powdered sugar
- ½ teaspoon lemon peel, grated
- 1 tablespoon lemon juice

Dissolve yeast in water and let sit 5 minutes. Heat milk in a saucepan on stovetop. Add sugar and butter, stirring to dissolve. Pour milk mixture into a large mixing bowl. Stir in salt, cinnamon, nutmeg and cardamom. Add 2 cups flour, eggs and oil. Beat until smooth. In a separate bowl combine fruit with ½ cup flour. Stir fruit mixture into flour mixture. Gradually add enough flour to make a stiff dough.

Knead with dough hook or by hand on a floured board until dough is smooth and elastic, about 10 minutes. Add only enough flour to prevent the dough from becoming too sticky. Dough should be soft. Let dough rise until doubled.

Punch dough down and form into 1–1½ inch balls and place on a greased baking sheet. Cut a cross on top of each ball with a knife or scissors. Cross should be no more than ⅛-inch deep.

Combine egg yolk and 3 tablespoons water. Brush buns lightly with diluted egg mixture. Cover and let rise in warm place.

Preheat oven to 375 degrees. Place dough onto baking sheet and bake about 20 minutes.

Lemon Glaze: Combine powdered sugar, lemon peel and lemon juice. Add a few drops of water if glaze is too thick. Cool slightly. Pour glaze into crosses on buns.

Hot Cross Buns

(low fat)

- 2 cups warm (110 to 115-degree) water
- 4 tablespoons nonfat powdered milk
- 2 tablespoons active dry yeast
- ⅓ cup honey
- 2 teaspoons cinnamon
- ⅙ teaspoon cloves
- ½ teaspoon nutmeg
- ½ teaspoon salt
- ¼ teaspoon cardamom
- 2½ to 3 cups plus 2 to 2½ cups all-purpose flour
- 4 tablespoons pumpkin
- 3 eggs or ¾ cup egg whites
- ⅔ cup currants or raisins
- 1 teaspoon lemon peel, grated
- ⅓ cup nuts, chopped (optional)
- ½ to 1 cup whole wheat flour
- ½ cup oatmeal

Egg Wash:

- 1 egg white, beaten
- 3 tablespoons water

Icing:

- 1 cup powdered sugar
- 2 teaspoons lemon juice
- 1 teaspoon water

Combine water, nonfat powdered milk, yeast and honey. Mix with an electric mixer. Add cinnamon, cloves, nutmeg, salt, cardamom, and 2½ to 3 cups all-purpose flour. Mix for 2 minutes. Stir in pumpkin, eggs, currents, lemon peel, nuts, whole wheat flour, oatmeal, and 2 to 2½ cups all-purpose flour. Mix until dough is smooth and elastic and comes away from the bowl. Dough should still be sticky though, so rolls spread a little when rising. Roll dough into balls. Place balls in greased pan. Combine egg and water. Spread egg wash over balls. Let dough rise until doubled.

Preheat oven to 350 degrees. Bake about 25 minutes.

Icing: Combine powdered sugar, lemon juice and water. Beat until smooth. Make a cross of icing on top of cooled buns.

Old-fashioned Cinnamon Rolls

- ½ cup buttermilk, warm
- ½ cup warm water (110 to 115 degrees)
- 1 tablespoon active dry yeast
- 3 to 3½ cups flour
- ¼ cup sugar
- 1 teaspoon salt
- 3 tablespoons margarine, melted or oil
- 1 egg

Glaze:

- ¼ cup margarine or butter
- 1 teaspoon vanilla
- ¼ cup buttermilk
- 4 cups powdered sugar

Combine buttermilk, water and yeast, let sit 5 minutes. Add half of flour along with remaining ingredients, mix 3 minutes. Add remaining flour. Mix well and turn out onto a floured surface. Knead for 5 minutes by hand. Place in a greased bowl turning once to grease top. Cover and let rise until double. To make filling, combine melted margarine or butter, brown sugar, cinnamon and raisins. Punch dough down. Roll dough out, spread with filling. Roll dough in a jelly roll fashion, pinching seams together. Cut roll in 1½ inch thickness and place 1½ inches apart in a greased 9x13 inch pan. Let rise until double. Preheat oven to 350 degrees. Bake for 15 to 20 minutes or until golden brown. To make icing, heat together the margarine and buttermilk until margarine is melted. Beat in vanilla and powdered sugar. If too sweet, add 1 teaspoon salt. Cool slightly and frost while still warm.

Variation: For lower fat use water in place of buttermilk, use 2 tablespoons oil or margarine instead of 3 tablespoons. Replace egg with 2 egg whites. Replace sugar with 2 tablespoons brown sugar for less sweetness.

Filling:

- ¾ cup melted margarine or butter
- 1½ cups brown sugar
- 1 cup raisins
- 2 tablespoons cinnamon

Combine ingredients. Cool cinnamon rolls slightly before glazing.

Sticky Buns

- 2¼ cups brown sugar
- 1 cup butter or margarine
- ¼ cup corn syrup
- 1 cup chopped nuts, optional

Combine all ingredients in a saucepan. Heat, mix just until butter melts. Spread into a greased 9x13 inch pan. Place rolls on top of sticky bun mixture. Bake as directed. After baking, turn pan over so sticky mixture is on top of rolls. Serve warm or cold.

Grandma's Cinnamon Rolls

- 3 tablespoons active dry yeast
- 1 cup warm water (110 to 115 degrees)
- 6 to 7 cups flour
- 2 cups buttermilk
- ¾ cup margarine, melted or oil
- ¾ cup brown sugar
- 2 teaspoons salt
- 3 eggs
- 1½ teaspoons vanilla
- ¼ teaspoon cinnamon
- ¼ teaspoon nutmeg

Filling:

- 1½ cups melted margarine or butter
- 3 cups brown sugar
- 2 cups raisins
- 4 tablespoons cinnamon

Frosting:

- ½ cup buttermilk
- 1 teaspoon vanilla
- 3 cups powdered sugar
- Dash of salt

Combine liquid and yeast and let sit 5 minutes. Add half the flour along with remaining ingredients. Mix for 3 minutes, then add remaining flour. Mix well and turn out onto floured surface. Knead for 5 minutes by hand. Place in a greased bowl turning once to grease top. Cover and let rise until double. Punch dough down. Roll dough out, spread with filling. Roll dough in a jelly roll fashion pinching seams together. Cut roll in 1½-inch sections and place in a large greased pan. Place rolls 1½ inches apart. Let rise until double. Bake at 350 degrees for 15–20 minutes or until golden brown. Cool slightly and frost while still warm.

Variation: ***Puffs:*** After dough has risen once, shape into balls of soft dough and place in greased muffin tins filling muffin tin ½ full. Cut down into dough with floured scissors approximately 1½ inch in an "X" cut. Sprinkle cinnamon, sugar, margarine or butter into the cut, raisins, nuts or applesauce (optional) into the cut. Let rise and bake. While puffs are still warm, drizzle glaze over tops.

Whole Wheat Cinnamon Rolls

(low fat or fat free)

- 2 tablespoons active dry yeast
- 4 cups warm water
- ½ cup nonfat powdered milk
- 1 cup oats
- ½ cup multi-grain
- ½ cup honey or sugar
- ¼ cup brown sugar
- ½ teaspoon salt
- 2 eggs or ½ cup egg substitute
- 2 cups whole wheat flour
- ¼ cup pumpkin
- 1 cup raisins, optional
- 2½ to 3 cups all-purpose flour

Fat-Free Frosting:

- ½ cup buttermilk or water
- 2½ to 3 cups powdered sugar
- 1 teaspoon maple flavoring

Combine all ingredients; mix until dough is no longer sticky but still soft, approximately 3 minutes. Can store in refrigerator until ready to use or let rise once and roll out for cinnamon rolls, use vegetable spray instead of butter or omit all together. Spread on a cinnamon/honey mixture or fruit filling, cut and let rise. Preheat oven to 350 degrees. Bake for 20 to 25 minutes.

To make frosting, combine ingredients until of right consistency.

Variation: Vanilla may replace maple flavoring.

Sticky Buns

(fat free)

- 1 cup orange or apple juice concentrate
- 1 cup honey
- 2 tablespoons cornstarch

(You can spread onto cinnamon rolls in place of cinnamon/honey mixture). Heat together orange juice concentrate, honey and cornstarch. Cook until thicker. Place a little in greased muffin tins, place cut cinnamon rolls into muffin tins to rise, or put mixture into a greased baking pan placing cinnamon rolls on top. Let rise and bake. Immediately after baking run a knife along the edges of pan and invert onto a plate.

Whole Wheat Cinnamon or Sweet Roll

(low fat)

- 2 tablespoons active dry yeast
- 1 cup water, warm
- 1 cup skim milk, warm
- ¼ cup margarine
- ½ cup honey
- ½ teaspoon salt
- 4 cups whole wheat flour, or a mixture of 3 cups whole wheat flour plus 1 cup oats
- 1 egg, beaten
- 2 egg whites
- 2 to 2½ cups all-purpose flour
- ½ cup raisins, optional

Filling:

- ½ cup brown sugar
- 2 teaspoons cinnamon
- ¾ cup raisins or currants

Glaze:

- 2 cups powdered sugar
- ½ teaspoon vanilla
- 3 tablespoons buttermilk or water

Dissolve yeast in water and set aside for 5 minutes. In a separate bowl combine milk, margarine, honey and salt. Stir in 2 cups whole wheat flour to make a soft batter. Add yeast, beaten egg and egg whites, beating well. Stir in enough remaining flour to make a soft dough. Place dough in a greased bowl, turning to grease top. Cover and let rise until doubled in size, about 1½ hours.

Grease a cookie sheet or baking pan. Divide dough into 2 parts. Roll 1 part to ¼-inch thickness in a rectangular shape. Spread with filling of your choice, or make a filling combining brown sugar, cinnamon and raisins or currants. Roll up tightly, beginning at wide side. Seal well by pinching edges of roll together. Slice ¾-inch thick and arrange slices on cookie sheet or baking pan. Repeat with remaining dough. Let rise 30–45 minutes.

Preheat oven to 350 degrees. Bake for 20 minutes. Combine powdered sugar, vanilla and buttermilk or water to make a glaze. Spread glaze over warm cinnamon rolls.

Oat Bran Cinnamon Rolls

(fat & sugar free)

- 2 tablespoons (2 packages) active dry yeast
- 2½ cups very warm water
- 4 tablespoons nonfat dry milk
- 4 egg whites or ½ cup egg substitute
- ½ teaspoon salt
- ½ cup apple juice concentrate
- ½ cup pumpkin
- ½ cup oatmeal
- ½ cup oat bran
- ¼ cup whole wheat flour
- ¾ teaspoon cinnamon
- 1 cup raisins
- 4½ to 5½ cups all-purpose flour

Filling:

- ½ cup apple juice concentrate
- 2 teaspoons cinnamon

Glaze:

- ¼ cup apple juice concentrate
- ¼ cup orange juice concentrate
- 1 teaspoon cornstarch

Dissolve yeast in water and set aside for 5 minutes. Add nonfat dry milk, egg whites, salt, apple juice concentrate, pumpkin, oatmeal, oat bran, whole wheat flour, cinnamon, raisins, and 3 cups all-purpose flour. Mix for 2 minutes. Add remaining flour, mixing into a soft dough. Refrigerate dough for at least 4 hours. Dough will last 3 days in refrigerator.

Spray baking pan with vegetable oil spray. Roll out dough as needed for cinnamon rolls. Spray dough lightly with vegetable oil spray. To make filling combine apple juice concentrate and cinnamon. Spread filling over dough. Roll dough up tightly and slice into rolls. Place rolls in pan. Spray tops of cinnamon rolls with vegetable oil spray. Let rolls rise until doubled in size.

Preheat oven to 350 degrees. Bake for 20–25 minutes. Make glaze by combining apple and orange juice concentrates and cornstarch in a microwavable container and microwaving until thick. Spread over warm rolls.

Variations:

1. Replace pumpkin with ½ oil and add 2 eggs.
2. Substitute honey for apple juice concentrate.
3. Make a filling with dried or unsweetened fruit, chopped (plums, apples, cherries, apricots, etc.).
4. ***Fat Free Glaze:*** Combine ½ cup buttermilk, 2½ to 3 cups powdered sugar, and 1 teaspoon vanilla or lemon extract. Spread over warm rolls.

Oat Bran Cinnamon Rolls

(cholesterol free)

Dough is best made the night before. Roll out in morning.

- 2½ tablespoons active dry yeast
- 4 cups warm water
- ½ to ⅔ cup honey
- ⅓ cup nonfat powdered dry milk
- ½ cup egg whites
- 1 cup oatmeal
- 1 cup oat bran
- 1 cup oil
- ¼ cup pumpkin
- 2½ teaspoons salt, optional
- 1 cup raisins, optional
- 6 to 8 cups flour

Frosting:

- ½ cup buttermilk
- 2½ to 3 cups powdered sugar
- 1 teaspoon vanilla or lemon extract

Dissolve yeast in water. Add honey, nonfat powdered milk, egg whites, oatmeal, oat bran, oil, pumpkin, salt, raisins and 4 cups flour. Mix for 3 minutes. Gradually add remaining flour to make a very soft dough. Store dough in a large container and let rise in refrigerator. Dough will keep up to 4 days.

Grease a baking sheet. Roll dough out for cinnamon rolls, adding flour if too sticky. Can spread over dough a mixture of honey, margarine and cinnamon or a mixture of apple juice concentrate, brown sugar and cinnamon. Roll dough up tightly and slice. Place slices on baking sheet. Let rise.

Preheat oven to 350 degrees. Bake for 20–25 minutes. Make frosting by combining buttermilk, powdered sugar and vanilla. Spread frosting over warm rolls.

Variation: A filling of fruit jam (raspberry, apple, strawberry, etc.) can be used.

Old-fashioned Strudel

- 2¾ cups flour
- ¼ teaspoon salt
- 1 egg
- 2 tablespoons oil, margarine or butter, melted
- ¾ cup warm water
- ½ cup butter or margarine, melted
- ½ cup plus 1 cup bread crumbs
- Powdered sugar

Combine flour and salt. Make a well in center of flour mixture. Add the egg, oil and water to the well. Mix to make a sticky dough. Knead dough on a floured surface or in a heavy duty mixer, gradually adding flour as needed until dough is soft and elastic. Cover dough with a bowl and allow to rest for 30 minutes. Meanwhile, line a large cookie sheet with greased aluminum foil or grease/butter a deep baking pan. This helps to keep oven clean in case of spill over.

Preheat oven to 400 degrees. Place dough on a clean floured tablecloth. Roll out dough into as large a square as possible. Place hands palm down so as not to tear dough and stretch dough, moving around the table, into a very large rectangle that is thin enough to read through it. Brush dough with melted butter. Sprinkle dough with ½ cup bread crumbs. Add fruit filling of your choice:

1. ***Apple Filling:*** 4 cups apple (peeled cored, and thinly sliced), 1 tablespoon lemon juice, ¼ cup brown sugar, ¼ cup granulated sugar, 1 teaspoon or more cinnamon, ¾ cup raisins (optional), and ¾ cup nuts, chopped (optional).
2. ***Cherry Filling:*** 4 cups pie cherries (pitted), ½ cup sugar, and a dash nutmeg.
3. ***Blueberry Filling:*** 4 cups blueberries, ½ cup sugar, and a dash nutmeg.
4. ***Peach or Apricot Filling:*** 4 cups fruit (cut up) and ¾ to 1 cup sugar.

Spoon fruit in an even row down one end and 2 inches from edge of dough. Sprinkle 1 cup bread crumbs over fruit filling. Trim any thick parts on corners of dough with scissors. Using the tablecloth, lift dough and fold in the two parallel sides of dough toward the center to enclose the filling. Roll dough like a jelly roll, allowing dough to roll over and over on itself until completely rolled. Place dough on cookie sheet or baking pan. Spray top of strudel with vegetable oil spray, or brush with melted butter or margarine. Bake until pastry is golden brown, about 40–45 minutes. Cool. Sprinkle with powdered sugar.

Cookies

Who doesn't like the aroma of fresh baked cookies drifting through the house; warm cookies fresh from the oven? Some people like them soft and moist, other like them thick, crisp or chewy. Cookies come frosted, unfrosted, big or small; chock full of grains, fruits and spices. There's nothing quite like a homemade cookie. Cookies bring back happy memories of years gone by, Grandma, as likely as not, made her reputation with a single recipe; but today, even a beginner can make a dozen different kinds of cookies that would have made Grandma gasp.

The recipes in this chapter will help you and your family build up lots of happy cookie memories. Possibilities for varying cookie recipes are endless; fruits, nuts and grains, all may be added with little or no change to the rest of the recipe. By using whole grain ingredients, and reducing the fat, cookies are not only delicious but good for you too.

The advantage most of these recipes gives you is that their calories are not empty. Rolled oats, nonfat dry milk, wheat germ, cereal, seeds, nuts and fruits are just some of the nutritious extras that can be added to cookies. Also, the fat can be reduced in a recipe by half by adding a binder such as mashed banana, pumpkin, applesauce, etc. The cookies will have more of a cake texture but will still be delicious.

There are five types of cookies:

1. ***Rolled:*** a moderately soft dough, chilled, rolled thin and cut out.
2. ***Drop:*** a softer dough, dropped from a tablespoon.
3. ***Ice box:*** a moderately soft dough; shaped in baking a roll and rolled up in wax paper or Saran wrap; chilled until firm in refrigerator and sliced thin with a sharp knife.
4. ***Pressed:*** a moderately soft dough, put through a cookie press to form definite shapes.
5. ***Bars:*** dough baked in a sheet pan and cut into bars after baking.

The process of mixing cookies is very similar to that for cakes, except that less liquid or none at all is used except for the eggs. Whatever type of cookie, a soft dough gives the tenderest product.

Care of Cookies

Never put more than one kind of cookie together in a jar as there will be an undesirable interchange of flavors.

Cranberry Cookies

- 1 cup brown sugar
- ¾ cup sugar
- ½ cup margarine
- ¼ cup buttermilk
- 2 tablespoons orange juice
- 1 egg
- 3 cups all-purpose flour
  –or–
  2 cups all-purpose flour
  plus 1 cup whole wheat flour
- ½ teaspoon baking soda
- 1 teaspoon baking powder
- ½ teaspoon salt, optional
- 2 cups cranberries, chopped
- 1 cup nuts, chopped

Grease cookie sheets. Preheat oven to 375 degrees. Cream together sugars and margarine. Add buttermilk, orange juice and egg, mixing well. Add, remaining ingredients, mixing well.

Drop by tablespoons about 2 inches apart onto cookie sheets. Bake for 10–15 minutes. Remove to rack to cool.

After cooling, cookies can be glazed with Brown Butter Glaze or Fat-free Glaze. Yield: About 3 dozen cookies.

Brown Butter Glaze:

Brown ⅓ cup margarine. Let cool. Add 2 cups powdered sugar and 2–4 tablespoons water.

Fat-free Glaze:

Combine ⅓ cup orange juice, 2 cups powdered sugar and 2–4 tablespoons water.

Washington Cranapple Cookies

This makes a delicious holiday recipe.

- 1 cup fresh or thawed frozen cranberries, chopped
- 1 cup apples, chopped
- ¾ cup sugar
- ½ cup shortening
- ½ cup margarine
- 1¼ cups brown sugar
- 2 eggs
- 1¾ cups flour
- 1 teaspoon salt
- 1 teaspoon baking powder
- 1 teaspoon baking soda
- 1 teaspoon cinnamon
- 1 teaspoon nutmeg
- ⅓ cup buttermilk
- 1 teaspoon vanilla
- 1½ teaspoons orange peel, grated
- 3 cups oatmeal
- 1 cup nuts, chopped

Combine cranberries, apples and sugar. Set aside for 30 minutes. In a separate bowl, cream together shortening, margarine and brown sugar. Add eggs and beat until well blended. Stir in remaining ingredients. Preheat oven to 375–400 degrees. Grease cookie sheets. Add apple and cranberry mixture to the flour mixture and mix well. Drop by tablespoonfuls onto cookie sheets. Bake for 10 minutes. Yield: About 2 dozen cookies.

Cranberry Oatmeal Cookies

- ½ cup shortening plus ½ cup margarine
- 1½ cups brown sugar
- 2 eggs
- ½ cup buttermilk
- 1 teaspoon nutmeg
- 3 cups oats
- 1½ cups fresh cranberries, chopped
- ½ cup walnuts, chopped

Grease cookie sheets. Preheat oven to 375 degrees. Cream together shortening, margarine and sugar. Beat in eggs. Stir in buttermilk. Add remaining ingredients, mixing well. Drop by tablespoonfuls about 2 inches apart on cookie sheets. Bake for about 10 minutes. Yield: About 3 dozen cookies.

Granola Cookies

- ¾ cup margarine
- ½ cup sugar
- 2 eggs
- ¼ cup molasses
- ¼ cup buttermilk
- ½ teaspoon baking soda
- 1 teaspoon cinnamon
- 2 cups flour
- 1 teaspoon or less salt
- 2 cups No Bake Granola (page 241)

Grease cookie sheets. Preheat oven to 375 degrees. Cream margarine and sugar together. Beat in eggs, molasses and buttermilk. Mix in baking soda and cinnamon. Add and mix well flour, salt and No Bake Granola. Drop by tablespoonfuls onto cookie sheets. Bake 8–10 minutes. Yield: About 2½ dozen cookies.

Holiday Fruit Cookies

- ½ cup shortening
- ½ cup margarine
- 2 cups brown sugar
- 1 teaspoon vanilla, brandy or sherry
- 2 eggs
- ½ cup buttermilk
- 1 teaspoon baking soda
- 1 teaspoon baking powder
- 4 cups all-purpose flour *–or–*
  2 cups all-purpose flour plus 2 cups whole wheat flour
- 1 cup candied cherries, chopped
- 1 cup candied fruit, chopped
- 2 cups dates, prunes or raisins, chopped
- 1 cup nuts, chopped

Cream together shortening, margarine, brown sugar and vanilla, brandy or sherry. Add eggs and beat until fluffy. Stir in buttermilk. Add, mixing well, baking soda, baking powder, flour, cherries, candied fruit, fresh fruit and nuts. Chill dough.

Grease cookie sheets. Preheat oven to 350 degrees. Drop dough by tablespoonfuls onto cookie sheets. Bake for 20 minutes. Yield: About 4 dozen cookies.

Variation: Top cookies with chopped red or green candied cherries before baking.

Christmas Drop Cookies

(fat free)

These cookies improve with age.

- 1 pound dates, chopped
- ½ cup walnuts, chopped
- ½ cup maraschino cherries, chopped
- 1 cup sugar
- 1 teaspoon vanilla
- 3 stiffly beaten egg whites
- 1 cup flour

Grease cookie sheets. Preheat oven to 350 degrees. Combine dates, cherries and walnuts. Stir in sugar and vanilla. Add egg whites and flour alternately to the fruit and nut mixture. (If mixture becomes too dry, add a few drops of maraschino cherry juice.) Drop by teaspoonfuls onto cookie sheets. Top each cookie with pieces of cherry. Bake until lightly browned, about 20 minutes. Store in airtight container. Yield: About 3½ dozen cookies.

Hermits

This recipe dates back to the 1880's.

- ½ cup shortening
- ½ cup margarine
- 1¾ cups brown sugar
- 2 eggs
- 3½ cups flour
- 1 teaspoon nutmeg
- 2 teaspoons cinnamon
- 1 teaspoon baking powder
- 1 teaspoon baking soda
- ⅓ teaspoon salt
- ½ cup buttermilk
- 1 cup nuts, chopped
- 1 cup raisins or other dried fruit, chopped
- 1 cup dates, chopped

Grease cookie sheet. Preheat oven to 375 degrees. Cream together shortening, margarine and sugar. Add eggs and beat well. Mix in flour, nutmeg, cinnamon, baking powder, baking soda and salt alternately with buttermilk. Stir in nuts and fruits. Drop by tablespoonfuls onto cookie sheet. Bake for 12–15 minutes. Yield: About 3 dozen cookies.

Hermits
(low fat, milk free)

- ½ cup dried apricots or apple, chopped
- ½ cup dried dates or prunes, chopped
- ½ cup raisins, chopped
- ¾ cup water
- ½ cup margarine
- ½ cup brown sugar
- ½ cup granulated sugar
- 1 egg
- 1 tablespoon lemon juice
- 1½ cups oatmeal
- 2 tablespoons wheat germ
- 2 cups flour
- 1 teaspoon baking soda
- 1 teaspoon baking powder
- ½ teaspoon salt
- ½ cup nuts, chopped

Combine dried fruit and water in a saucepan and simmer for 5 minutes until thick. Set aside and let cool.

Meanwhile, beat together until light and fluffy margarine and sugars. Beat in egg and lemon juice. Add oatmeal, wheat germ, flour, baking soda, baking powder, salt and nuts.

Add cooled fruit mixture and mix well. Chill dough. Preheat oven to 350 degrees. Grease cookie sheets. Drop dough by tablespoonfuls onto cookie sheets.

Bake for 12–15 minutes. Cool cookies on racks. Store in tightly covered container. Yield: About 2½ dozen cookies.

Old-fashioned Cookies

This recipe easily makes a large variety of cookies to satisfy everyone.

- 1½ cups brown sugar
- 1¼ cups granulated sugar
- 2 cups margarine, or 1 cup margarine plus 1 cup shortening
- 4 eggs
- 1 teaspoon salt
- 2 teaspoons baking soda
- 1 tablespoon cream of tartar
- 5½ to 6 cups flour
- ¼ cup buttermilk

Preheat oven to 375 degrees. Lightly grease cookie sheets. Cream together sugars and margarine until fluffy. Add eggs, mixing well. Combine dry ingredients in a separate bowl. Stir dry mixture into sugar mixture alternately with buttermilk and mix well. Drop by teaspoonfuls about 2 inches apart on cookie sheets. Bake for 10–15 minutes. Yield: About 9 dozen cookies.

Variations: Omit cream of tartar and 1½ teaspoon baking soda; substitute 2 tablespoons baking powder combined with ½ teaspoon baking soda.

Chocolate Cookies: Add 2 tablespoons cocoa to 2 cups dough.

Chocolate Chip and Nut Cookies: Add ¾ cup chocolate chips and ¾ cup chopped nuts to 2 cups dough.

Coconut Cookies: Add 2 cups coconut and ½ teaspoon almond extract to 2 cups dough. Shape 1-inch balls and flatten on cookie sheet. Top each with a candied cherry.

Cranberry Orange Cookies: Add ⅓ cup more sugar, 1 teaspoon grated orange peel, and 2 tablespoons orange juice to 2 cups dough.

Fruit Cookies: Add 1 cup chopped fruit, ½ teaspoon cinnamon and ¼ teaspoon cloves to 2 cups dough. If using dry fruit, soak in water until soft, then drain.

Ginger Cookies: Add 2 T. dark molasses and ¾ to 1 teaspoon ginger to 2 cups dough. Shape 1-inch balls, dipping fingers into water occasionally to prevent dough from sticking to fingers.

Orange Cookies: Add 1 teaspoon grated orange peel and 2 tablespoons orange juice to 2 cups dough. A little additional sugar may be added.

Pecan Balls: Add 1 cup chopped pecans and 1 teaspoon vanilla to 2 cups dough. Shape into 1-inch balls.

Chocolate Chip Cookies

This is a crisp cookie.

- ½ cup margarine
- ½ cup shortening
- ¾ cup brown sugar
- ½ cup sugar
- 1 egg
- 1 teaspoon vanilla
- 1½ tablespoons buttermilk
- ½ teaspoon salt
- 1 teaspoon baking soda
- ½ teaspoon cream of tartar
- 2 cups plus 2 tablespoons flour
- 1 cup chocolate chips
- ½ cup nuts, chopped

Preheat oven to 375 degrees. Cream margarine, shortening and sugars together. Add, beating well, egg, vanilla and buttermilk. Add remaining ingredients, mixing well. Drop by tablespoonfuls onto ungreased cookie sheets and bake until light golden brown, about 8–10 minutes. Cool 1 minute before removing to racks to cool. Yield: About 2½ dozen cookies.

Variations:

1. For a softer cookie, reduce flour to 1¾ cups, omit buttermilk and cream of tartar, and increase vanilla to 1½ teaspoons.

2. ***Chocolate-Chocolate Chip Cookies:*** Add 2 tablespoons cocoa to dry ingredients.

Chocolate Chip Cookies

(lower sugar, lower fat)

- ¼ cup margarine
- 2 tablespoons apple juice concentrate, Fruit Sweet, or honey
- 1 egg
- 1 teaspoon vanilla
- ¾ cup flour
- ¼ teaspoon baking soda
- ¼ teaspoon cream of tartar
- ¼ teaspoon salt
- ½ cup low-fat chocolate chips or mini chocolate chips

Grease cookie sheets. Preheat oven to 375 degrees. Cream together margarine and sweetener. Beat in egg and vanilla. Combine dry ingredients with cream mixture, mixing thoroughly. Drop by tablespoonfuls about 2 inches apart on cookie sheets. Bake 8–10 minutes. Yield: About 1½ dozen cookies.

Chocolate Chunk Krinkles

The cookie chocolate lovers can't get enough of.

3 beaten eggs
½ cup oil
1½ cups sugar
4 ounces unsweetened chocolate, melted
2 teaspoons baking powder
½ teaspoon salt
2 cups flour
¾ cup semisweet chocolate chips or chunks
¾ cup nuts, chopped (optional)
2 teaspoons vanilla
Powdered sugar

Combine eggs, oil, sugar and chocolate, beating well. Add baking powder, salt and flour, mixing well. Stir in chocolate chips or chunks, nuts and vanilla. Chill dough for several hours.

Preheat oven to 375 degrees. Lightly grease cookie sheets. Shape dough into 1-inch balls and roll in powdered sugar. Bake on cookie sheets until edges are set and tops are cracked, about 8–10 minutes. Do not overbake.

Cool on wire racks. After cookies cool, additional powdered sugar may be sprinkled on top. Yield: About 3½ dozen cookies.

Variation: To reduce fat, replace unsweetened chocolate with ½ cup cocoa, reduce flour to 1⅔ cups, and reduce baking powder to 1½ teaspoons. Reduce chocolate chips to ½ cups or use mini chocolate chips.

Notes:

Grandma's Favorite Peanut Butter Cookies

Always a favorite with everyone.

½	cup margarine	1	tablespoon vanilla
½	cup shortening	2	beaten eggs
1	cup brown sugar	1	teaspoon baking soda
1	cup granulated sugar	¾	teaspoon salt
1	cup peanut butter	2½	to 3 cups flour

Cream together margarine, shortening, sugars, peanut butter and vanilla. Add eggs. Mix in baking soda, salt and flour. Lightly grease cookie sheet.

Preheat oven to 375 degrees. Hand roll dough into balls, place on cookie sheet and flatten with a fork in a crisscross pattern, dipping fork in flour to reduce stickiness. Bake for 10–12 minutes. Yield: About 4½ dozen cookies.

Variations:

Egg Free Cookies: Omit eggs to make delicious shortbread peanut butter cookies.

Lower Fat Cookies: Omit shortening. Substitute granulated and brown sugars with ½ cup honey plus ½ cup brown sugar. Replace 1 egg with 2 egg whites or omit eggs altogether. Reduce soda to ½ teaspoon and add ¾ teaspoon baking powder.

Note: Dough may be chilled several hours before baking.

Notes:

Monster on a Diet Cookie

(low fat)

These cookies are fun for kids to make and taste good too.

- 2 tablespoons oil
- 2 tablespoons low fat peanut butter
- ½ cup brown sugar
- 1 tablespoon buttermilk
- 1 egg
- 1 teaspoon vanilla
- 2 tablespoons cocoa
- ½ cup flour
- ½ cup whole wheat flour, or ¼ cup whole wheat flour plus ¼ cup oatmeal
- ½ teaspoon baking soda
- ¼ teaspoon salt
- ½ cup chocolate chips
- ½ cup M&Ms
- ½ cup nuts, chopped

Preheat oven to 375 degrees. Cream oil, peanut butter, sugar and buttermilk together. Beat in egg, vanilla and cocoa. Stir in remaining ingredients, mixing thoroughly. Drop dough by teaspoonfuls onto ungreased cookie sheet. Bake for about 10 minutes. Yield: About 1½ dozen cookies.

Chocolate Chip Peanut Butter Cookies

(wheat free)

Even if you can have wheat in your diet, these are a very delicious cookie.

- ¾ cup margarine
- ¾ cup shortening
- 1½ cups peanut butter
- 1½ cups granulated sugar
- 1½ cups brown sugar
- 3 beaten eggs
- 9 cups cornflakes or Rice Krispies
- 3½ cups oatmeal
- 1½ teaspoons baking soda
- 1½ teaspoons baking powder
- 1 cup chocolate chips
- 1 cup nuts, chopped

Lightly grease cookie sheet. Preheat oven to 375 degrees. Cream together margarine, shortening, peanut butter and sugars. Add eggs. Stir in cereal and oatmeal. Stir in remaining ingredients, mixing well. Drop dough by tablespoonfuls onto cookie sheet, pressing each cookie slightly. Bake for 9–10 minutes. Yield: About 6 dozen cookies.

Icebox Cookies
(milk & egg free)

- 1 cup softened margarine
- ¾ cup brown sugar
- 2 cups flour
- ½ cup nuts, chopped

Combine margarine and sugar. Stir in flour and nuts, mixing well. With well-floured hands form dough into a log 1½-inches in diameter. Wrap in plastic wrap and chill in refrigerator for several hours or overnight. Grease cookie sheets. Preheat oven to 375 degrees. Cut log into thin slices. Bake for 10–12 minutes. Yield: About 2 dozen cookies.

Old-fashioned Icebox Cookies

- ½ cup shortening
- ½ cup margarine, softened
- 1¾ cups brown sugar
- 2 eggs
- 3 cups all-purpose flour, or 2 all-purpose flour plus 1 cup whole wheat flour
- 1 tablespoon baking powder
- ½ teaspoon salt
- 1 cup nuts, chopped
- ¾ teaspoons cinnamon or grated lemon rind, optional
- 1 teaspoon vanilla

Cream together shortening, margarine, sugar and eggs. Stir in remaining ingredients, mixing well. Roll dough into logs and refrigerate overnight.

Grease cookie sheets. Preheat oven to 375 degrees. Cut logs into thin slices. Bake until golden brown, about 8–10 minutes. Cool cookies on wire rack. Yield: About 4 dozen cookies.

Whole Wheat Snickerdoodles

- ½ cup margarine
- ¾ cup brown sugar
- 1 egg
- 1 teaspoon vanilla
- 1½ cups whole wheat flour
- ½ teaspoon baking soda
- 1 teaspoon cream of tartar
- ¼ teaspoon salt

Topping:

- 1 teaspoon cinnamon
- 4 tablespoons sugar

Preheat oven to 375 degrees. Cream until fluffy margarine and sugar. Beat in egg. Add, mixing well, vanilla, flour, baking soda, cream of tartar and salt. Mix cinnamon and sugar. Form dough into 1-inch balls. Roll balls in cinnamon and sugar mixture. Flatten cookies slightly with the bottom of a drinking glass. Bake on an ungreased cookie sheet for 8–10 minutes. Yield: About 2½ dozen cookies.

Original Snickerdoodles

These are a tasty and crisp cookie, a favorite in our family.

- ½ cup margarine
- ½ cup shortening
- 1½ cups sugar
- 2 eggs
- 2¾ cups flour
- 2 teaspoons cream of tartar
- 1 teaspoon baking soda
- ¼ teaspoon salt

Topping:

- 4 tablespoons sugar
- 4 teaspoons cinnamon

Preheat oven to 400 degrees. Lightly grease cookie sheet. Cream together margarine, shortening and sugar. Beat in eggs. Mix in flour, cream of tartar, baking soda and salt. Combine sugar and cinnamon. Shape dough into 1-inch balls. Roll balls in the cinnamon and sugar mixture. Place cookies about 2 inches apart on a cookie sheet. Bake for 8–10 minutes. These cookies puff up at first and then flatten out. Cool cookies on wire rack. Yield: About 2 dozen cookies.

Snickerdoodles

(fat free)

1¾ cups sugar
½ cup honey or Karo syrup
3 egg whites
2 tablespoons buttermilk or water
2 teaspoons vanilla
3 cups flour
2 teaspoons soda

Topping:

2 teaspoons cinnamon
¼ cup sugar

Spray cookie sheets with vegetable oil spray. Preheat oven to 375 degrees. Combine sugar, honey and egg whites. Add buttermilk or water and vanilla, mixing well. Combine flour and baking soda and add to sugar mixture.

Mix cinnamon and sugar. Form dough into 1-inch balls. Roll balls in cinnamon-sugar mixture. Bake for 8–9 minutes. Yield: About 4 dozen cookies.

Variations:

Fat Free Ginger Cookies: Substitute molasses for honey. Add 2 teaspoons cinnamon, 1½ teaspoons ginger and ¼ teaspoon cloves.

Fat Free Lemon Cookies: Replace vanilla with 1 teaspoon lemon juice and add 1 tablespoon grated lemon peel.

Notes:

Buttermilk Sugar Cookies

- ½ cup shortening
- ½ cup margarine
- 2 cups sugar
- 1 teaspoon vanilla
- 2 eggs
- ½ teaspoon salt
- 1 teaspoon nutmeg
- 1 teaspoon orange rind, grated
- 1 teaspoon baking soda
- 1 tablespoon baking powder
- 4½ to 5 cups flour
- ¾ cup buttermilk

Preheat oven to 400 degrees. Grease cookie sheets. Cream shortening, margarine, sugar, and vanilla. Beat in eggs.

In a separate bowl combine salt, nutmeg, orange rind, baking soda, baking powder, and flour. Stir dry ingredients into the shortening mixture alternately with the buttermilk.

Form dough into balls and flatten slightly with the bottom of a glass dipped in water. Sprinkle with sugar before baking or frost after baking.

For a soft cookie, bake 8–10 minutes. Bake 11–12 minutes for a crisp cookie. Cool cookies on a rack. Yield: About 5½ dozen cookies.

Variation: For egg-free cookies, omit eggs and increase buttermilk to 1 cup.

Cookie Frosting (fat free):

This frosting dries to a shiny, hard finish and won't stick together when stacked in a container, which makes it excellent for all frosted cookies.

- 1 cup powdered sugar
- 2 teaspoons vanilla
- 2 teaspoons corn syrup

Combine sugar, vanilla and corn syrup until of spreadable consistency. Spread over cookies.

Sugar Cookies

(no cholesterol, lower fat)

1 cup sugar
¾ cup oil
2 eggs or 4 egg whites
1 tablespoon instant nonfat powdered milk
1 teaspoon vanilla
1 teaspoon orange rind, grated
2 cups all-purpose flour
½ cup whole wheat flour
¾ teaspoon salt
1½ teaspoon baking powder

Lightly grease cookie sheets. Preheat oven to 375 degrees. Combine together sugar and oil. Add eggs, powdered milk, vanilla and orange rind. Stir in and mix well flours, salt and baking powder. Shape dough into 1-inch balls. Balls may be dipped in sugar, or in a cinnamon and sugar or nutmeg and sugar mixture. Flatten balls as thinly as possible with a glass bottom dipped in flour or with a fork. Bake for 10–12 minutes. Yield: About 4 dozen cookies.

Susie's Raspberry Filled Sugar Cookies

½ cup shortening
½ cup margarine
1⅓ cups sugar
2 eggs
2 teaspoons vanilla
¼ teaspoon nutmeg
¼ teaspoon cinnamon
½ salt
2½ teaspoons baking powder
2½ to 3 cups flour
1 teaspoon raspberry jam

Preheat oven to 375 degrees. Lightly grease cookie sheets. Cream together shortening, margarine and sugar until fluffy. Beat in, mixing well, eggs, vanilla, nutmeg, cinnamon, salt, baking powder and flour. Form dough into 1-inch balls and flatten with the bottom of a glass dipped in flour. Place raspberry jam between 2 unbaked flattened cookies and pinch cookie edges together. Place cookies on prepared cookie sheet. Bake 8–10 minutes. Remove from oven and sprinkle powdered sugar over cookies. Yield: About 2 dozen cookies.

Variations: 1 egg plus 1 tablespoon of 2% milk can replace 2 eggs, or omit milk and add 2 teaspoons baking powder and increase flour to 3 cups. Chill dough for 1 hour.

Molasses Spice Sugar Cookies

- ½ cup shortening
- ¼ cup margarine
- 1 cup brown sugar
- 1 beaten egg
- ¼ cup molasses
- 2 cups flour
- 2 teaspoons baking soda
- 1 teaspoon cinnamon
- ¾ teaspoon ginger
- ½ teaspoon cloves
- ¼ teaspoon salt

Grease cookie sheets. Preheat oven to 375 degrees. Cream together shortening, margarine and sugar. Add remaining ingredients, mixing well. Form dough into 1-inch balls. Roll balls in granulated sugar. Bake on cookie sheets for 10–12 minutes. Bake longer for a crisp cookie. Underbake for a chewy cookie. The cookies will puff up and then flatten while baking. Yield: About 3½ dozen cookies.

Whole Wheat Honey Cookies

(egg & milk free)

- 1½ cups margarine
- 1 cup honey
- 1 cup hot water
- 3 cups whole wheat flour
- 3½ cups oatmeal
- 1 cup raisins, optional
- 1 cup nuts, chopped (optional)

Lightly grease cookie sheets. Preheat oven to 350 degrees. Cream together margarine and honey. Stir in hot water. Stir in, 1 cup at a time, flour. Add, mixing completely, oatmeal, raisins and nuts. Drop dough by tablespoonfuls onto cookie sheet. Bake for 10–15 minutes. Store cookies in an airtight container to keep moist. Yield: About 4 dozen cookies.

Honey & Spice Cookies

- 1 cup margarine
- ½ cup brown sugar
- ½ cup honey
- 3 eggs
- 1 teaspoon vanilla
- 3 cups flour
- 1 teaspoon baking soda
- ¼ teaspoon baking powder
- ½ teaspoon salt
- 1½ teaspoons cinnamon
- ½ teaspoon nutmeg
- 1½ to 2 cups dates or raisins, chopped
- ¾ cup nuts, chopped

Lightly grease cookie sheet. Preheat oven to 350 degrees. Cream margarine, sugar and honey together. Beat in eggs and vanilla. Add remaining ingredients, mixing well. Drop dough by tablespoonfuls onto cookie sheets. Bake for 12–15 minutes. Yield: About 3 dozen cookies.

Cocoa Chewies

(fat free)

You would never guess that these are fat free, they are so yummy. These are the most popular cookies that I make.

- 5 cups powdered sugar
- ½ to ⅔ cups flour
- 1 cup cocoa
- ½ to ¾ cups egg whites

Line cookie sheets with parchment paper, waxed paper, or lightly grease. Preheat oven to 350 degrees. Combine sugar, flour and cocoa. Add egg whites slowly, mixing well. Drop cookies by tablespoonfuls onto cookie sheets. Bake about 12–15 minutes. Cookies will puff up while baking. Store in airtight container to prevent cookies from drying out. Yield: About 3 dozen cookies.

Variation (for a smaller batch):

- 3¾ cups powdered sugar
- ¾ cup cocoa
- ⅓ to ½ cup flour
- ½ cup egg whites (about 4 egg whites)

Combine sugar, cocoa and flour. Add egg whites, mixing well. Yield: About 2 dozen cookies.

Cocoa Cookies

(fat free)

- 2 egg whites
- ¼ cup honey or corn syrup
- 1 tablespoon water
- 1 teaspoon vanilla
- 2½ cups Fat Free Baking Mix (page 235)

Grease cookie sheets. Preheat oven to 350 degrees. Combine all ingredients, mixing well. Roll dough into balls, then roll in sugar to coat. Flatten each cookie with the bottom of a drinking glass. Bake for 6–8 minutes. Let cool on cookie sheet for 5 minutes before transferring cookies to a rack to finish cooling. Store in an airtight container or cookies will dry out. Yield: About 2 dozen cookies.

Coconut Cookies

(fat, sugar & wheat free)

- 1 cup (2 large) mashed bananas
- ¾ cups orange juice
- ½ cup apple juice concentrate
- 1 cup raisins
- 2 cups grated unsweetened coconut
- 2 teaspoons baking powder
- 1 teaspoon baking soda
- 1¾ cups brown rice flour
- ½ cup oatmeal, optional
- 1 teaspoon vanilla

Grease cookie sheets. Preheat oven to 350 degrees. Combine all ingredients, mixing well. Drop dough by tablespoonfuls onto cookie sheets. Bake until cookies are golden brown, about 12–15 minutes. Yield: About 2 dozen cookies.

Cornflake Macaroons

(fat & wheat free)

- 3 egg whites
- 1 cup sugar
- ¼ teaspoon almond extract
- ¼ teaspoon vanilla extract
- 1½ cups flaked coconut
- 3 cups cornflakes

Grease cookie sheet well. Preheat oven to 300 degrees. Beat egg whites until stiff but not dry. Gradually add sugar. Add almond and vanilla extracts. Fold in coconut and cornflakes. Drop by teaspoonfuls onto cookie sheet and bake for 20 minutes. Remove from cookie sheet immediately and cool on rack. Yield: About 3½ dozen cookies.

Low Fat Cornflake Macaroons

(wheat free)

- 3 egg whites
- 1 cup powdered sugar
- ⅛ teaspoon salt
- 1 cup flaked coconut
- 2 cups cornflakes
- ½ cup nuts, chopped

Grease cookie sheet well. Preheat oven to 300 degrees. Beat egg whites until stiff but not dry. Gradually add sugar. Add salt. Fold in coconut and cornflakes. Drop by teaspoonfuls onto cookie sheet and bake for about 20 minutes. Remove from cookie sheet immediately and cool on rack. Yield: About 3½ dozen cookies.

Molasses Crinkle Cookies

- 1 cup margarine or butter
- 1 cup brown sugar
- 1 egg
- ¼ cup molasses
- ½ cup nonfat dry milk
- 2 teaspoons baking soda
- ¼ teaspoon salt
- ½ teaspoon cloves
- 1 teaspoon cinnamon
- 1 teaspoon ginger
- ¼ cup wheat germ
- 2¼ cups flour

Grease cookie sheets well. Preheat oven to 375 degrees. Cream butter and brown sugar until smooth and light. Beat in egg until fluffy. Add molasses and dry milk, beat well. Blend in soda, salt and spices. Stir in wheat germ and beat for 1 minute. Stir in flour until blended. Form dough into 2-inch balls. Roll balls in sugar and place on cookie sheet. Sprinkle each ball with a few drops of water. Bake for 14 minutes. Cool on wire rack. Yield: About 4 dozen cookies.

Molasses Crisps

(wheat free)

- ¾ cup margarine
- 1 cup brown sugar
- 1 egg
- ⅓ cup molasses
- 1 cup nonfat powdered milk
- ¼ teaspoon salt
- 1 teaspoon ginger
- 1 teaspoon nutmeg
- 1 teaspoon cinnamon
- 2 teaspoons baking soda
- 2½ cups rye flour
- ½ cup oats or 1 cup finely chopped nuts, optional

Lightly grease cookie sheets. Preheat oven to 375 degrees. Combine margarine and brown sugar and beat until fluffy. Stir in egg. Add remaining ingredients and mix well. Shape dough into 1-inch balls. Roll balls in sugar and place on cookie sheets about 2 inches apart. Bake for 10–12 minutes. Yield: About 4 dozen cookies.

Molasses Gingerbread Cookies

(egg & milk free, low fat)

This recipe makes a large batch.

- 1/3 cup margarine
- 1 cup brown sugar
- 1½ cups molasses
- 2/3 cup cold water
- 2 teaspoons baking soda
- 1 teaspoon salt
- 1 teaspoon cinnamon
- 1 teaspoon cloves
- 1 teaspoon nutmeg
- 1 teaspoon allspice
- 6 to 7 cups flour

Cream margarine, sugar, molasses and water together. Blend in, mixing well, baking soda, salt, cinnamon, cloves, nutmeg, allspice and flour. Chill dough for several hours or overnight.

Grease cookie sheets. Preheat oven to 350 degrees. Roll dough out on a lightly floured surface. Make shapes with cookie cutters. Space cookies on cookie sheets (they will spread a little while baking). Bake for 10–12 minutes. Yield: About 8 dozen cookies.

Variation: For a more gingerbread-like cookie, omit allspice and add 1 teaspoon ginger.

Old-fashioned Gingersnap Cookies

- ¼ cup margarine
- ½ cup shortening
- 1 cup sugar
- 1 egg
- 1 teaspoon cinnamon
- 1 tablespoon ginger
- ½ teaspoon salt
- 2 teaspoons baking soda
- 2 cups flour

Cream margarine, shortening and sugar together. Beat in egg, cinnamon, ginger and salt. Blend in baking soda and flour. Preheat oven to 350 degrees. Lightly grease cookie sheets. Form dough into small balls. Roll balls in granulated sugar. Bake until tops turn crinkly and brown, about 12–15 minutes. Yield: About 3 dozen cookies.

Oat Bran Ginger Cookies

(low fat)

These are a soft and chewy cookie.

- ¼ cup margarine
- ¼ cup oil
- ¾ cup brown sugar
- ½ cup honey or a mixture of honey and molasses
- 2 egg whites or egg substitute
- 3 cups oat bran
- ¾ cups flour
- 1 teaspoon baking soda
- ¼ teaspoon baking powder
- 1½ teaspoons ginger
- ½ plus 1 teaspoon cinnamon
- ¼ cup sugar

Preheat oven to 350 degrees. Lightly grease cookie sheet. Combine margarine, oil, sugar and honey; beat until fluffy. Add, beating well, oat bran, flour, baking soda, baking powder, ginger and ½ teaspoon cinnamon. Shape dough into 1-inch balls.

In a separate bowl, mix together 1 teaspoon cinnamon and sugar. Roll balls in cinnamon and sugar mixture and place on cookie sheet. Press each ball into a flat cookie.

Bake until lightly browned, about 10–13 minutes. Cool cookies for 1 minute before removing from cookie sheet. Finish cooling cookies on a wire rack. Store cookies in an airtight container. Yield: About 3 dozen cookies.

Variation: ½ teaspoon cinnamon may be omitted from cookie dough and ginger increased to 2 teaspoons.

Oatmeal Applesauce Cookies

(fat free)

1¼ cups granulated sugar
1¼ cups brown sugar
1 cup applesauce
½ cup egg whites
1 tablespoon vanilla
3¾ cups flour
4½ cups oats
½ tablespoon baking soda
½ tablespoon baking powder
¾ teaspoon salt
2 teaspoons cinnamon
¾ cup raisins, optional

Lightly grease or line cookie sheets with waxed or parchment paper. Preheat oven to 350 degrees. Combine and mix well sugars, applesauce, egg whites and vanilla. Add remaining ingredients, mixing well. Drop by tablespoonfuls onto cookie sheets. Flatten with wet fingers. Bake about 8 minutes. Yield: About 3½ dozen cookies.

Banana Oatmeal Cookies

(low fat or fat free)

1 cup ripe bananas
1 cup granulated sugar
1 cup brown sugar
2 eggs or egg substitute
1 teaspoon vanilla
1 teaspoon lemon juice
½ teaspoon salt, optional
1 teaspoon baking soda
¼ teaspoon baking powder
1½ cups flour
3 cups oatmeal
1 cup raisins
1 cup nuts, chopped (optional)

Grease cookie sheets. Preheat oven to 350 degrees. Cream together bananas and sugars. Beat in eggs, vanilla and lemon juice. Mix in remaining ingredients. Drop batter by tablespoonfuls onto cookie sheets. Bake for 15 minutes. Yield: About 3 dozen cookies.

Oatmeal Chocolate Chip Cookies

- ½ cup shortening
- ½ cup margarine
- ¾ cup brown sugar
- ¾ cup granulated sugar
- 1½ teaspoons vanilla
- 2 eggs
- ¾ cup flour
- ¾ cup whole wheat flour
- 1 teaspoon baking soda
- ½ teaspoon salt
- ¼ teaspoon cinnamon
- 2 cups oatmeal
- ½ cup nuts, chopped
- 1 cup chocolate chips

Preheat oven to 375 degrees. Cream together until fluffy shortening, margarine, sugars and vanilla. Add eggs and beat lightly. Stir in and mix well flours, baking soda, salt, cinnamon and oatmeal. Stir in nuts and chocolate chips. Drop by tablespoonfuls onto ungreased cookie sheet. Bake for 8–10 minutes. Yield: About 2½ dozen cookies.

Oatmeal Cookies

(wheat free)

- 2 cups oatmeal
- ¾ cup brown sugar
- ⅓ cup oil
- 2 egg whites
- ¼ teaspoon salt
- ½ teaspoon vanilla
- ½ cup nuts, chopped
- ½ cup raisins, dried dates, or candied fruits, chopped

Lightly grease cookie sheets. Preheat oven to 325 degrees. Combine oatmeal, brown sugar and oil. In a separate bowl beat egg whites until frothy and add to the oatmeal mixture. Mix in salt, vanilla, nuts and raisins. Drop by tablespoonfuls onto cookie sheets. Bake for 15 minutes. Cool before removing cookies from cookie sheet. Yield: About 1½ dozen cookies.

Original Oatmeal Cookies

- 1¼ cups softened margarine
- ¾ cup brown sugar
- ½ cup granulated sugar
- 1 egg
- 1 teaspoon vanilla
- 1½ cups flour
- 1 teaspoon baking soda
- ½ teaspoon salt, optional
- 1 teaspoon cinnamon
- 3 cups oatmeal

Preheat oven to 375 degrees. Cream margarine and sugars. Beat in egg and vanilla. Mix in flour, baking soda, salt and cinnamon. Stir in oatmeal. Drop by tablespoonfuls onto ungreased cookie sheet. Bake 8–9 minutes for a chewy cookie, 10–11 minutes for a crisp cookie. Yield: About 2½ dozen cookies.

Variations:

1. Add 1 cup raisins and 1 cup chopped nuts.
2. Omit cinnamon and add chocolate chips.
3. Margarine can be reduced to 1 cup and add a second egg.
4. For a slightly different chewy cookie, use ½ cup shortening and ½ cup margarine. Add 2 eggs, increase flour to 2 cups. Add ¾ cup chopped nuts or sunflower seeds and 1 teaspoon baking powder. Add ¼ teaspoon cinnamon, optional.

Old-fashioned Oatmeal Raisin Cookies

- 1 cup brown sugar
- 2 eggs
- ¾ cup oil
- 1¼ teaspoons baking soda
- 3 tablespoons buttermilk
- 1 teaspoon cinnamon
- ½ teaspoon nutmeg
- ½ teaspoon salt
- 2 teaspoons vanilla
- 1 cup dates or raisins, chopped
- 4 cups oats
- 1 cup flour
- 1 cup nuts, chopped

Grease cookie sheets. Preheat oven to 350 degrees. Beat sugar, eggs and oil together. Dissolve baking soda in buttermilk and mix into the egg mixture. Add remaining ingredients in the order given and mix well. Drop by tablespoonfuls onto cookie sheets. Bake for 12–15 minutes. Yield: About 2½ dozen cookies.

Oatmeal Scotchies

The combination of butterscotch, brown sugar and coconut gives these cookies a delicious flavor.

- ½ cup margarine
- ½ cup shortening
- 1½ cups brown sugar
- 1 teaspoon vanilla
- 2 eggs
- 1½ cups flour
- 1 teaspoon baking soda
- 1 teaspoon salt
- 2⅓ cups oats
- 1 cup butterscotch chips
- ¾ cup nuts, chopped
- ½ cup coconut

Grease cookie sheets. Preheat oven to 375 degrees. Cream until fluffy margarine, shortening, sugar and and vanilla. Add eggs and blend lightly. Stir in and mix well flour, baking soda, salt and oats. Add, mixing well, butterscotch chips, nuts and coconut. Drop by tablespoonfuls onto cookie sheets. Press slightly to flatten. Bake for about 9 minutes. Yield: About 2½ dozen cookies.

Old-fashioned Oatmeal Cookies

(low fat, lower sugar)

- ½ cup light margarine or ⅓ cup oil
- ¼ cup granulated sugar
- ¼ cup brown sugar
- ¼ cup egg substitute or 2 egg whites
- 1 teaspoon vanilla
- 2 cups oatmeal
- ⅓ cup whole wheat flour
- ⅓ cup all-purpose flour
- ¼ teaspoon salt
- 2 teaspoons baking powder
- 1 teaspoon cinnamon, optional
- ½ cup raisins

Grease cookie sheets. Preheat oven to 375 degrees. Cream together margarine and sugars. Beat in egg and vanilla. Stir in remaining ingredients, mixing lightly until well combined. Drop batter by tablespoonfuls onto cookie sheets. Bake for 10–12 minutes. Yield: About 1½ dozen cookies.

Chewy Oatmeal Cookies

- ¼ cup margarine
- ¼ cup shortening
- ½ cup brown sugar
- ½ cup granulated sugar
- ½ teaspoon vanilla
- 1 egg
- 1 cup flour
- 1 cup oatmeal
- ½ teaspoon baking powder
- ½ teaspoon baking soda
- ¼ teaspoon salt
- ⅛ teaspoon cinnamon, optional
- ½ cup nuts, chopped

Preheat oven to 375 degrees. Cream together margarine, shortening, sugars and vanilla. Beat in egg and mix well. Add remaining ingredients, mixing well. Roll dough into balls and place balls on ungreased cookie sheets. Sugar may be sprinkled on top of cookies before baking, or combine 3 tablespoons sugar and ½ teaspoon cinnamon. Sprinkle cinnamon and sugar mixture over cookies. Bake for 10–12 minutes. Yield: About 1½ dozen cookies.

Variation: Divide batter in half. Form balls with half the dough and sprinkle cinnamon and mixture balls on cookie sheets before baking. Add chocolate chips to other half of the dough, form balls, place on cookie sheets, and bake.

Grandma's Molasses Oatmeal Raisin Cookies

With a slight hint of cinnamon and the wonderful flavor of molasses, these are so delicious!

- ½ cup margarine
- ¾ teaspoon cinnamon
- 2 tablespoons molasses
- ½ cup brown sugar
- ⅓ cup sugar
- 1 egg
- 1 cup flour
- 1 teaspoon baking soda
- ¼ teaspoon salt
- 1 cup oatmeal
- ¾ cup raisins or dates, chopped
- ½ cup nuts, chopped (optional)

Lightly grease cookie sheets. Preheat oven to 350 degrees. Cream together margarine, cinnamon, molasses, sugars, and egg. Add flour, baking soda and salt, and mix well. Stir in remaining ingredients, mixing well. Drop by tablespoonfuls onto cookie sheets. Bake for 8–10 minutes. Yield: About 1½ dozen cookies.

Oatmeal Cocoa Cookies

(egg free, lower fat)

- ¾ cup margarine
- 1½ cups brown sugar
- ½ cup cocoa
- 2 teaspoons vanilla
- ½ cup buttermilk or skim milk
- 1½ cups oatmeal
- 1 cup flour
- ⅔ cup whole wheat flour
- 2½ teaspoons baking powder
- ¼ teaspoon baking soda
- ¼ salt
- 1 cup nuts, chopped (optional)

Grease cookie sheets. Preheat oven to 400 degrees. Cream together margarine and sugar. Mix in cocoa, vanilla and milk. Add remaining ingredients, mixing well. Drop by tablespoonfuls onto cookie sheets. Bake until cookies feel firm to the touch, about 8–10 minutes. Yield: About 2½ dozen cookies.

Oatmeal Fig Cookies

- 1 cup figs, coarsely chopped
- ½ cup hot water
- 1 cup flour
- 1½ cups whole wheat flour
- ¼ cup instant nonfat powdered milk
- 1 teaspoon baking soda
- 1½ teaspoons cinnamon
- ½ teaspoon nutmeg
- ½ teaspoon salt
- 3 cups oats
- ½ cup walnuts, chopped
- ½ cup oil
- 1 cup brown sugar
- ¼ cup buttermilk
- 2 eggs

Cover figs with hot water and let stand 10 minutes. Drain water and reserve for later use. Grease cookie sheets with vegetable oil spray. Preheat oven to 350 degrees. Mix dry ingredients together. Mix oil, brown sugar, buttermilk and eggs together. Add liquid mixture to the dry ingredients. Add reserved figs and water. Drop dough by teaspoonfuls onto cookie sheets. Bake for 10 minutes. Yield: About 4 dozen cookies.

Dried Fruit Oatmeal Cookies

- ½ cup softened margarine
- ¾ cup brown sugar
- 1 large or 2 small eggs
- ½ teaspoon baking soda
- 1 tablespoon warm buttermilk
- ¾ cup flour
- ½ teaspoon salt
- 1½ teaspoons vanilla
- 1½ cups oatmeal
- 1½ cups dried fruits, chopped

Grease cookie sheets. Preheat oven to 375 degrees. Cream together margarine and sugar. Beat in eggs. In a separate bowl dissolve baking soda in warm buttermilk. Stir buttermilk mixture into margarine mixture. Stir in flour, salt, vanilla, oatmeal and dried fruits. Drop by tablespoonfuls onto cookie sheets. Dip bottom of a glass in cold water and flatten dough to make thin cookies. Sprinkle tops with sugar. Bake for 8–10 minutes. Remove from cookie sheets and cool on a rack. Yield: About 2 dozen cookies.

Raisin Oatmeal Cookies

- ½ cup shortening
- ½ cup margarine
- 2 cups brown sugar
- 2 eggs
- 2½ tablespoons lemon juice
- 1 teaspoon salt
- 1 teaspoon baking soda
- 2 cups flour
- 3 cups oatmeal
- 1¼ cups raisins
- ½ cup nuts, chopped

Grease cookie sheets. Preheat oven to 375 degrees. Cream until fluffy shortening, margarine and sugar. Add eggs and lemon juice and beat lightly. Add salt, baking soda, flour and oatmeal and mix well. Stir in raisins and nuts. Drop by tablespoonfuls onto cookie sheets. Press down slightly to flatten. Bake for 8–9 minutes. Yield: About 3½ dozen cookies.

Raisin Oatmeal Cookies
(low fat)

- 1 cup low-fat margarine or ½ cup oil
- ¾ cup brown sugar
- ¾ cup granulated sugar
- 1 teaspoon vanilla
- 4 egg whites or egg substitute for 2 eggs
- 1 teaspoon salt
- 1 teaspoon baking powder
- 1 teaspoon baking soda
- 2 tablespoons buttermilk
- 2 cups flour
- 3 cups oats
- ½ cup raisins or dates, chopped
- ½ teaspoon cinnamon, (optional)
- ½ cup nuts, chopped (optional)

Grease cookie sheets. Preheat oven to 375 degrees. Beat together margarine, sugars and vanilla. Beat in remaining ingredients and mix well. Drop by tablespoonfuls onto cookie sheets. Bake for 10–12 minutes. Yield: About 2 dozen cookies.

Honey Cookies

- ½ cup oil or margarine
- 1 cup honey
- 1 teaspoon vanilla
- 2 eggs or egg substitute
- 1¾ cups whole wheat flour
- 2 cups oatmeal
- ½ teaspoon baking soda
- ½ teaspoon baking powder
- ¼ teaspoon salt
- 1 teaspoon cinnamon
- ½ cup apples, chopped
- 1 cup raisins, dates, or dried fruit, chopped
- ½ cup nuts, chopped (optional)

Grease cookie sheets. Preheat oven to 350 degrees. Cream together margarine and honey. Beat in remaining ingredients. Drop by table-spoonfuls onto cookie sheets. Bake for 10–12 minutes. Yield: About 2 dozen cookies.

Honey Apple Cookies

- ½ cup oil
- ¾ cup brown sugar
- ⅓ cup honey
- 1 egg
- ⅓ cup buttermilk
- 1¼ to 1½ cups all-purpose flour
- ¾ cup whole wheat flour
- 2 cups oatmeal
- ¾ cup nuts or sunflower seeds, chopped
- 1½ teaspoons baking powder
- ¼ teaspoon baking soda
- 1 teaspoon orange peel, grated
- ¼ teaspoon nutmeg
- 1 teaspoon cinnamon
- ¼ teaspoon salt
- 1 cup apples, chopped

Grease cookie sheets. Preheat oven to 375 degrees. Cream together oil and sugar. Beat in honey, egg and buttermilk. Add flours, oatmeal, nuts or seeds, baking powder and soda, orange peel, nutmeg, cinnamon and salt, mixing well. Stir in apples. Drop by tablespoonfuls onto cookie sheets. Bake for 10–13 minutes. Yield: About 2 dozen cookies.

Applesauce Cookies

- ½ cup softened margarine
- ¼ cup shortening
- ½ cup brown sugar
- ¼ cup granulated sugar
- 1 egg
- 1 cup applesauce
- 1 teaspoon vanilla
- 1 tablespoon lemon juice
- 1 teaspoon salt
- 1 teaspoon cinnamon
- ¼ teaspoon allspice
- ⅓ teaspoon cloves
- 1 teaspoon baking soda
- ½ teaspoon baking powder
- 2 cups flour
- 1 cup oatmeal
- ½ cup raisins
- ½ nuts, chopped

Grease cookie sheets. Preheat oven to 375 degrees. Cream together margarine, shortening and sugars. Add remaining ingredients, mixing well. Drop batter by tablespoonfuls onto cookie sheets. Bake for 10–12 minutes. Yield: About 2 dozen cookies.

Variation: To reduce fat, omit shortening.

Applesauce Cookies

(fat & sugar free)

1½ cups applesauce
⅓ cup apple juice concentrate
1½ tablespoons nonfat powdered milk
⅓ cup egg whites
1½ teaspoons vanilla
½ teaspoon salt
1 teaspoon cinnamon
¾ teaspoon nutmeg
½ teaspoon allspice
1½ teaspoons baking soda
¾ cup flour
1 cup oatmeal
¾ cup whole wheat flour
½ cup oat bran
1 cup raisins

Combine all ingredients, mixing well. Dough will be more like a cake batter. Let dough sit 5 minutes.

Meanwhile, preheat oven to 350 degrees. Grease cookies sheets or line with waxed or parchment paper.

Drop dough by tablespoonfuls onto cookie sheets and spread each cookie a little in a circle. Bake for 10–12 minutes. Yield: About 2½ dozen cookies.

Apple Meringue Kisses

(fat free)

2 egg whites
1⅓ cups sugar
¼ teaspoon salt
½ teaspoon almond extract
½ cup finely apple, chopped
¼ cup finely glazed or candied cherries, chopped

Grease cookie sheets. Preheat oven to 325 degrees. Beat egg whites until stiff but not dry. Continue to beat and add sugar and salt. Fold in extract and fruit. Drop by teaspoonfuls well apart on cookie sheets. Bake for 15 minutes. Cool 5 minutes before removing from cookie sheets. Cool on rack. Store in an airtight bag or container. Yield: About 3 dozen cookies.

Apple Nut Cookies
(lower fat)

- 1/3 cup margarine
- ½ cup brown sugar
- 1 egg
- 1 cup all-purpose flour
- ½ cup whole wheat flour
- 1 teaspoon baking powder
- ½ teaspoon baking soda
- ½ teaspoon salt, optional
- 1 teaspoon cinnamon
- ¼ teaspoon nutmeg
- 3 tablespoons buttermilk
- ¼ cup raisins
- ½ cup nuts, chopped
- 2½ cups apples, chopped

Grease cookie sheets. Preheat oven to 375 degrees. Cream margarine and sugar together. Add egg, beating well. In a separate bowl combine flours, baking powder and soda, salt, cinnamon and nutmeg. Stir dry mixture into batter alternately with buttermilk. Stir in raisins, nuts and apples. Drop by tablespoonfuls onto cookie sheets and bake for 10–12 minutes. Yield: About 2 dozen cookies.

Molasses Apple Cookies

- ½ cup shortening
- ½ cup margarine
- 1½ cups brown sugar
- ¼ cup molasses
- 3 eggs
- 1 tablespoon cinnamon
- ½ teaspoon nutmeg
- ½ teaspoon cloves
- ½ teaspoon salt
- 1 teaspoon baking powder
- 3½ cups flour
- 1 cup finely apples, chopped
- 1 cup nuts, chopped

Grease cookie sheets. Preheat oven to 375 degrees. Cream together shortening, margarine, sugar and molasses. Beat in eggs. In a separate bowl combine cinnamon, nutmeg, cloves, salt, baking powder and flour. Mix dry ingredients with shortening mixture. Stir in apples and nuts. Drop by tablespoonfuls onto cookie sheets and bake for 12–15 minutes. Yield: About 3½ dozen cookies.

Apple Cookies

(lower fat)

- ¼ cup shortening
- ¼ cup margarine
- 1¾ cups brown sugar
- 1 egg
- 1 teaspoon salt
- 1 teaspoon cinnamon
- 1 teaspoon nutmeg
- ½ teaspoon cloves
- 1 teaspoon baking soda
- ⅓ cup buttermilk
- 2 cups flour
- ½ cup raisins
- 1 cup apple, grated
- ½ cup nuts, chopped

Grease cookie sheets. Preheat oven to 400 degrees. Cream together shortening, margarine and sugar. Beat in egg. Combine remaining ingredients in a separate bowl. Mix dry ingredients with shortening mixture. Stir in raisins, apple and nuts. Drop by tablespoonfuls onto cookie sheets and bake for 11–14 minutes. Yield: About 2½ dozen cookies.

Oat Bran Raisin Cookies

(low fat)

- ¾ cup brown sugar
- ⅓ cup honey
- 3 tablespoons margarine, softened
- 2½ tablespoons oil
- 2 egg whites
- 1¼ cups oat bran
- 1 cup oatmeal
- 1 cup flour
- ½ teaspoon baking soda
- ¼ teaspoon baking powder
- ½ cup raisins

Preheat oven to 350 degrees. Lightly grease cookie sheet. Beat together sugar, honey, margarine and oil until light and fluffy. Add egg whites and beat until well blended. Gradually add remaining ingredients and mix well. Roll into 1 or 2-inch balls. Drop onto cookie sheet. Press into flat cookies. Bake until golden brown, about 10–12 minutes. Cool for 1 minute before placing cookies on a rack to cool. Store cookies in a covered container. Yield: About 3½ dozen cookies.

Bran Cookies

(fat free)

- 1¾ cups flour
- 1 teaspoon baking soda
- ½ teaspoon baking powder
- ½ teaspoon salt
- ¾ teaspoon cinnamon
- 1 cup brown sugar
- ¼ cup sugar
- 3 egg whites
- 2 teaspoons vanilla
- ¼ cup oat bran or wheat bran
- 1 cup bran flakes or other grain flakes

Preheat oven to 385 degrees. Spray cookie sheets with vegetable oil spray. Mix together flour, baking soda, baking powder, salt, and cinnamon. In a separate bowl, combine sugars. Add egg whites and vanilla and mix well. Stir in dry ingredients. Drop by tablespoonfuls onto cookie sheet. Bake for 10–12 minutes. Yield: About 2½ dozen cookies.

Zucchini Brownies

(low fat, egg free)

- 2 cups flour
- 1¼ cups sugar
- 1½ teaspoons baking soda
- 1 teaspoon salt
- ¼ cup cocoa
- ½ cup nuts, chopped (optional)
- ¼ cup oil
- 2 cups grated zucchini
- 2 teaspoons vanilla

Preheat oven to 350 degrees. Grease 9 x 13-inch rectangular baking pan. Mix together flour, sugar, baking soda, salt, cocoa and nuts. Add, mixing until moistened, oil, zucchini and vanilla. Pour batter into prepared pan and bake for 25 minutes. Cool before cutting into squares.

Honey Brownies

(wheat free)

- 1/3 cup margarine, melted
- 1/3 cup cocoa
- 1 cup honey
- 2 eggs
- 1 tablespoon vanilla
- ½ teaspoon salt
- ¾ cup oat flour
- 1½ teaspoons baking powder
- ½ cup nuts, chopped

Preheat oven to 350 degrees. Grease an 8-inch square pan. Heat together margarine and cocoa, mixing until thoroughly combined. In a bowl combine honey, eggs, salt, oat flour, baking powder and nuts. Add cocoa mixture. Pour batter into pan. Bake for 20–25 minutes. Center will still be soft. Cool and cut.

'Frosted' Chocolate Brownies

- ½ cup margarine or butter
- ½ cup oil
- 1 cup hot water
- 1/3 cup cocoa
- 2 cups sugar
- 2 cups flour
- 2 teaspoons vanilla
- 1 teaspoon baking soda dissolved in ½ cup buttermilk
- 2 eggs
- ¾ nuts, chopped (optional)

Preheat oven to 350 degrees. Grease an 11 x 16-inch pan. Combine margarine, oil and hot water. Mix with cocoa, sugar and flour. In a separate bowl, combine buttermilk mixture with eggs and vanilla, then stir into margarine and cocoa mixture. Beat well. Pour batter into pan and bake for 20 minutes. While cake is still warm, spread with Buttermilk Icing.

Buttermilk Icing:

- ½ cup butter or margarine
- 1/3 cup buttermilk
- 1 box (1 pound) powdered sugar
- ¼ cup cocoa
- 1 teaspoon vanilla
- 1 cup nuts, chopped

Combine butter and buttermilk in a saucepan and heat on stovetop. Stir in powdered sugar, cocoa and vanilla. Spread icing over warm cake and sprinkle nuts on top.

Brownies
(milk & wheat free)

These brownies are delicious and keep well for several days—if they have a chance!

- 2 squares (2 ounces) unsweetened chocolate
- 1/3 cup butter or margarine
- 1/3 cup brown sugar
- 1/3 cup granulated sugar
- 2 eggs
- ½ cup brown rice flour
- 2 tablespoons cornstarch
- 1 teaspoon baking powder
- ½ teaspoon salt
- ½ cup nuts, chopped

Melt chocolate and butter or margarine in a saucepan. Cool slightly. Meanwhile, grease an 8-inch square baking pan and preheat oven to 350 degrees. Stir into chocolate mixture granulated sugar, brown sugars and eggs. This mixture will be quite stiff. In a separate bowl, combine brown rice flour, cornstarch, baking powder, and salt. Stir rice flour mixture into chocolate mixture along with nuts. Pour batter into baking pan and bake for 30 minutes. A dull crust will form on top as the brownies bake. Cool brownies in the pan.

Variation: To reduce fat, replace chocolate with 6 tablespoons cocoa, increase margarine to ½ cup, and reduce rice flour to 1/3 cup.

Fudgy Walnut Brownies

- 1 cup margarine, melted
- 2 cups sugar
- 2 teaspoons vanilla
- 1/8 teaspoon maple extract
- 4 eggs
- 1/3 cup cocoa
- 1 cup flour
- ½ teaspoon salt
- 1 cup chocolate chips
- 1 cup nuts, chopped

Preheat oven to 350 degrees. Grease a 9 x 13 x 2-inch pan that has been lined with waxed or parchment paper. Cream margarine, sugar, vanilla and maple extracts together. Beat in eggs. Add remaining ingredients one at a time, beating well. Pour batter into baking pan. Bake until brownies start to pull away from the pan, about 25–30 minutes. Be careful not to overbake. Let brownies cool in pan before cutting.

Cocoa Brownies

(lower fat)

- 2 eggs
- 1 teaspoon vanilla
- 1 cup evaporated skim milk
- 1 cup unsweetened applesauce
- 2 cups flour
- 1 cup brown sugar
- ¾ cup granulated sugar
- ½ cup cocoa
- 1¼ teaspoons baking soda
- 1 teaspoon baking powder
- ¼ teaspoon salt, optional

Stir in the applesauce mixture until just moistened. Do not overmix. Preheat oven to 350 degrees. Grease a 9 x 12-inch baking pan. Mix together eggs, vanilla, milk and applesauce. In a separate bowl combine remaining ingredients. Combine dry ingredients with batter. Pour into baking pan. Bake for 35–40 minutes. Sprinkle powdered sugar on top, or leave plain. Cool before cutting.

Brownies

(fat free)

- 2 egg whites, lightly beaten
- ¾ cup evaporated skim milk or buttermilk
- ¼ cup honey or corn syrup
- 1 teaspoon vanilla
- 2 cups Fat Free Baking Mix (page 235)

Preheat oven to 350 degrees. Coat an 8 x 8 x 2-inch baking pan with nonstick vegetable oil cooking spray. Combine all ingredients and beat until well blended. Pour batter into pan. Bake for 30–35 minutes.

Variation: 1 cup of mini marshmallows can be sprinkled over top before baking.

Fruit Bars

(fat & sugar free)

This is a family favorite, deliciously full of fruits and nuts.

- 3 bananas, mashed
- ½ cup applesauce
- ¾ tablespoon cinnamon
- ¾ tablespoon lemon juice
- 1 tablespoon vanilla
- 1½ cups apple juice
- 1½ cups apple concentrate
- ½ cup water
- ¾ cup egg whites
- ½ cup flour
- 1½ cups oat bran
- 3 cups oatmeal
- 2 cups whole wheat flour
- 2 tablespoons baking powder
- 1½ teaspoons baking soda
- ¾ to 1 cup raisins
- ¾ to 1 cup yellow raisins or other dried fruit
- ¾ to 1 cup dates, chopped
- ¾ cup nuts, chopped (optional)

Combine bananas, applesauce, cinnamon, lemon juice, vanilla, apple juice, apple concentrate and water. Stir in egg whites, mixing lightly. Stir in remaining ingredients. Mix together for about 1 minute. Let batter sit in bowl for 5 minutes.

Meanwhile, preheat oven to 350 degrees. Grease a baking pan (for thicker bars), a half-sheet pan or a cookie sheet (for thinner bars) with vegetable oil or spray. Smooth batter into baking pan or onto baking sheet.

Bake until batter pulls away from pan sides and feels firm to the touch, checking often, about 20 minutes. Do not overbake.

Yield: One-half sheet pan or two 9 x 12-inch pans.

Molasses Fruit Bars

(lower fat)

- 1/3 cup oil or 3 tablespoons margarine plus 2½ tablespoons oil
- ½ cup brown sugar
- ½ cup granulated sugar
- ¼ cup molasses
- ¼ cup water
- 1 teaspoon vanilla
- 2 teaspoons cinnamon
- ¼ teaspoon nutmeg
- 1/8 teaspoon mace or allspice
- ¼ teaspoon salt
- 1 egg
- 3 to 3¼ cups all-purpose flour, or a mixture of 2½ cups white and ¾ cup whole wheat flours
- ½ teaspoon baking soda
- 2 cups raisins, chopped apricots or apples, or a combination of dried fruits

Cream together margarine and/or oil and sugars. Beat in molasses, water, vanilla, cinnamon, nutmeg, mace or allspice, salt, egg, flour and baking soda. Stir in raisins or dried fruit. Chill dough for at least one hour.

Preheat oven to 350 degrees. Grease cookie sheets. Roll dough into logs 14 inches long by 1 inch in diameter. Brush tops with buttermilk. Bake for 15 minutes. Cool in pan for 15 minutes. Cut logs diagonally into 1-inch bars.

Variations: Water can be replaced with ¼ cup orange juice and granulated sugar reduced to ¼ cup.

Notes:

Cookie Jar Fruit Bars

Very delicious, a holiday favorite.

- ¾ cup raisins, chopped
- ½ cup dates or additional raisins, chopped
- ¼ cup orange juice or 2 tablespoons brandy plus 2 tablespoons orange juice
- ½ cup soft margarine, butter, or shortening
- ½ cup brown sugar
- ½ cup granulated sugar
- 1 beaten egg
- 1 teaspoon vanilla
- 1 teaspoon cinnamon
- ¼ teaspoon nutmeg
- ½ teaspoon baking soda
- 2 to 2¼ cups all-purpose flour, or a mixture of 1½ cups all-purpose flour plus ½ cup whole wheat flour
- 1 cup nuts, chopped

Place a small quantity of flour in a food processor. Add raisins, dates, brandy and orange juice.

In a separate bowl beat together margarine and sugars. Add egg and vanilla and beat until fluffy. Beat in remaining ingredients. Stir in raisin mixture. Chill dough at least 1½ hours or overnight.

Preheat oven to 375 degrees. Grease baking sheets. Divide dough into three or four equal parts. Place two portions on a baking sheet.

Using floured hands, shape each portion into a log about 11 inches long, 1½ inches wide, and 1½ inches thick. Use a pastry brush to brush tops of logs with buttermilk.

Bake until lightly browned, about 15–20 minutes. Bars will feel soft but will firm up when cooled. Cool 10 minutes before removing from baking sheets. Use a sharp knife to cut logs diagonally into 1-inch bars. Let bars cool.

Grandpa's Fruit Bars

This recipes makes a cake-like bar.

- 2 cups raisins
- 1½ cups chopped glazed fruit
- ½ cup unsweetened orange or pineapple juice
- 1 cup nuts, chopped
- 2 teaspoons vanilla
- 1 cup margarine or butter
- 1 cup brown sugar
- 1 cup granulated sugar
- 2 beaten eggs
- 2 teaspoons cinnamon
- 4½ cups all-purpose flour, or a mixture of all-purpose and whole wheat flours
- 2 teaspoons baking powder
- 1 teaspoon baking soda

Soak 2 cups of raisins for 10 minutes. Drain raisins and combine with glazed fruit, fruit juice, nuts and vanilla. Let sit while preparing the remaining ingredients.

In a separate bowl cream margarine, sugars and eggs together. Beat in remaining ingredients. Mix well. Add fruit mixture, blending well. Refrigerate for two hours or overnight.

Preheat oven to 400 degrees. Grease an 11 x 16 x 1-inch pan or a 15½ x 10½ x 1-inch pan. Bake until lightly browned, about 15–20 minutes.

When cool, cut into 1½ x 3-inch bars. Powdered sugar can be sprinkled on top or icing drizzled on top.

Variation: The recipe can be halved using the same sized pan to make a more bar-like cookie.

Buttermilk Pumpkin Cake or Bars

(low fat)

- 1¼ cups brown sugar
- ½ cup oil, or ¼ cup shortening and ¼ cup margarine
- ¼ cup molasses
- ¾ cup buttermilk
- ½ cup pumpkin, squash or sweet potato, cooked and mashed
- 2 eggs or egg substitute
- ½ teaspoon cinnamon
- ½ teaspoon allspice
- 1 teaspoon orange peel, grated
- 1 teaspoon baking powder
- ¾ teaspoon baking soda
- ¼ teaspoon salt
- 2½ cups all-purpose flour
- ¼ cup nuts, chopped (optional)

Preheat oven to 350 degrees. Grease a 13 x 9 x 2-inch baking pan. Beat sugar, oil, molasses, buttermilk, and pumpkin together for 2 minutes. Stir in eggs and then the remaining ingredients and beat for 2–3 minutes. Pour into baking pan. Bake for 30–35 minutes.

Variations:

1. To make bars, spread batter in a jelly roll pan.
2. Whole wheat flour can replace a portion of the all-purpose flour.

Pumpkin Cookies

(milk & egg free)

- ½ cup margarine
- ½ cup brown sugar
- ½ cup granulated sugar
- ½ cup shortening
- 1 cup pumpkin
- 1 teaspoon baking powder
- 2 cups flour
- 1 teaspoon baking soda
- 1 teaspoon cinnamon
- 1 teaspoon vanilla

Lightly grease cookie sheets. Preheat oven to 350 degrees. Cream together margarine, sugars and shortening. Add remaining ingredients, mixing well. Drop batter by tablespoonfuls onto cookie sheets. Bake for 8–10 minutes. Yield: About 2½ dozen cookies.

Delicious Pumpkin Bars

- 2 cups flour
- 2 teaspoons baking powder
- ½ teaspoon salt
- 2 teaspoons cinnamon
- 1 teaspoon baking soda
- 2 cups sugar
- 1 cup oil
- 4 eggs
- 2 cups pumpkin, cooked and mashed

Grease a 12 x 15-inch jelly roll pan. Preheat oven to 350 degrees. Combine all ingredients and beat well. Pour batter into pan and bake for about 25 minutes. Meanwhile, make Cream Cheese Frosting.

Cream Cheese Frosting:

- 6 ounces cream cheese, softened
- 1 tablespoon margarine, softened
- 1 teaspoon vanilla
- 1¾ cups powdered sugar
- Nuts, chopped (optional)

Mix well. Spread over cooled pumpkin bars. Chopped nuts may be sprinkled over frosting.

Variation: To lower fat content, use fat-free cream cheese.

Pumpkin Bar Cookies

(lower fat)

- ¼ cup oil
- 1 cup brown sugar
- 2 eggs
- ⅔ cup cooked, mashed pumpkin
- ½ teaspoon salt
- ½ teaspoon cinnamon
- ½ teaspoon ginger
- ½ teaspoon nutmeg
- ¾ cup flour
- ½ teaspoon baking soda
- ½ cup dates or raisins, chopped
- ½ cup nuts, chopped

Grease a 9 x 9-inch baking pan. Preheat oven to 350 degrees. Cream oil and sugar together. Beat in eggs. Add, mixing well, pumpkin, salt, cinnamon, ginger, nutmeg, flour and baking soda. Stir in dates or raisins and nuts. Pour mixture into baking pan. Bake for about 30 minutes. Cool for 5 minutes. Remove from pan and cool on a rack. Frost or sprinkle powdered sugar on top.

Lemon Bars

If you like lemon pie, you'll love the tartness of these delicious bars.

- 1 cup flour
- ¼ cup sugar
- ½ cup margarine, softened
- 2 eggs, beaten
- 3 tablespoons lemon juice
- 1 teaspoon lemon rind, grated
- 1 cup sugar
- ½ teaspoon baking powder
- 2½ teaspoons flour

Preheat oven to 350 degrees. To make crust, mix together flour, sugar and margarine. Press mixture into an 8 or 9-inch square baking pan. Bake until lightly browned, about 15 minutes. Meanwhile, mix together remaining ingredients. Pour batter over the hot crust. Bake until lightly browned, about 15–20 minutes. Cut into squares while warm. When cool, sprinkle powdered sugar on top.

Variations: For reduced fat in the crust, reduce margarine to ¼ cup and add 2 teaspoons buttermilk. To reduce fat in the filling, reduce eggs to 1 egg plus 1 egg white.

Date Bars

(low fat, sugar free)

- 2 eggs
- Pinch of salt
- 2 tablespoons boiling water
- ½ cup whole wheat flour
- ½ cup all-purpose flour
- 2 teaspoons baking powder
- 1 teaspoon maple extract
- ⅓ cup walnuts, chopped
- 30 medium-sized dates, chopped

Grease an 8-inch-square baking pan. Preheat oven to 350 degrees. Beat eggs and salt together until light. Add boiling water and beat well. Stir in remaining ingredients. Bake for 15–20 minutes. Turn out on a rack to cool. Cut and serve bars while warm.

Walnut Bars

This is similar to pecan pie. Great for family gatherings!

- 1 cup margarine
- 2 cups flour
- ¼ teaspoon salt
- ½ cup powdered sugar
- ½ cup melted margarine
- 2 tablespoons flour
- 4 eggs
- 1⅓ cups brown sugar
- 1⅓ cups corn syrup
- 2 teaspoons lemon juice
- 1½ teaspoons grated lemon peel

Grease a 9 x 13 x 2-inch baking pan. Preheat oven to 350 degrees. To make crust, cream together margarine, flour, salt and sugar. Mix until dough clings together. Press into baking pan. Bake until lightly browned, about 10 minutes.

For filling, mix together margarine and flour. Add, beating well, eggs, brown sugar, corn syrup, lemon juice and lemon peel. Spread walnuts over baked crust. Pour liquid mixture over the walnuts. Bake until golden brown and set, about 20–25 minutes. Cool before cutting into bars.

Nut Bars
(lower fat)

- ½ cup margarine
- ¼ cup sugar
- 1 egg
- ½ teaspoon vanilla
- 1½ cups flour
- Dash of salt
- 4 egg whites
- 2½ cups nuts, chopped
- 1 cup sugar
- 1½ teaspoons cinnamon

Grease a 9 x 13 x 2-inch baking pan. Preheat oven to 350 degrees. To make the base crust, cream together margarine and sugar. Beat in egg, vanilla, flour and salt. Spread this base into the baking pan. Bake for about 15 minutes.

Meanwhile, make the filling. Beat egg whites until foamy. Stir in nuts, sugar and cinnamon. Pour mixture into a saucepan and cook over low heat until sugar dissolves. Increase temperature until the mixture leaves sides of the pan, stirring constantly. Remove from heat before mixture becomes dry. Spread over the base. Bake 15 minutes. Cut into bars when cool.

Raspberry or Apricot Nut Bars
(low fat)

- ½ cup margarine
- ¼ cup sugar
- 1 egg
- ½ teaspoon vanilla
- 1½ cups flour
- 1 cup apricot or raspberry jam
- 2 egg whites
- ½ cup sugar
- ½ cup nuts, chopped

Grease a 9 x 13 x 2-inch baking pan. Preheat oven to 350 degrees. To make the base crust, cream together margarine and sugar. Beat in egg, vanilla and flour. Spread this base into the baking pan. Spread raspberry jam over unbaked crust base. In a separate bowl, beat egg whites. Gradually add sugar. Beat until mixture forms into peaks. Fold in nuts. Spread over jam covered base. Bake until firm, about 35–40 minutes. Cool slightly before cutting into bars.

Notes:

Desserts

"Feast or famine?" I say neither. There are times in life to celebrate, when creating and serving a rich and luscious dessert is just what is needed to share our joy and bounty on a special occasion. Who could imagine a wedding without a tiered cake or Thanksgiving without sweet, rich pies? But, on a daily basis, this kind of excess can contribute to dietary related diseases such as cancer and heart disease. So, in this section, as in all the others, you will find my traditional recipes for your favorite desserts, as well as my modified versions. These will give you alternatives for delicious and *nutritious* treats that you can feel good about eating and serving every day.

One of the secrets to my success, and I suggest you do the same: unless someone asks, I don't tell that my goodies are low in fat or sugar. A lot of people have endured well-intentioned but tasteless (or worse!) substitutes for their favorite desserts, only to find themselves attempting to choke down something with the texture of a dog biscuit and the taste of sawdust! Understandably, some people's minds and mouths shut tight as steel traps when offered another opportunity to try something that's healthy for them. In this case, what they don't know really *can't* hurt them! After they exclaim how much they enjoyed one of these healthy snacks, *then* you can share our little secret!

Recipes for delicious desserts that are low in fat and free of sugar are found in this chapter. When baking a cake lower in fat, I've found spraying pans with vegetable spray and lining them with waxed paper keeps cakes from sticking to pans. Most of the fat in pies and cobblers are found in the crust. I've reduced the fat in most of the recipes by at least half with satisfactory results. When making frosting for cakes, replace most of the fat with buttermilk. This adds a wonderful taste to frostings. I find fruit fillings can be used successfully in sugar-free cakes and a sugar-free whipped topping is excellent.

Don't be afraid to experiment with your favorite recipe. That's how most of my recipes came about. Also, I find it's very helpful to write down any changes you make in a recipe as you make it so as not to forget what you did later if the recipe is a success. Don't depend on your memory as I've done and then found I couldn't remember what I added or didn't add. Go ahead and enjoy making and eating these healthy goodies.

It's fun to experiment and you may even come up with some good substitutes of your own. In a lot of my recipes, I've shown the original recipe and then the reduced fat recipe. You can do the same with a favorite recipe you have. Give it a try.

Notes:

Oven Temperatures

Pie Shells: 425 degrees for 15 minutes.

Berry and Fruit Fillings: 425 degrees for 10–15 minutes, reduce oven temperature to 350 degrees and continue baking for 30–40 minutes.

Custard Fillings in Unbaked Pie Shells: 425 degrees for 10–15 minutes; reduce oven temperature to 350 degrees and continue baking for 20–30 minutes.

Dough for several piecrusts stored in plastic bags or airtight containers will keep in the refrigerator or freezer for later use.

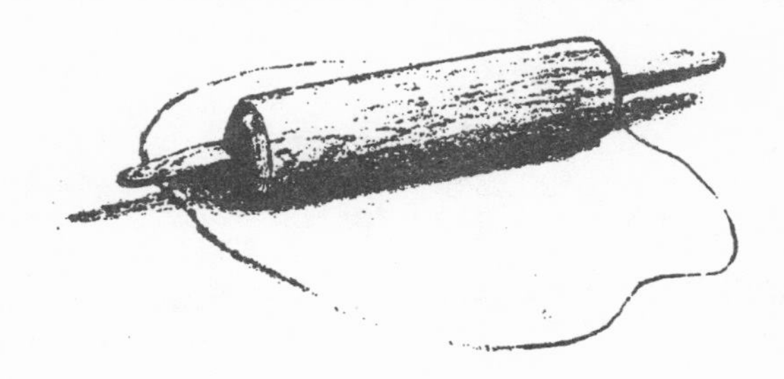

Old-fashioned Pie Crust

One 9-inch pie crust:

- 1 cup flour
- ⅓ teaspoon salt
- ⅓ teaspoon sugar
- ⅓ cup shortening
- 3 tablespoons cold water

Four 9-inch pie crusts:

- 4 cups flour
- 1½ teaspoons salt
- 1½ teaspoons sugar
- 1⅓ cups shortening, or 1¼ cups to reduce fat
- ¾ cup cold water

Mix thoroughly flour, salt and sugar. Cut in shortening until dough is texture of coarse cornmeal or small peas. Sprinkle water a little at a time over the dough while tossing quickly with a fork until particles stick together; 2 to 4 tablespoons of water are required for each cup of flour. Form dough into a ball. Dough may be wrapped and chilled for 1 hour. Use as little flour as possible to lightly flour rolling surface. Roll dough out to make pie crust. Prick crust surface all over with a fork before baking.

Pie Crust
(no cholesterol)

3 cups flour
1 teaspoon salt
1 teaspoon sugar
2 egg whites
1 teaspoon vinegar
1 cup cold oil
⅓ cup cold water

Combine flour, salt and sugar. In a separate bowl, combine egg whites, vinegar, oil, and water. Add egg mixture to flour mixture. Mix until well combined. Divide dough into three portions. For easier rolling, roll crust between two pieces of floured waxed paper. Yield: Three 9-inch pie crusts.

Pie Crust
(low fat)

1½ cups flour
1 teaspoon sugar
¼ teaspoon salt, optional
½ cup margarine

Combine flour, sugar and salt. Add margarine and mix until crumbly. Roll out dough between two pieces of floured waxed paper. Yield: One 9-inch pie crust.

No Fail Pie Crust

Five 9-inch pie crusts:
4 cups flour
1 teaspoon salt
1 teaspoon sugar
1¾ cups shortening
1 egg, beaten
1 tablespoon vinegar
½ cup cold water

Thoroughly mix flour, salt and sugar. Cut in shortening. In a separate bowl combine egg, vinegar and water. Mix thoroughly. Add egg mixture to flour mixture and add more water if needed. Form dough into a ball. Dough may be placed in plastic wrap and chilled in refrigerator for 30 minutes. Roll dough out to make pie crust.

Variation: Reduce shortening to 1¼ cups for a lower fat pie crust.

Whole Wheat Pie Crust with Wheat Germ

- 2 cups whole wheat flour
- 2 teaspoons sugar
- 1 teaspoon salt
- ½ cup chopped nuts, optional
- ½ cup toasted wheat germ
- 1 teaspoon lemon peel, grated
- ½ cup oil, chilled
- 6 tablespoons ice water

Combine flour, sugar, salt, nuts, wheat germ, and lemon peel. In a separate bowl combine oil and ice water. Gradually pour oil and water mixture over the flour mixture. Mix until combined. Work the dough into two balls. Flatten one ball and store it in the refrigerator. Roll out the second ball between two pieces of floured waxed paper until large enough to fill a 9-inch pie pan. Remove top layer of waxed paper. Flip crust into pie pan and remove the remaining layer of waxed paper. Form dough to fit pie pan. Refrigerate while preparing pie filling.

Fill pie crust with filling. For top crust, remove remaining dough ball from refrigerator. Roll out dough between two pieces of floured waxed paper. Remove top layer of waxed paper and flip onto pie. Carefully trim edges. Pinch bottom and top crusts together with fingers. Bake according to the type of pie.

Whole Wheat No Roll Pastry Shell

- ¾ cup all-purpose flour
- ¾ cup whole wheat flour
- 1 teaspoon salt
- 1 teaspoon sugar
- ½ cup cold oil
- ¼ cup whole, 2% or skim milk

Combine flours, salt and sugar. In a separate bowl, whisk together oil and milk. Pour oil mixture over flour mixture. Mix with a fork until completely dampened. Press evenly and firmly with fingers to line bottom of pie pan. Press dough up the sides of pie pan to partly cover the rim. Make sure dough is pressed to an equal thickness.

For a prebaked pie crust, preheat oven to 425 degrees. Bake crust for 12–15 minutes. Cool crust. Fill as desired.

For an unbaked pie crust, preheat oven to 400 degrees. Fill pie crust as desired and bake for 15 minutes. Reduce oven temperature to 350 degrees and continue baking until the filling tests done.

Prebaked Pie Crust

(wheat free)

½ cup cornstarch
½ teaspoon salt
½ cup finely milled rye flour
½ cup fine cottage cheese
½ cup cold butter or shortening

Sift together cornstarch, salt and rye flour. Work in, as for pastry, cottage cheese and butter or shortening. Wrap and chill dough in refrigerator for at least 30 minutes. Preheat oven to 425 degrees. Pat dough to line a 9-inch pie pan. Prick bottom and sides with a fork. Bake pie crust for 12 minutes.

Fresh Berry Pie

4 cups fresh blackberries, loganberries, boysenberries and/or blueberries
1 9-inch unbaked pie shell plus crust for top
½ cup honey
¼ cup brown sugar
4 to 5 tablespoons flour
1 teaspoon lemon juice
¼ teaspoon nutmeg, optional
¼ teaspoon cinnamon, optional
Dash salt

Place half the berries into pie shell. Combine honey, brown sugar, flour, nutmeg, cinnamon, lemon juice, and salt. Pour half the honey mixture over berries in pie shell. Top with remaining berries and then remaining honey mixture. Preheat oven to 425 degrees. Cover with pie crust. Trim edges and seal top and bottom crusts together with fingers. Make slits in top for steam to escape. Bake for 15 minutes. Reduce oven temperature to 350 degrees and continue to bake for 25–30 minutes.

Variations:

1. Use maximum amount of flour if berries are juicy.
2. Omit lemon juice in wild berry pie.
3. Use nutmeg and cinnamon with blueberries.

Strawberry Pie
(sugar free)

- 1 package (3 ounces) sugar-free vanilla pudding & pie mix (not instant)
- 1 package (3 ounces) sugar-free strawberry gelatin
- 2½ cups cold water
- Fresh strawberries
- 1 9-inch prebaked pie crust

In a medium saucepan combine vanilla pudding, strawberry gelatin and water. Cook over medium heat until slightly thickened. Remove from heat and let cool. Meanwhile, arrange strawberries in pie crust. Pour cooled pudding mixture over strawberries in pie crust. Serve with sugar-free homemade or store-bought light whipped topping.

Whipped Topping #1 (fat & sugar free):

- ½ teaspoon gelatin dissolved in 1 tablespoon warm water
- ¼ cup frozen apple juice concentrate
- ⅓ cup instant nonfat dry milk
- ½ teaspoon vanilla
- ½ teaspoon lemon juice

Combine ingredients and beat until stiff.

Whipped Topping #2 (fat & sugar free):

- ¾ cup evaporated skim milk
- ¼ cup apple juice plus 8 packets of *Equal* or ¼ cup apple juice concentrate
- 1 teaspoon vanilla
- ½ teaspoon lemon peel
- Pinch of nutmeg

Combine all the ingredients in a deep, narrow bowl. Freeze until partially frozen, about 1½ hours. Beat at highest speed until stiff. Immediately spoon over fresh fruit, pie, or other dessert.

Peach Cobbler

(low fat)

- 1 can (21 ounces) peach pie filling
- 1 teaspoon nutmeg
- 1 can (16 ounces) peach slices
- Juice from peaches, optional
- ½ cup brown sugar
- ½ cup flour
- ½ cup oatmeal
- ¼ cup margarine
- 1 cup sugar, or a ½ cup sugar plus ⅓ cup honey
- ½ cup margarine
- ½ cup buttermilk
- ½ cup egg substitute
- ¼ cup fat free sour cream
- 1 tablespoon vanilla
- 2½ cups all-purpose flour
- ½ cup whole wheat flour
- 1 teaspoon baking powder
- 1 teaspoon baking soda
- ⅓ teaspoon salt

Grease a 13 x 9-inch pan. Combine peach pie filling, nutmeg and peach slices. Set aside. In a separate bowl, combine brown sugar, flour, oatmeal, and margarine. Mix until crumbly. Set aside.

In a separate bowl, combine sugar and margarine. Stir in buttermilk. Add egg substitute, sour cream and vanilla. Beat for about 2 minutes. Add flours, baking powder, baking soda, and salt. Mix well.

Preheat oven to 350 degrees. Spread half the batter in pan. Spread peaches on top. Drop spoonfuls of remaining batter over the peaches but do not spread. Sprinkle top with brown sugar and oat mixture. Bake for 60–70 minutes. Cool. Pie can be glazed.

Glaze: Combine ½ cup powdered sugar and 1 tablespoon buttermilk. Drizzle over slightly warm cobbler.

Easy Apple or Peach Crisp

(milk, egg & fat free)

- 3 cups apples or peaches, peeled and sliced
- 3 tablespoons lemon juice
- ½ cup brown sugar
- 1½ teaspoons cinnamon
- ½ cup oatmeal

Preheat oven to 375 degrees. Combine peaches and lemon juice. Arrange fruit in a baking dish. In a separate bowl, combine brown sugar, cinnamon and oatmeal. Sprinkle brown sugar mixture over the fruit. Bake for 30 minutes.

Apple Crisp

- 6 to 8 apples, peeled, cored and sliced (about 6 cups)
- ¼ cup water
- 1 tablespoon lemon juice
- 1 teaspoon cinnamon
- 1 cup oatmeal
- ¾ cup flour
- ½ to ¾ cup brown sugar
- ⅓ cup margarine

Combine apples, water, lemon juice, and cinnamon. Spread mixture over the bottom of a 2-quart baking dish. Preheat oven to 375 degrees. Mix together until crumbly oatmeal, flour, brown sugar, and margarine. Sprinkle oatmeal mixture over apples in baking dish. Bake for 30–40 minutes. Topping

Variations:

1. For a fat and sugar free recipe, substitute water with ½ to ¾ cup apple juice concentrate.
2. Raisins can be added.
3. Substitute ⅓ to ½ cup apple juice concentrate for margarine and sugar.
4. Substitute all-purpose flour with whole wheat flour.

Apple Pie
(sugar free)

Filling:

6 cups apples, peeled, cored and sliced
½ to 1 cup apple juice concentrate
3 tablespoons flour
1½ teaspoons cinnamon
1 tablespoon orange juice concentrate
Dash nutmeg

Pie Crust:

¾ cup shortening
2 cups flour
½ teaspoon salt

To make pie crust, combine shortening, flour and salt. Mix until crumbly. Add water a tablespoon at a time and mix until dough clings together. Divide dough in half. Roll half the dough out on a floured surface to fit a 9-inch pie pan. Carefully line pan with dough and trim. Roll out remaining dough for top crust.

Preheat oven to 400 degrees. Combine apples, apple juice concentrate, flour, cinnamon, orange juice concentrate, and nutmeg. Pour mixture into unbaked pie shell. Top with dough for crust. Cut slits so steam can escape. Crimp and seal edges. Bake for 45 minutes.

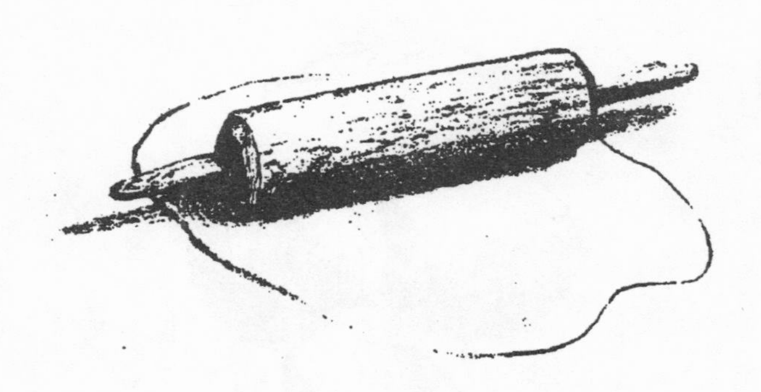

Old-fashioned Lemon Meringue Pie

1½ cups sugar
5 tablespoons cornstarch
2 tablespoons flour
¼ teaspoon salt
1½ plus ½ cups cold water
3 egg yolks
½ cup lemon juice
2 teaspoons lemon peel, grated
2 tablespoons margarine, optional
1 prebaked 9-inch pie crust

In a large microwavable bowl, or a 2 or 3-quart saucepan, combine sugar, cornstarch, flour, salt, ½ cup water, and egg yolks. Add lemon juice, grated lemon peel and 1½ cups cold water. Mix thoroughly.

In microwave: Microwave on high for 2 minutes, stir well, and microwave on high for 2 more minutes. Continue to microwave 1 minute at a time and stir until mixture comes to a boil and becomes thick. Total microwaving time is about 8 minutes. If desired, stir in optional margarine. Let mixture sit for 5 minutes. Stir. Pour mixture into prebaked pie crust. Spread meringue over top.

On stovetop: Cook over medium heat, stirring constantly, until mixture comes to a full boil. If desired, add optional margarine. Let mixture sit for 5 minutes. Stir. Pour mixture into prebaked pie crust. Spread meringue over top.

Meringue:

3 egg whites
4 to 6 tablespoons sugar or sweetener to taste

Preheat oven to 350 degrees. Beat egg whites until foamy. Gradually add sugar or sweetener. Beat until whites stand up in peaks. Spread evenly over top and edges of pie crust. Bake until medium brown, about 15 minutes.

Variations (in case of allergies):

1. ***Corn free:*** Use ½ cup plus 3 tablespoons flour.
2. ***Wheat free:*** Use 6 tablespoons of cornstarch.

Buttermilk Lemon Pie

This recipe makes a delicious but unusual pie.

- 1 unbaked 9-inch pie crust, unbaked
- 2 cups sugar
- 3 tablespoons flour
- ¼ teaspoon nutmeg
- ¼ cup margarine or butter, melted
- 3 eggs, lightly beaten
- 1 cup buttermilk
- ¼ cup lemon juice
- 1 teaspoon vanilla

Preheat oven to 400 degrees. Combine sugar, flour and nutmeg. Add margarine or butter and beat until creamy. Stir in eggs, lemon juice and vanilla. Pour into pie crust. Bake for 10 minutes. Reduce oven temperature to 325 degrees and bake for 30 additional minutes.

Old-fashioned, Two Crusted Lemon Pie

This lemon pie uses fewer eggs and you don't have to separate them as in other recipes.

- ¼ cup cornstarch
- ¼ cup water
- 1½ cup boiling water
- 2 tablespoons lemon peel, grated
- 1 tablespoon butter or margarine
- 1½ cups plus 1 tablespoon sugar
- ¼ cup lemon juice
- 2 eggs
- 1 unbaked 9-inch pie crust
- 1 tablespoon milk

In a medium saucepan dissolve cornstarch in ¼ cup water. Cook until thick and clear. Add 1½ cups boiling water. Remove from heat. Add lemon peel and butter or margarine. Let mixture cool.

When cool, add 1½ cups sugar, lemon juice and eggs. Mix well. Pour mixture into pie crust. Preheat oven to 375 degrees. Cover pie with a top crust. Pinch top and bottom crusts together with fingers. Cut slits in top crust to let steam escape and brush with milk. Sprinkle 1 tablespoon sugar over top crust. Bake for 30 minutes. Increase oven temperature to 425 degrees and continue baking for 10 minutes.

Lemon Cream Pie

(egg free)

A combination of flour and cornstarch results in a smoother, sturdier pie filling.

1½	cups sugar	1	teaspoon lemon peel, grated
7	tablespoons cornstarch		Yellow food coloring, optional
½	teaspoon salt	1	teaspoon gelatin
1½	cups boiling water	¼	cup cold water
3	tablespoons margarine	½	cup evaporated milk
½	cup lemon juice	1	prebaked 9-inch pie crust

In a medium saucepan combine sugar, cornstarch and salt. Slowly add boiling water. Cook, stirring constantly, until mixture is thick and smooth. Stir in margarine, lemon juice, grated lemon, and food coloring. Set aside 1 cup of mixture for use as a glaze.

In a small saucepan combine gelatin and cold water. Heat until dissolved. Add to the remaining lemon filling mixture. Stir in milk and continue to stir until cooled. Pour into prebaked 9-inch pie crust. Cover top of pie with the reserved glaze mixture. Chill thoroughly.

Variations:

1. Substitute 5 tablespoons cornstarch plus ¼ cup flour for 7 tablespoons cornstarch.

2. For corn-free pie, substitute cornstarch with flour: 2 tablespoons flour equals 1 tablespoon cornstarch or 4 tablespoons tapioca.

Lemon or Lime Pie

(egg free)

1	15-ounce can sweetened condensed milk	1	tablespoon grated lemon or lime rind
⅓	cup lemon or lime juice	¼	teaspoon salt

Bake a 9-inch pie crust. Cool. Meanwhile, combine milk, juice, rind, and salt. Stir until thickened. Pour into prebaked pie crust. Chill for at least 3 hours before serving.

This is the traditional dessert we all love. Each recipe has been changed slightly, but still retains the wonderful flavor and smoothness we all love.

Pumpkin Pie I

- 1 unbaked 9-inch pie shell
- 1 can (16 ounces) pumpkin
- 2 teaspoons pumpkin pie spice
- ½ teaspoon salt
- ¾ cup brown sugar or ½ cup honey
- 1 can (12 ounces) evaporated milk
- 2 eggs, beaten

Preheat oven to 425 degrees. Combine all ingredients and pour into pie shell. Bake for 15 minutes. Reduce oven temperature to 350 degrees and bake for additional 30 minutes. Cool before cutting.

Variation: For an egg-free pie, omit eggs and add 2 tablespoons cornstarch and 2 tablespoons flour.

Homemade Pumpkin Pie Spice (for one 9-inch pie):

- 1 teaspoon cinnamon
- ½ teaspoon ginger or allspice
- ½ teaspoon nutmeg

Pumpkin Pie II

- 1 unbaked 9-inch pie shell
- 1 cup whole or 2% milk
- 2 eggs
- 1¾ cups pumpkin
- ½ cup brown sugar or ⅓ cup honey
- 1½ teaspoon cinnamon
- ¼ teaspoon ginger
- ¼ teaspoon nutmeg
- ¼ teaspoon salt

Preheat oven to 425 degrees. Combine eggs with milk and beat for 1 minute. Combine remaining ingredients and pour into pie shell. Bake for 15 minutes. Reduce oven temperature to 350 degrees and bake for additional 30 minutes. Cool before cutting.

Fat Free Pumpkin Pie I

- 1 unbaked 9-inch pie shell
- 1 can (16 ounces) pumpkin
- ¾ cup sugar
- 2 teaspoons pumpkin pie spice
- ½ teaspoon salt
- 1 can (12 ounces) evaporated skim milk
- 3 egg whites, slightly beaten, or ½ cup egg substitute

Preheat oven to 425 degrees. Combine all ingredients and pour into pie shell. Bake for 15 minutes. Reduce oven temperature to 350 degrees and bake for additional 30 minutes. Cool before cutting.

Fat Free Pumpkin Pie II

- 1 unbaked 9-inch pie shell
- 1 can (16 ounces) pumpkin
- 1 can (14 ounces) fat free sweetened condensed milk
- 4 egg whites, slightly beaten
- 2 teaspoons pumpkin pie spice
- ½ teaspoon salt

Preheat oven to 425 degrees. Combine all ingredients and pour into pie shell. Bake for 15 minutes. Reduce oven temperature to 350 degrees and bake for additional 30 minutes. Cool before cutting.

Fat Free Pumpkin Pie Topping:

- ⅓ cup fat free vanilla yogurt
- 1 tablespoon sugar
- 2 teaspoons lemon juice

Combine ingredients. Chill.

Whipped Topping for Pumpkin Pie (fat free):

- ½ cup instant nonfat powdered milk
- ½ cup ice water
- 2 tablespoons lemon juice
- ¼ cup sugar
- ½ teaspoon vanilla

Combine milk, water and lemon juice. Beat until stiff. Fold in sugar and vanilla.

Tofu Pumpkin Pie

(low fat)

2	packages (each 10.5 ounces) silken, soft, tofu, drained	¼	teaspoon salt
2	egg whites	2	teaspoons cinnamon
1½	cups canned pumpkin	½	teaspoon nutmeg
½	cup sugar	½	teaspoon ginger
		1	unbaked 9-inch pie crust

Preheat oven to 425 degrees. Process all ingredients in a blender until thoroughly combined. Pour mixture into pie crust. Bake for 15 minutes. Reduce oven temperature to 350 degrees and continue baking for 50 minutes. Pie is completely baked when a toothpick inserted into pie is almost clean when removed.

Original Pumpkin Cheesecake

Crust:
- 1 cup graham cracker crumbs
- ¼ cup sugar
- ¼ cup butter or margarine, melted

Filling:
- 2 packages (each 8 ounces) cream cheese, softened
- 1 cup brown sugar
- 1 can (16 ounces) pumpkin
- 2 teaspoons cornstarch
- 1¼ teaspoons cinnamon
- ½ teaspoon nutmeg
- 4 eggs
- 1½ teaspoons sherry, optional

Topping:
- 2 cups sour cream (about 16 ounces)
- ¼ cup sugar
- 1 teaspoon vanilla
- 1 teaspoon sherry or bourbon, optional

Preheat oven to 350 degrees. Combine crumbs, sugar and butter. Press cracker mixture into bottom and 1 inch up sides of a 9-inch springform pan. Bake for about 6 minutes. Crust does not need to brown. Let crust cool.

Meanwhile, beat cream cheese until smooth. Stir in brown sugar. Blend in pumpkin, cornstarch, cinnamon and nutmeg. Add eggs one at a time. Beat mixture until smooth and creamy. Pour mixture into cooled crust. Bake in 350 degree oven until center is slightly soft to the touch, about 45–55 minutes.

To make topping, beat sour cream, sugar, vanilla, and sherry together. Spread over top of baked cheesecake. Return to 350 degree oven and bake 10 minutes. Cool on wire rack before removing sides of pan. Chill cake in refrigerator.

Variation: Replace cinnamon and nutmeg with 2 teaspoons pumpkin pie spice.

Original Pumpkin Cheesecake

(fat free)

Crust: Spray springform pan with vegetable oil spray. Coat pan with wheat bran or make a crust with lower fat corn oil margarine or oil.

Follow directions for Original Pumpkin Cheesecake with the following modifications.

Filling:

1. Use fat-free cream cheese.
2. Replace 4 eggs with ¾ cup egg substitute.

Topping:

1. Use fat-free sour cream.
2. Reduce sugar to 3 tablespoons.
3. Reduce vanilla to ½ teaspoon.
4. Reduce sherry or bourbon, if included, to ½ teaspoon.

Cheesecake

(low fat)

- ½ to ¾ cup graham cracker crumbs
- 2 packages (each 8 ounces) nonfat cream cheese
- ½ cup sugar
- 1 tablespoon flour
- ½ cup nonfat sour cream
- 3 egg whites
- 1 teaspoon vanilla extract
- 2 cups strawberries, blueberries, peaches, or other fruit, sliced (optional)

Spray 9-inch pie pan with nonstick vegetable oil spray. Coat pie pan with graham cracker crumbs and set aside. Preheat oven to 325 degrees. Combine cream cheese, sugar and flour. Beat until creamy. Beat in sour cream, egg whites and vanilla. Pour mixture into graham cracker crust. Bake until top cracks, about 40 minutes. Cool on a wire rack. Refrigerate cooled cheesecake for at least 3 hours before serving. Cover cheesecake with fruit before serving.

Pecan Cheesecake Pie

- 1 package (8 ounces) cream cheese
- 4 eggs
- ⅔ cup sugar
- 2 teaspoons vanilla
- 1 9-inch unbaked pie crust
- 1¼ cups pecans, chopped
- 1 cup corn syrup
- ¼ teaspoon salt

Combine cream cheese, 1 egg, ⅓ cup sugar, and 1 teaspoon vanilla. Beat until fluffy. Spread mixture over bottom of pie crust. Sprinkle chopped pecans over mixture in pie shell. Preheat oven to 350 degrees. Beat 3 eggs until well mixed but not foamy. In a separate bowl combine corn syrup, ⅓ cup sugar, 1 teaspoon vanilla, and salt. Add corn syrup mixture to the beaten eggs and mix well. Pour corn syrup and egg mixture over the pecans in pie shell. Bake until nuts are slightly browned, about 40 minutes. Top will rise like a soufflé and sink as it bakes.

Variation: For lower fat, use fat-free cream cheese and reduce chopped pecans to ¾ cup.

Cocoa Cream Pie

(egg free)

- 1 cup sugar
- ⅓ cup cocoa
- ⅓ cup cornstarch
- ¼ teaspoon salt
- 3 cups milk
- 3 tablespoons margarine or butter
- 1½ teaspoons vanilla
- 1 prebaked 9-inch pie crust

Combine in a medium saucepan sugar, cocoa, cornstarch, and salt. Gradually blend in milk. Stir until smooth. Cook over medium heat, stirring constantly, until mixture comes to a boil. Boil and stir for 3 minutes. Remove from heat. Blend in margarine or butter and vanilla. Pour mixture into pie crust. Cover pie with plastic wrap and chill for 3 or 4 hours before serving. Pie may be topped with whipped topping, cherry pie filling, or fresh blueberries.

Variation: Substitute ⅓ cup cornstarch with a mixture of 5 tablespoons cornstarch plus ¼ cup flour.

Old-fashioned Chocolate Cake

- 1 cup margarine or butter
- 1½ cups granulated sugar or a mixture of granulated and brown sugars
- 2 eggs
- 1 teaspoon vanilla
- 1¾ cups flour
- ½ cup cocoa
- 1¼ teaspoons baking soda
- ½ salt
- 1 cup buttermilk
- Cocoa Butter Cream Frosting

Preheat oven to 350 degrees. Grease a 9 x 13-inch pan or two 8 or 9-inch pans. Combine margarine, eggs and vanilla. Beat for 3 minutes. In a separate bowl combine flour, cocoa, baking soda, and salt. Add, alternately with buttermilk, flour mixture to margarine mixture. Mix well. Pour batter into pan. Bake for 30–35 minutes. Frost with Coca Butter Cream Frosting.

Variation: For lower fat, substitute ½ cup egg substitute for eggs or egg whites and reduce cocoa to ¼ cup, margarine to ¼ cup, and buttermilk to ¾ cup.

Cocoa Butter Cream Frosting:

- ⅓ cup margarine, softened
- 2¾ cups powdered sugar
- ⅓ cup buttermilk
- 1 teaspoon vanilla
- Dash salt

Combine all ingredients and mix until of spreading consistency.

Chocolate Cake

(no cholesterol, low fat, egg & milk free)

- ¼ cup cocoa
- 1 cup brown sugar
- 1 cup water
- ½ cup oil
- 1 tablespoon vanilla
- 1½ cups flour
- 1 teaspoon baking soda
- ½ teaspoon baking powder

Preheat oven to 350 degrees. Grease two 8-inch pans. Combine cocoa, brown sugar, water, oil, and vanilla. Mix well. Stir in flour, baking soda, baking powder. Pour batter into pans. Bake for 50 minutes.

Chocolate Layer Cake

(fat free)

4 egg whites
¾ cup evaporated skim milk or buttermilk
¼ cup honey or corn syrup
1 teaspoon vanilla
2 cups Fat Free Baking Mix (page 235)
Raspberry jam for frosting plus fresh raspberries for top of cake, or Fluffy Frosting

Preheat oven to 350 degrees. Coat two 8-inch round cake pans with vegetable oil spray. Beat egg whites until soft peaks foam. In a separate bowl combine milk, corn syrup and vanilla. Beat in baking mix until blended. Fold in one-fourth of the egg whites until blended. Gently fold in remaining egg whites just until incorporated. Divide batter evenly between the two pans. Bake for about 20 minutes. Cool cakes in pans for 15 minutes. Turn cakes out onto racks to cool.

Spread one layer with raspberry jam and sprinkle fresh raspberries over top layer, or frost with a Fluffy Frosting.

Fluffy Frosting (fat free):

¾ cup sugar
3 tablespoon water
2 teaspoons corn syrup
½ teaspoon vanilla
½ teaspoon salt
1 egg white

Combine ingredients and beat until blended. Pour mixture into top of double boiler placed over boiling water. Beat at high speed until soft peaks form for 4–5 minutes. Spread frosting over cake or cupcakes.

Classic American Chocolate Cake

(milk free)

- ¾ cup margarine or butter
- 1¾ cups sugar, or a mixture of granulated and brown sugars
- 3 eggs
- 1 teaspoon vanilla
- 2 cups flour
- ⅔ cup cocoa
- 1¼ teaspoons baking soda
- ¼ teaspoon baking powder
- ¾ teaspoon salt
- 1¾ cups water

Preheat oven to 350 degrees. Grease and flour two 9-inch pans. Combine margarine, sugar, eggs, and vanilla. Beat for 3 minutes. In a separate bowl combine flour, cocoa, baking soda, baking powder, and salt. Add, alternately with water, flour mixture to the margarine mixture. Mix until well combined. Pour batter into pans. Bake until a toothpick inserted in the center of cake comes out clean, about 30–35 minutes. Cool in pans for 5 minutes. Turn cakes out onto racks to cool.

Chocolate Cake

(egg & milk free)

- ⅔ cup oil
- 2 tablespoons white vinegar
- 1 tablespoon vanilla
- 2 cups cold water
- 2 teaspoons baking soda
- 3 cups flour
- 2 cups sugar
- ⅓ cup cocoa
- 1 teaspoon salt

Preheat oven to 350 degrees. Grease a 9 x 13-inch pan. Combine oil, vinegar, vanilla, cold water, and baking soda. Stir in flour, sugar, cocoa, and salt. Mix well. Pour batter into pan. Bake for 30–40 minutes.

Chocolate Cake
(gluten & wheat free)

- ½ cup shortening, margarine or oil
- 1¼ cups sugar
- 4 eggs
- ⅓ cup cocoa
- ⅓ cup water
- 2 tablespoons cornstarch
- 2 teaspoons potato flour
- 1⅓ cup brown rice flour
- 1 teaspoon salt
- 1½ teaspoons baking soda
- 1 teaspoon baking powder
- ½ cup buttermilk

Preheat oven to 350 degrees. Grease two 8 or 9-inch pans and line with waxed paper. Combine shortening and sugar. Add eggs, cocoa and water, beating well after each addition. In a separate bowl combine cornstarch, flours, salt, baking soda, and baking powder. Add flour mixture to shortening mixture alternately with buttermilk and mix well. Pour batter into pans and bake for 40 minutes. Loosen edges, invert cake onto racks, remove waxed paper, and cool cakes.

Notes:

Chocolate Cupcakes
(fat free)

2	egg whites, lightly beaten	1	teaspoon vanilla
¾	cup water	2½	cups Fat Free Baking Mix (page 235)
½	cup honey or light corn syrup		

Preheat oven to 350 degrees. Line muffin cups with cupcake liners. Combine all ingredients and mix well. Fill muffin cups about two-thirds full. Bake for 20–25 minutes. Top cooled cupcakes with icing.

Icing (fat free):

1	cup powdered sugar		Liquid (orange juice, lemon juice, etc.)
½	teaspoon vanilla		

Combine sugar and vanilla with enough liquid to make a spreadable frosting. Spread over cake or cupcakes.

Vanilla Icing (fat free):

⅓	cup egg whites	1½	teaspoons vanilla
3	to 3½ cups powdered sugar	¼	teaspoon salt

Whip egg whites until foamy. Add powdered sugar, vanilla and salt. Mix well and spread on cake or cupcakes. Store cake or cupcakes in a covered container, if possible.

Chocolate Icing (fat free):

⅓	cup egg whites	1½	teaspoons vanilla
3	to 3¼ cups powdered sugar	¼	teaspoon salt
¼	cup cocoa		

Whip egg whites until foamy. Add powdered sugar, cocoa, vanilla, and salt. Mix well and spread on cake or cupcakes. Store cake or cupcakes in a covered container, if possible.

Baked Icing:

This icing is spread on a cake before baking and bakes with the cake.

1	egg white	2	tablespoons cocoa (optional)
⅛	teaspoon salt	½	cup nuts, chopped (optional)
½	cup brown sugar		

Combine egg white and salt. Whip until stiff. Beat in brown sugar and fold in cocoa. Spread mixture over cake batter in pan. Chopped nuts may be sprinkled over the icing. Bake as indicated in cake recipe for no longer than 25 minutes.

German Chocolate Cake

- 2 cups sugar
- ½ cup oil
- ½ cup margarine
- 4 eggs
- 1 teaspoon vanilla
- ¼ teaspoon salt
- ½ cup cocoa
- 1 cup buttermilk
- 3½ cups flour
- Coconut Pecan Frosting

Preheat oven to 350 degrees. Grease two 8 or 9-inch pans. Combine sugar, oil and margarine. Beat until fluffy. Beat in eggs one at a time. Stir in vanilla, salt, cocoa, buttermilk, and flour. Beat well. Pour batter into pans and bake for about 25 minutes. Frost cooled cake with Coconut Pecan Frosting.

Coconut Pecan Frosting:

- 1 egg
- ⅔ cup (5 ounces) evaporated milk
- ⅔ cup sugar
- ¼ cup margarine
- 1⅓ cups coconut
- ½ cup pecans, chopped

In a microwavable container combine egg, milk, sugar, and margarine. Microwave until thick and bubbly. When cool stir in coconut and pecans.

Devil's Food Cake
(milk free)

1½ cups flour
1 cup granulated sugar
⅓ cup brown sugar
¾ teaspoon salt
1¼ teaspoons baking soda
¼ teaspoon baking powder
½ cup cocoa
¾ cup warm water
1 teaspoon vanilla
½ cup margarine, softened, or oil
2 eggs
½ cup nuts, chopped (optional)
Brown Sugar Frosting

Preheat oven to 350 degrees. Grease two 8 or 9-inch cake pans. Combine flour, sugars, salt, baking soda, baking powder, and cocoa. In a separate bowl combine warm water, vanilla and margarine. Add water mixture to flour mixture and beat for 2 minutes. Stir in 2 eggs and beat for 2 more minutes. Stir in nuts. Pour batter into pans and bake for 30–40 minutes. Remove cake from oven and let stand for 5 minutes. Invert cakes onto racks to cool. Frost cooled cakes with Brown Sugar Frosting.

Variations: To make a cake that is also wheat and gluten free, replace flour with the following:

1 cup brown rice flour
½ cup cornstarch
½ teaspoon baking powder
3 eggs

Brown Sugar Frosting (fat free):

1 egg white
1 cup brown sugar
3 tablespoons water

Combine egg white, brown sugar and water in the top of double boiler over hot water. Beat until mixture holds its shape. Spread over cooled cake.

Angel Food Cake

(fat & milk free)

- 1¾ cups (12–14) egg whites
- 2 teaspoons cream of tartar
- ¼ salt, optional
- 1½ cups sugar, divided
- 1 teaspoon vanilla extract
- ½ teaspoon almond extract
- ¾ cup flour

Preheat oven to 350 degrees. Beat egg whites, cream of tartar and salt until soft peaks form. Gradually add ¾ cup sugar a little at a time. Beating on high speed, add vanilla and almond extracts and continue beating until stiff peaks form.

In a separate bowl combine flour and ¾ cup sugar. Fold flour mixture into egg white mixture a little at a time until just blended. Pour batter into ungreased 10-inch tube pan. Cut through batter gently to remove any air bubbles. Bake until crust is golden and cracks are dry, about 30–35 minutes. Invert pan over a bottle or funnel and let cool completely. Remove cooled cake from pan.

Variation: To make Cocoa Angel Food Cake, add ¼ cup cocoa to the flour mixture.

Lemon Poppyseed Cake

- 1¼ cups sugar
- ⅓ cup oil
- 2 eggs
- 2 teaspoons vanilla
- 1 tablespoon lemon rind, grated
- 3 cups flour
- 1 teaspoon baking soda
- 1 teaspoon baking powder
- ¼ teaspoon salt
- 3 tablespoons poppy seeds
- 1¼ cups buttermilk
- 3 tablespoons lemon juice

Preheat oven to 350 degrees. Grease a 10 or 12-inch bundt or tube pan. Combine sugar and oil. Beat in eggs, vanilla and lemon rind. Add flour, baking soda, baking powder, salt, and poppy seeds. Mix well. Stir in buttermilk and lemon juice. Beat 1–2 minutes. Pour batter in pan. Bake for 45 minutes. Cool in pan 10 minutes. Turn cake out to cool on a wire rack. While still warm, brush or drizzle glaze over cake.

Variations: For a low fat or fat free recipe:

1. Replace oil with ½ cup unsweetened applesauce, or reduce oil to 2 tablespoons and add ⅓ cup unsweetened applesauce.
2. Replace eggs with ½ cup egg substitute or 4 egg whites.
3. Replace buttermilk with skim milk and increase lemon juice to 4 tablespoons.

Glaze (fat free):

- ½ cup powdered sugar
- 1 teaspoon lemon rind, grated
- 1 teaspoon skim or buttermilk
- 2 teaspoons fresh lemon juice

Combine ingredients and drizzle over warm Lemon Poppyseed Cake.

Buttermilk Blackberry Cake

Buttermilk gives cakes a light, fine crumb and a rich flavor.

- 1 cup margarine, butter or oil
- 1 cup brown sugar
- 3 eggs
- 1 cup blackberry or raspberry preserves
- ½ teaspoon nutmeg, optional
- ½ teaspoon ground cloves, optional
- 1 teaspoon cinnamon, optional
- 1 tablespoon baking soda dissolved in 1 cup buttermilk
- 2 cups flour

Preheat oven to 350 degrees. Grease three 8-inch layer pans or a bundt pan. Combine margarine and sugar. Beat in eggs. Add preserves. Stir in nutmeg, cloves and cinnamon. Stir baking soda and buttermilk mixture into batter. Add flour and beat well. Pour batter into pans. Bake for 20–25 minutes. Frost with Caramel Frosting.

Caramel Frosting:

- 3½ to 4 cups brown sugar
- ½ cup water
- 4 tablespoons margarine or butter
- 8 marshmallows
- 1 teaspoon vanilla

Combine brown sugar and water in a saucepan. Bring to a boil and simmer for 1 minute. Remove from heat. Add margarine, marshmallows and vanilla. Beat until thick.

Berry or Fruit Buttermilk Cake

(low fat)

- ⅓ cup margarine or oil
- 1 cup sugar
- 1 egg or 1 egg white
- ½ teaspoon vanilla
- ½ teaspoon lemon juice
- ½ teaspoon almond extract
- 2 cups flour
- ¼ teaspoon salt
- 2 teaspoons baking powder
- ½ teaspoon baking soda
- 1 cup buttermilk
- Vanilla icing
- Raspberries for top of cake

Preheat oven to 350 degrees. Grease 9 x 13-inch pan or two layer pans. Combine margarine and sugar. Beat in egg, vanilla, lemon juice, and almond extract. In a separate bowl combine flour, salt, baking powder, and baking soda. Add flour mixture, alternately with buttermilk, to margarine mixture. Beat for 3 minutes. Pour batter into pan and bake for 25–30 minutes. While cake is still warm, frost with Vanilla Icing and sprinkle raspberries on top.

Notes:

Buttermilk White Cake
(low fat)

- ¼ cup margarine
- ¼ cup shortening
- 1⅓ cups buttermilk
- 1 teaspoon vanilla
- 2 cups sugar
- 2½ cups flour
- 1 teaspoon baking powder
- ½ teaspoon baking soda
- 4 egg whites

Preheat oven to 350 degrees. Grease two 8 or 9-inch pans or one 9 x 13 x 2-inch pan. Combine margarine, shortening, buttermilk, vanilla, and sugar. Stir in flour, baking powder and baking soda. Add egg whites and beat for 2 or 3 minutes. Pour batter in pans and bake for 30–35 minutes. Spread Lemon Filling or Banana Filling on bottom layer and frost with a frosting of your choice.

Lemon Filling (low fat, egg free):

- ¾ cup sugar
- 3 tablespoons cornstarch
- ¼ teaspoon salt
- ⅔ cup water
- 1 teaspoon lemon peel, grated
- ¼ cup lemon juice
- 1 tablespoon margarine
- 1 or 2 drops yellow food coloring

Combine sugar, cornstarch, salt, water, lemon peel, and lemon juice. Cook over medium heat stirring often, or microwave until mixture thickens and boils for 1 minute. Remove from heat. Stir in margarine and food coloring. Spread filling between cake layers or use in pie.

Variation: For a less tart filling, replace ¼ cup lemon juice with 3 tablespoons lemon juice plus 1 tablespoon orange juice.

Banana Filling (egg free):

- 3 tablespoons cornstarch or 6 tablespoons flour
- ⅓ cup sugar
- ⅛ teaspoon salt
- ½ cup cold milk
- 1 teaspoon vanilla
- 1½ cups hot milk
- 1 or 2 bananas, sliced

Combine cornstarch or flour, sugar and salt. Add cold milk and mix well. Stir in vanilla. Gradually add hot milk. Cook on stovetop or in microwave, stirring every minute or two, until thick. Let cool slightly. Add banana slices. Spread filling over bottom layer of cake.

Old-fashioned Buttermilk Cake

- 1 cup margarine or butter, softened
- 2 cups sugar
- 4 eggs
- 3 cups flour
- 2 teaspoons baking powder
- ½ teaspoon baking soda
- ½ teaspoon salt
- 2 cups buttermilk
- 1 teaspoon vanilla

Preheat oven to 350 degrees. Grease and flour three 8-inch cake pans. Cream margarine or butter and sugar and beat until fluffy. Add eggs, beating well after each egg. Beginning and ending with flour, add flour, baking powder, baking soda, and salt, and buttermilk. Add vanilla and beat well. Pour batter in cake pans and bake for 25–30 minutes. Cool cake and frost.

Quick & Fluffy Frosting (fat free):

- 1 egg white
- ¾ cup sugar
- 1 tablespoon corn syrup
- ¼ teaspoon cream of tartar
- Dash of salt
- 1 teaspoon vanilla
- ¼ cup water, boiling

Beat egg white until stiff. Gradually add while stirring constantly sugar, corn syrup, cream of tartar, salt, and vanilla. Slowly add boiling water and beat until stiff peaks form.

Old-fashioned Buttermilk Cake

(low fat)

- 1 teaspoon baking powder
- ¾ teaspoon baking soda
- 1¾ cups buttermilk
- ¼ cup shortening
- ¼ cup margarine or butter
- 1½ cups sugar
- ½ teaspoon salt
- 1 teaspoon vanilla
- 3 cups cake flour or 2¾ cups all-purpose flour
- 3 egg whites, beaten stiffly

Preheat oven to 375 degrees. Grease a layer or loaf pan. Dissolve baking powder and baking soda in buttermilk. In a separate bowl combine shortening, margarine and sugar. Add salt and vanilla. Stir in ½ cup flour. Add remaining flour alternately with buttermilk mixture. Fold in egg whites. Pour batter into pans and bake for 25–30 minutes.

Buttermilk Orange Cake

- 1 cup sugar
- ¾ cup oil or margarine
- 2 eggs
- 2¼ cups flour
- 1 teaspoon baking powder
- 1 teaspoon baking soda
- ¼ teaspoon salt
- 1 cup buttermilk
- 2 orange rinds, grated
- 1 cup nuts, chopped

Topping:

- 2 oranges, juiced
- ½ cup sugar

Preheat oven to 375 degrees. Grease a bundt pan. Combine sugar and oil or margarine. Add eggs and beat well. Mix in flour, baking soda, baking powder, and salt. Stir in buttermilk, orange rind and nuts. Pour batter into pan. Bake for 30–35 minutes.

Variation: To make Buttermilk Cranberry Cake, add 1 cup chopped dates and 1 cup whole cranberries when adding buttermilk, orange rind and nuts.

Notes:

Old-fashioned Buttermilk Pound Cake

- 2 cups sugar
- ½ cup margarine, softened
- ½ cup oil
- 4 eggs
- ½ teaspoon baking soda
- 1 cup buttermilk
- 3 cups flour
- ¼ teaspoon salt
- 2 teaspoons baking powder
- 2 teaspoons lemon juice
- 1 teaspoon almond extract

Preheat oven to 350 degrees. Grease and flour a 10-inch tube pan. Cream sugar, margarine and oil, beating well. Add eggs, beating after each addition. In a small bowl dissolve baking soda in buttermilk. In a separate bowl, combine flour, salt and baking powder. Beginning and ending with flour mixture, add flour mixture to sugar mixture, alternating with buttermilk mixture. Beat for 2 minutes. Stir in lemon juice and almond extract. Pour batter into tube pan. Bake for 1 hour. Cool in pan for 10 minutes. Remove from pan onto rack and continue cooling. While still warm, cake may be glazed with Lemon Glaze.

Variation: To make Lemon Pound Cake, omit margarine, increase oil to ¾ cup, replace buttermilk with 2 additional tablespoons of lemon juice, add ¾ cup orange juice or apricot nectar, omit baking soda, and increase baking powder to 1 tablespoon.

Lemon Glaze (fat free):

- 1½ cups powdered sugar
- ⅓ to ½ cup lemon juice

Combine ingredients and beat to spreading consistency. Glaze cake while still warm.

Buttermilk Coffee Cake
(no cholesterol, low fat)

- 1 cup granulated sugar
- ¼ cup margarine, softened
- ½ cup egg whites or ½ cup egg substitute
- ¾ cup buttermilk
- 1 teaspoon vanilla
- 2 cups flour
- 1 teaspoon baking powder
- 1 teaspoon baking soda
- ½ teaspoon salt

Topping:

- ½ cup oatmeal
- Nuts, chopped (optional)
- ⅓ cup brown sugar
- 1 teaspoon cinnamon

Grease a 10-inch tube pan or 9 x 12-inch cake pan. Cream granulated sugar and margarine. Beat in egg whites, buttermilk and vanilla. In a separate bowl combine flour, baking powder, baking soda, and salt. Stir flour mixture into sugar mixture. Preheat oven to 350 degrees. Make topping by combining oatmeal, chopped nuts, brown sugar, and cinnamon. Pour half the cake batter into pan, sprinkle half the topping over batter in pan, and repeat for remaining batter. Bake until toothpick inserted in center of cake comes out clean, about 40–50 minutes.

Coffee Cake
(milk & sugar free)

- ½ cup bananas, mashed
- ⅓ cup margarine, softened
- 3 eggs
- 1 teaspoon vanilla
- 1 teaspoon orange peel, grated
- ¼ cup apple juice concentrate
- 1 cup water
- 3 cups flour
- 1 teaspoon baking soda
- 2 teaspoons baking powder
- 1½ cups dates, chopped

Topping:

- ¼ cup dates, chopped
- ¼ cup nuts, chopped
- ¼ cup flaked unsweetened coconut or oatmeal
- ½ teaspoon cinnamon

Preheat oven to 350 degrees. Grease a 9 x 13-inch pan. Cream banana and margarine. Beat until fluffy. Beat in eggs, vanilla, orange peel, apple juice, water, flour, baking soda and powder. Stir in dates. Pour batter into pan. In a separate bowl combine topping ingredients and sprinkle over batter in pan. Bake 20–25 minutes.

Coffee Cake
(sugar free)

- ½ cup banana, mashed
- ½ cup margarine, softened
- 3 large eggs
- 1 teaspoon vanilla
- 1 teaspoon orange extract
- 1¼ cups water
- 2½ cups all-purpose flour
- ½ cup whole wheat flour
- 1 teaspoon baking soda
- 2 teaspoons baking powder
- 1½ cups dates, chopped
- ¼ cup unsweetened coconut

Topping:

- ¼ cup dates, chopped
- ¼ cup nuts, chopped

Preheat oven to 350 degrees. Grease and flour a 9 x 13-inch baking dish. Combine bananas and margarine. Beat in eggs, vanilla, orange extract, and water. In a separate bowl combine flours, baking soda, baking powder. Stir flour mixture into bananas mixture. Stir in coconut. Spoon batter into baking dish. Combine dates and nuts and sprinkle over batter in pan. Bake for 20–25 minutes.

Apple Coffee Cake
(fat free)

- 1 cup applesauce
- 1¼ cups brown sugar
- ½ cup egg substitute or 4 egg whites
- 1 teaspoon vanilla
- 1½ cups all-purpose flour
- ½ cup whole wheat flour
- 1½ teaspoons baking soda
- ½ teaspoon cinnamon
- 1½ cups apple, grated
- ½ cup raisins, optional

Preheat oven to 350 degrees. Grease a 9-inch bundt or tube pan. Combine applesauce, brown sugar, egg substitute, and vanilla. In a separate bowl combine flours, baking soda and cinnamon. Stir flour mixture into applesauce mixture. Fold in apple and raisins. Bake for 45 minutes.

Cranapple Bars or Cake

(sugar free)

- ½ cup unsweetened applesauce
- ½ cup unsweetened apple juice concentrate
- ¼ cup oil
- 3 eggs
- ½ tablespoon orange or lemon peel, grated
- 1½ cups all-purpose flour
- 3 tablespoons whole wheat flour
- ¼ cup oatmeal
- 1 teaspoon baking soda
- 2 teaspoons baking powder
- 1 teaspoon nutmeg
- 1½ teaspoon cinnamon
- ½ cup cranberries
- 1 cup raisins, optional
- ½ cup nuts, chopped (optional)

Topping:

- ¼ cup nuts, chopped
- 1 teaspoon cinnamon

Preheat oven to 350 degrees. Grease a 9 x 13 x 2-inch pan. Combine applesauce, apple juice and oil. Stir in eggs, orange or lemon peel, flours, oatmeal, baking soda and powder. Mix well. Stir in nutmeg, cinnamon, cranberries, raisins, and nuts. Pour batter into pan. Combine nuts and cinnamon. Sprinkle over batter in pan. Bake for 20 minutes.

Pumpkin Cake

(low fat, egg & milk free)

- ¼ cup margarine, shortening or oil
- 1 cup brown sugar
- 1 cup pumpkin
- ⅓ cup orange juice
- 1½ cups all-purpose flour
- ¼ cup whole wheat flour
- 2 tablespoons cornstarch
- 1 teaspoon cinnamon
- 1 teaspoon pumpkin pie spice (or ½ teaspoon nutmeg plus ½ teaspoon allspice)
- 1 teaspoon baking soda
- 1 teaspoon baking powder
- ½ teaspoon salt
- 1 cup dried fruits, chopped (optional)
- 1 cup nuts, chopped (optional)

Preheat oven to 350 degrees. Grease a loaf or bundt pan. Combine margarine and brown sugar. Mix in pumpkin and orange juice. In a separate bowl combine flours, cornstarch, cinnamon, pumpkin pie spice, baking soda, baking powder, and salt. Stir flour mixture into margarine mixture. Mix well. Dried fruits and nuts may be stirred in if desired. Bake for 1 hour.

Old-fashioned Pumpkin Cake

- ½ cup butter or margarine
- 1½ cups sugar
- 2 eggs
- 1 cup pumpkin
- ⅔ cup buttermilk
- 1¾ cups flour
- 2 teaspoons pumpkin pie spice
- 2 teaspoons baking powder
- 1 teaspoon baking soda
- ¾ teaspoon salt

Preheat oven to 350 degrees. Grease a 10-inch bundt pan or two 8-inch cake pans. Combine butter and sugar. Add eggs, pumpkin and buttermilk. Beat well. In a separate bowl combine flour, pumpkin pie spice, baking powder and soda, and salt. Add flour mixture to butter mixture. Mix well. Pour batter into pan. Bake for 30–40 minutes.

Old-fashioned Banana Cream Cake

- ¾ cup margarine or butter, softened
- 1½ cups sugar
- 2 large or 3 small eggs
- 3 bananas (about 1 cup), mashed
- ½ cup buttermilk
- 1½ teaspoons vanilla
- 2 cups flour
- 1 teaspoon baking powder
- 1 teaspoon baking soda
- ½ teaspoon salt
- Whipped topping for between Layers and to frost cake
- 1 banana, sliced, for top of cake
- ½ cup nuts, chopped, for top of cake

Preheat oven to 350 degrees. Grease and flour two 8 or 9-inch cake pans. Combine margarine or butter and sugar. Beat until light and fluffy. Stir in eggs and beat well. Add bananas, buttermilk and vanilla. In a separate bowl combine flour, baking powder, baking soda, and salt. Stir flour mixture into banana mixture. Pour batter into cake pans and bake for 35–40 minutes. Cool cake in pans for 5 minutes before turning out onto wire racks to completely cool. Spread whipped topping on bottom layer. Frost cake with whipped topping. Slice banana and arrange on top of cake. Sprinkle nuts on top.

Banana Cake

(sugar free)

- 1 cup bananas, mashed
- ¼ cup buttermilk
- ¼ cup shortening
- 1 egg
- ½ teaspoon vanilla
- ¾ cup apple juice concentrate
- 1 cup flour
- 1 teaspoon baking powder
- ½ teaspoon baking soda

Preheat oven to 350 degrees. Grease an 8 or 9-inch cake pan. Combine banana, buttermilk, shortening, egg, vanilla, and apple juice concentrate. Stir in flour, baking powder and soda. Bake for 25–30 minutes.

Banana Cake

(gluten & wheat free)

- ½ cup shortening, margarine or oil
- 1 cup sugar
- 4 eggs
- 1 cup bananas, mashed
- 1 teaspoon vanilla
- 1½ cups rice flour
- ½ cup cornstarch
- 1½ teaspoons baking soda
- 1½ teaspoons baking powder
- ¾ teaspoon salt
- ½ cup buttermilk

Preheat oven to 350 degrees. Grease two 8 or 9-inch cake pans and line with waxed paper. Combine shortening and sugar. Add, beating after every addition, eggs, bananas and vanilla. In a separate bowl combine flour, cornstarch, baking soda, baking powder, and salt. Stir flour mixture alternately with buttermilk into banana mixture. Bake for about 40 minutes. Loosen edges, invert onto a wire rack, remove waxed paper, and cool.

Carrot, Apple or Pumpkin Cake I

(sugar free)

- ¾ cup oil
- 4 eggs
- 1 cup apple juice concentrate, thawed
- ½ cup applesauce or pumpkin
- 3 tablespoons *Fruit Sweet* or increase apple juice concentrate by 4 tablespoons
- 1¼ tablespoons cinnamon
- 1 tablespoon orange rind, grated
- 2½ cups all-purpose flour
- ½ cup whole wheat flour
- 1½ tablespoons baking powder
- ¾ tablespoon baking soda
- 1¼ cup apples, chopped, or grated carrots, chopped
- ½ cup nuts and/or raisins, chopped (optional)

Preheat oven to 350 degrees. Grease a 9 x 12 or 9 x 13-inch cake pan, or a quarter-sheet cake pan. Combine oil, eggs, apple juice, applesauce or pumpkin, and *Fruit Sweet*. Stir in cinnamon, orange rind, flours, baking powder, baking soda, apples or carrots, and nuts or raisins. Mix well. Pour batter into pan and bake for 35–40 minutes.

Carrot, Apple or Pumpkin Cake II

(low fat, egg & sugar free)

- 1 cup raisins
- 1 cup cold water
- ½ cup apple juice concentrate
- 2 tablespoons margarine
- 1 cup carrots or apples, grated
- 2 cups flour
- ¼ teaspoon salt
- 2 teaspoons baking soda
- 1 teaspoon cinnamon
- 1 teaspoon nutmeg
- 1 teaspoon ground cloves
- 1 cup nuts, chopped

In a large saucepan, combine raisins, water, apple juice, margarine, and carrots or apple. Bring to a boil and simmer for 20 minutes. Let cool.

Meanwhile, preheat oven to 350 degrees. Grease a 13 x 9½ x 2-inch pan. Add flour, salt, baking soda, spices, and nuts to the fruit mixture. Mix well. Pour batter into pan and bake for 35–40 minutes.

Variations:

1. Flour may consist of 1 cup all-purpose flour plus 1 cup whole wheat flour.

2. *Pumpkin Cake:* Omit grated carrots or apples. Add 1 cup pumpkin when adding dry ingredients.

Carrot Cake

(sugar free)

- 5 egg whites
- 5 egg yolks
- ½ cup oil
- 1½ teaspoons vanilla
- 2 cups (16 ounces) apple juice concentrate
- ¼ cup applesauce
- 2 or 3 carrots, grated
- ½ cup raisins and nuts, chopped
- 3 cups all-purpose flour
- 1 cup whole wheat flour
- 1 teaspoon allspice
- 1 tablespoon cinnamon
- Dash of salt
- 1 tablespoon baking powder
- 1½ teaspoons baking soda

Preheat oven to 350 degrees. Grease a quarter-sheet cake pan for a thicker cake, or a one-third sheet cake pan for a thinner cake, or bake in two one-quarter sheet cake pans. Beat egg whites until stiff. In a separate bowl cream together egg yolks and oil. Add vanilla, apple juice, applesauce, carrots, raisins and nuts. Stir in flours, allspice, cinnamon, salt, baking powder, and baking soda. Fold egg yolk mixture gently into egg white mixture. Pour batter into cake pan and bake for 40 minutes. Frost cooled cake with Sugar Free Icing and store in a cool place.

Variation: Frost with sugar free whipped topping.

Sugar Free Icing:

- 1 package (3 ounces) cream cheese
- ¾ cup apple juice concentrate
- 1 teaspoon vanilla

Combine ingredients. Spread on cooled cake.

Variation: If not sweet enough, add a couple of packages of *Equal* sweetener.

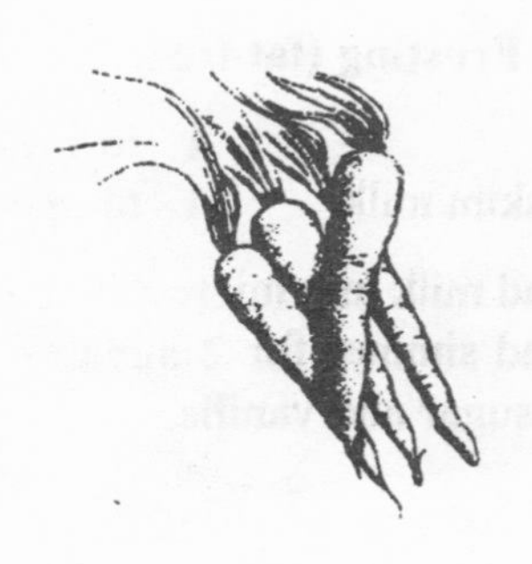

Honey Carrot or Apple Cake

(fat free)

1½ cups all-purpose flour
½ cup whole wheat flour
½ cup honey
½ cup unsweetened applesauce
½ cup brown sugar
1 cup egg substitute
2 teaspoons cinnamon
2 teaspoons orange peel, grated
1 teaspoon baking powder
1 teaspoon baking soda
3 cups carrot, grated
½ cup raisins
½ cup nuts, chopped (optional)

Preheat oven to 350 degrees. Grease a 9 x 13-inch pan or two 8 or 9-inch pans. Combine all ingredients and beat for 2 minutes. Bake for 30–40 minutes. Frost cooled cake with Fat Free Cream Cheese Honey Icing or Fat Free Honey Icing.

Fat Free Cream Cheese Honey Icing:

1 package (8 ounces) fat free cream cheese
⅓ cup honey
1 teaspoon vanilla

Beat cream cheese until smooth. Stir in honey and vanilla. Spread over cooled cake.

Fat Free Honey Icing:

1 cup honey
2 egg whites

Measure honey into a microwavable bowl. Microwave until heated to 238 degrees, about 5 minutes. Meanwhile, beat egg whites until stiff. Pour hot honey slowly into egg whites. Beat until of spreading consistency.

Old-fashioned Caramel Frosting (fat free):

1 cup brown sugar
⅔ cup buttermilk or skim milk
1 to 1½ cups powdered sugar
1 teaspoon vanilla

Combine brown sugar and milk in a microwavable container. Bring to a boil in the microwave and simmer for 2 minutes. Remove from microwave. Beat in powdered sugar and vanilla.

Old-fashioned Carrot Cake

- 1¼ cups oil
- 1 cup brown sugar
- 1 cup granulated sugar
- 2 teaspoons cinnamon
- 1 teaspoon allspice, optional
- 1 teaspoon salt
- 4 eggs
- 2½ cups all-purpose flour
- ½ cup whole wheat flour
- 2 teaspoons baking powder
- 1½ teaspoons baking soda
- 2 cups carrots, shredded
- 1 cup crushed pineapple with juice
- 1 teaspoon vanilla
- ½ cup walnuts, chopped
- ½ cup coconut
- ½ cup raisins, optional

Preheat oven to 350 degrees. Grease a bundt pan or 10 x 14 x 2-inch cake pan. Combine oil and sugars. Scrape bowl often as sugar sticks to bowl. Beat in eggs and remaining ingredients. Beat for about 2 minutes. Pour into pan and bake for 40 minutes. Cool and frost with Old-fashioned Cream Cheese Frosting.

Variation: For lower fat and sugar, replace oil, sugar and eggs in the recipe with:

- ⅔ cup oil
- 1 cup sugar
- ½ cup unsweetened applesauce
- ¾ cup egg substitute or egg whites

and increase baking powder to 1 tablespoon.

Old-fashioned Cream Cheese Frosting:

- 1 package (8 ounces) cream cheese
- 2 tablespoons butter or margarine, softened
- 2 teaspoons vanilla
- 4 cups powdered sugar
- Buttermilk, if needed
- Coconut, optional
- Nuts, chopped or sliced (optional)

Beat cream cheese until smooth. Mix in butter or margarine, vanilla, and sugar. Add buttermilk if needed for spreading consistency. Stir in coconut and nuts.

Cream Cheese Frosting (fat free or lower fat):

- 1 package (8 ounces) fat free cream cheese
- 4 tablespoons margarine or buttermilk
- 2 to 3 cups powdered sugar
- 2 teaspoons vanilla

Beat cream cheese until smooth. Add margarine or buttermilk, sugar, and vanilla. Beat well.

Zucchini and/or Carrot Cake

(egg & milk free)

This is a very heavy, chewy cake.

- ¼ cup honey
- 1 cup carrot or zucchini, grated
- 1 cup raisins or dates, chopped
- ¼ cup margarine
- 1½ cups very hot water
- 1 teaspoon cinnamon
- ½ teaspoon allspice
- ½ teaspoon nutmeg
- 2 teaspoons baking soda
- 1 teaspoon baking powder
- 1 cup all-purpose flour
- ½ cup wheat germ
- ½ cup bran of your choice
- ½ to 1 cup nuts, chopped, or sunflower seeds

Combine honey, carrot or zucchini, raisins or dates, margarine, and hot water. Set aside for 10 minutes. Preheat oven to 350 degrees. Grease a 13 x 9-inch pan. Stir in remaining ingredients and mix well. Pour batter into pan and bake for 20 minutes. Reduce oven temperature to 325 degrees and continue to bake until toothpick inserted in center comes out clean, about 40–50 minutes.

Apple/Carrot Cake

(low fat)

- 1 cup all-purpose flour
- 1 cup whole wheat flour
- 1 cup sugar
- 1 teaspoon baking powder
- 1 teaspoon baking soda
- ⅓ teaspoon salt
- 1 teaspoon cinnamon
- 1 cup apple juice
- ¼ cup oil
- 2 eggs or egg substitute
- 2 cups carrots, shredded
- 1 cup nuts, chopped
- 1 cup raisins, optional

Preheat oven to 350 degrees. Grease a 9 x 13-inch pan. Combine ingredients in the order given. Beat for 2 minutes. Pour into pan and bake for 30–40 minutes. Frost cooled cake with Fat Free Frosting.

Fat Free Frosting:

- ½ cup fat free yogurt
- 2 tablespoons buttermilk
- 1 teaspoon lemon juice or vanilla
- 1½ cups powdered sugar

Combine ingredients. Spread over cooled cake.

Fresh Apple Fruit Loaf

(egg & milk free)

1 cup brown sugar
½ cup oil
2 tablespoons sherry
1 teaspoon vanilla
1 cup mixed candied or dried fruit, coarsely chopped
1 cup fresh dates, pitted and cut in small pieces
1 cup raisins
1 cup nuts, chopped
2 teaspoons baking soda
1½ cups apples, coarsely shredded
2 cups flour
½ teaspoon salt
1 teaspoon cinnamon
¼ teaspoon nutmeg

Preheat oven to 350 degrees. Grease and flour a 5 by 9-inch loaf pan. Combine brown sugar, oil, sherry, and vanilla. Stir in candied or dried fruit, dates, raisins, and nuts. In a separate bowl, mix grated apple and baking soda. Stir apple mixture into fruit and nut mixture. Add flour, salt, cinnamon, and nutmeg. Blend thoroughly. Pour batter into loaf pan and bake for 1 hour and 25 minutes. Cool in pan for 5 minutes. Turn onto wire rack to continue cooling.

Apple Spice Cake

- 1 cup margarine, softened
- 1 cup brown sugar
- ½ cup granulated sugar
- 1 large or 2 small eggs
- 1½ cups unsweetened applesauce
- 2 teaspoons vanilla
- 2¼ cups all-purpose flour
- ½ cup whole wheat flour
- 2 teaspoons baking soda
- ½ teaspoon nutmeg
- 1½ teaspoons cinnamon
- ½ teaspoon mace, optional
- ½ teaspoon salt
- 1 cup raisins
- ¾ cup apple, chopped
- ½ cup nuts, chopped

Preheat oven to 350 degrees. Grease a 10-inch bundt or tube pan. Combine margarine and sugars. Beat until fluffy. Add eggs and then applesauce and vanilla. In a separate bowl, combine flours, baking soda, nutmeg, cinnamon, mace, and salt. Add flour mixture to egg mixture and beat for 2 minutes. Stir in raisins, apples and nuts. Pour batter into pan. Bake for 1 hour. Cool cake for 10 minutes in pan. Turn out on rack to finish cooling (the side that was up while baking should be on top). While cake is still slightly warm, brush tops and sides with glaze.

Variation: To reduce fat, replace eggs with egg substitute, substitute ½ cup oil for margarine, increase applesauce to 2 cups, and add 2 tablespoons wheat germ.

Apple Glaze:

- ¼ cup margarine
- ¼ cup brown sugar
- 2 tablespoons granulated sugar
- ¼ cup apple juice or cider
- 1 tablespoon orange peel, grated
- 4 tablespoons orange juice
- 2 tablespoons low fat or whole evaporated milk

Combine ingredients in a 1 quart saucepan. Heat to boiling, stirring constantly. Reduce heat and simmer 5 minutes, stirring frequently. Cool 5 minutes. Stir to reblend. Pour or brush on slightly cooled cake.

'Washington' Apple Cake

- ¼ cup buttermilk
- ½ cup oil
- 1 cup brown sugar
- ½ cup granulated sugar
- 2 teaspoons vanilla
- 2 eggs
- 4 cups apple, grated
- 2 cups all-purpose flour
- ½ cup whole wheat flour
- 2 teaspoons cinnamon
- 1 teaspoon salt
- 2 teaspoons baking powder
- ½ teaspoon baking soda
- ¾ cup nuts, chopped (optional)

Preheat oven to 350 degrees. Grease a 9 x 13-inch cake pan or a 10-inch bundt pan. Combine buttermilk, oil, sugars, vanilla, and eggs. Beat in apples, flours, cinnamon, salt, baking powder, and baking soda. Mix well. Pour into pan and bake for 45 minutes.

Variation: To reduce fat, reduce oil to ¼ cup, increase buttermilk to ½ cup, replace eggs with egg substitute or 4 egg whites, and omit nuts.

Apple Cake
(egg & milk free)

- ½ cup oil
- 1 cup granulated sugar
- 1 cup brown sugar
- 1 teaspoon cinnamon
- 2 teaspoons baking soda
- ½ teaspoon salt
- 2 teaspoons vanilla
- 1½ cups all-purpose flour
- ½ cup whole wheat flour
- 3 cups apples, chopped
- 1 cup raisins
- 1 cup nuts, chopped

Preheat oven to 350 degrees. Grease a 9 x 13-inch pan. Combine in order given oil, sugars, cinnamon, baking soda, salt, vanilla, and flours. Beat for 2 minutes. Stir in apple, raisins and nuts. Pour batter into pan and bake for 30 minutes.

Old-fashioned Applesauce Cake

- ¼ cup shortening
- ¼ cup margarine
- ¾ cup brown sugar
- ¾ cup granulated sugar
- 3 eggs
- ⅓ cup buttermilk
- 1 cup applesauce
- 1 teaspoon baking powder
- 1 teaspoon baking soda
- 1 teaspoon cinnamon
- ½ teaspoon allspice
- ¼ teaspoon nutmeg
- ½ teaspoon vanilla
- 2 cups all-purpose flour
- ¼ cup whole wheat flour
- 1 cup raisins and nuts, chopped (optional)

Preheat oven to 350 degrees. Grease a 9 x 13 x 2-inch cake pan. Cream shortening, margarine and sugars. Beat in eggs. Stir in remaining ingredients, except raisins and nuts, and beat for 1 minute. Stir in raisins and nuts. Pour batter into cake pan and bake for 30 minutes.

Seven Minute Frosting (fat free):

- 2 egg whites
- 1½ cups sugar
- ⅓ cup corn syrup
- ¼ teaspoon cream of tartar
- 6 tablespoons water
- ⅛ teaspoon salt
- 1 teaspoon vanilla

Combine egg whites, sugar, corn syrup, cream of tartar, water, and salt in top of double boiler over boiling water. Beat with electric mixer on high speed for about 7 minutes until frosting is thick and soft glossy peaks form. Remove from hot water. Stir in vanilla. After frosting cake, store cake in a covered container so frosting does not dry out. Yield: 2 cups.

Variations:

1. ***Seven Minute Lemon Frosting:*** Omit vanilla. Add 2 tablespoons lemon juice and ¼ teaspoon lemon rind, grated.
2. ***Seven Minute Orange Frosting:*** Omit vanilla. Add 1 tablespoon lemon juice, ¼ cup orange juice, and ½ teaspoon orange rind, grated.

Applesauce Cake

(egg free)

- ¾ cup oil
- 1 cup granulated sugar
- 1 cup brown sugar
- 3¼ cups unsweetened applesauce, heated
- 4 cups flour
- 2 tablespoons cocoa
- 4 teaspoons baking soda
- 2 teaspoons cinnamon
- 1¼ teaspoons salt
- ½ teaspoon nutmeg
- ½ teaspoon allspice
- ½ cup raisins
- ½ cup walnuts, chopped

Preheat oven to 350 degrees. Combine oil and sugars until well blended. Add hot applesauce and beat well. Gradually add, beating well after each addition, flour, cocoa, baking soda, cinnamon, salt, nutmeg, and allspice. Stir in raisins and walnuts. Pour batter into two 9-inch pans or 9 by 13-inch pans. Bake 25–30 minutes.

Applesauce Fruit Cake

(egg & milk free)

- 3 cups unsweetened applesauce
- 1 cup margarine
- 1 cup granulated sugar
- 1 cup brown sugar
- 4 cups flour
- ½ cup whole wheat flour, optional
- 1 tablespoon baking soda
- 1 teaspoon baking powder
- 2½ teaspoons cinnamon
- ½ teaspoon salt
- ½ teaspoon ground cloves
- 2 pounds mixed dates, whole and chopped
- 1 pound candied red cherries
- ¼ pound candied green cherries
- ¼ pound candied pineapple or mixed candied fruit of your choice
- 4 cups nuts, chopped

In a medium saucepan combine applesauce, margarine and sugars. Bring applesauce mixture to a boil over medium and boil for 5 minutes. Remove mixture from heat to cool.

Preheat oven to 250 degrees. Grease loaf pans or 1-pound tin cans, or line with parchment or waxed paper. When applesauce mixture is cool add flours, baking soda, baking powder, cinnamon, salt, cloves, dates, candied fruit, and nuts. Mix well. Pour batter equally into loaf pans or tin cans. Bake for 2½ hours. Cool in pans for 10 minutes. Remove cake from pans and continue cooling on rack. Wrap cooled cake in cheesecloth and saturate with apricot brandy or pineapple juice. Wrap in plastic wrap and then in aluminum foil. Store in refrigerator indefinitely.

Old-fashioned Gingerbread
(or Molasses Cake)

½ cup margarine
½ cup sugar
2 eggs
1 teaspoon baking soda dissolved in 1 cup boiling water
1 cup molasses
2 cups all-purpose flour
½ cup whole wheat flour
2 teaspoons baking powder
1½ teaspoons cinnamon
½ teaspoon ground cloves
1 teaspoon ginger
¼ teaspoon salt, optional

Preheat oven to 350 degrees. Grease a 9 x 13-inch or 9 x 9 x 2inch pan. Combine margarine and sugar. Beat in eggs. Add baking soda dissolved in water and molasses to egg mixture. In a separate bowl combine flours, baking powder, cinnamon, cloves, ginger, and salt. Add flour mixture to egg mixture and mix well. Pour batter into pan. Bake for 35–40 minutes.

May be frosted with a light icing or whipped topping, sprinkled with powdered sugar, or served plain.

Variation: For a low fat recipe reduce margarine to ¼ cup, reduce sugar to ¾ cup, add ⅓ buttermilk, and replace eggs with ½ cup egg substitute or egg whites.

Light Icing or Glaze:

2 tablespoons skim milk
1 tablespoon lemon juice
¼ teaspoon salt, optional
1 to 1½ cups powdered sugar

Combine ingredients. Add more liquid if needed for spreading consistency.

Variations:

1. Substitute skim milk and lemon juice with 3 tablespoons buttermilk.

2. ***Lemon Icing:*** Omit milk and add 3 tablespoons lemon juice and 1 teaspoon grated lemon rind.

3. ***Orange Icing:*** Omit milk and add 4 tablespoons orange juice and 1 teaspoon grated orange rind.

Gingerbread

(wheat free)

- 1¼ cups rye or rice flour
- 1¼ cups cornstarch
- 2 teaspoons baking soda
- 1 teaspoon cinnamon
- ¼ teaspoon ground cloves
- ¼ teaspoon ginger
- ½ cup sugar
- 1 cup molasses
- ½ cup butter
- 1 cup boiling water
- 2 eggs

Preheat oven to 325 degrees. Grease a 9 or 10-inch square pan Combine flour, cornstarch, baking soda, cinnamon, cloves, and ginger In a separate bowl combine sugar, molasses, butter, and boiling water Stir sugar mixture into flour mixture. Add eggs and beat well. Bake for 60 minutes.

Buttermilk Gingerbread

- 3 cups flour
- 1 teaspoon baking soda
- 1 teaspoon ginger
- 1 teaspoon cinnamon
- ¼ teaspoon salt
- 1 cup buttermilk
- 1 cup brown sugar
- ¾ cup molasses
- ¾ cup margarine, melted
- 2 eggs, beaten

Preheat oven to 350 degrees. Grease a 9 x 13-inch pan. Combine flour, baking soda, ginger, cinnamon, and salt. In a separate bowl combine brown sugar, molasses, margarine, and eggs. Stir sugar mixture into flour mixture alternately with the buttermilk. Pour batter into pan and bake for 40 minutes. Cool.

Buttermilk Spice Cake

(egg free)

- 2¼ cups flour
- 1⅓ cups sugar
- 1½ teaspoons baking soda
- 1 teaspoon baking powder
- ¼ teaspoon salt
- 1 teaspoon cinnamon
- ½ teaspoon ground cloves
- 1 teaspoon vanilla
- ½ cup oil or margarine, melted
- 1½ cups buttermilk

Preheat oven 350 degrees. Grease a 10-inch tube or bundt pan and dust lightly with brown sugar. Combine flour, sugar, baking soda, baking powder, salt, cinnamon, and cloves. In a separate bowl combine vanilla, oil or margarine, and buttermilk. Stir liquid ingredients into dry ingredients and mix well until batter is smooth. Pour batter into pan and bake for 1 hour. Cool in pan for 15 minutes, then turn out on rack to cool.

Variation: Substitute part of the sugar with brown sugar.

Old-fashioned Spice Cake

- ½ cup margarine
- ½ cup shortening
- 2 cups brown sugar
- 3 eggs
- 1 cup buttermilk
- 3 cups flour
- 2 teaspoons baking powder
- 1 teaspoon baking soda
- 2 teaspoons cinnamon
- 1 teaspoon nutmeg
- ¼ teaspoon ground cloves
- 1 cup raisins
- 1 cup nuts, chopped (optional)

Preheat oven to 350 degrees. Grease a 9 x 13 x 2-inch pan. Cream margarine, shortening and brown sugar. Add eggs and beat well. Stir in buttermilk. Mix in flour, baking powder, baking soda, cinnamon, nutmeg, cloves, nuts, and raisins. Bake for 45 minutes.

Whole Wheat Spice Cake

(low fat)

- 1/4 cup oil
- 2 cups pumpkin
- 1 cup maple syrup or honey
- 2 eggs
- 1/2 cup buttermilk or yogurt
- 3 1/2 cups whole wheat flour
- 1 tablespoon baking powder
- 1 1/4 teaspoons baking soda
- 1/2 teaspoon salt
- 1 teaspoon cinnamon
- 1/2 teaspoon allspice
- 3/4 teaspoon nutmeg
- 1 cup nuts and dates, chopped

Preheat oven to 350 degrees. Grease a 10-inch bundt or tube pan. Combine oil, pumpkin, syrup or honey, and extract. Stir in eggs and buttermilk or yogurt. In a separate bowl combine flour, baking powder, baking soda, salt, cinnamon, allspice, and nutmeg. Stir pumpkin mixture into flour mixture and mix well. Stir in nuts and dates. Pour batter into pan and bake for 45–55 minutes.

Variations:

1. 1 teaspoon maple extract can be added to the honey.
2. A combination of honey, molasses, and/or syrup can be substituted.

Spice Cake

(no cholesterol, egg & milk free, low fat)

- 1 cup honey or corn syrup
- 1 cup water
- 1 teaspoon salt
- 1/2 teaspoon ground cloves
- 1/2 teaspoon nutmeg
- 1 teaspoon cinnamon
- 1 tablespoon oil
- 1 teaspoon baking soda
- 2 cups flour or 1 cup all-purpose flour plus 1 cup whole wheat flour
- 1 1/2 teaspoons baking powder

In a saucepan combine honey or corn syrup, water, salt, cloves, nutmeg, and oil. Bring to a boil and simmer for 3 minutes. Let cool. Meanwhile, preheat oven to 350 degrees and grease a 9 or 10-inch tube pan.

Add baking soda to cooled mixture and stir to dissolve. Add flour and baking powder. Mix well. Pour batter in tube pan. Bake for 20 minutes. Reduce oven temperature to 325 degrees and continue baking for 40–50 minutes.

Spice Cake

(sugar free)

- 1 cup dates, chopped
- 1 cup prunes or apples, chopped
- 1 cup water
- ½ cup margarine
- 1 cup raisins
- 2 eggs
- 1 teaspoon baking soda
- ¼ teaspoon salt
- ½ cup all-purpose flour
- ½ cup whole wheat flour
- 1 cup nuts, chopped
- ¼ teaspoon cinnamon
- ¼ teaspoon nutmeg
- 1 teaspoon vanilla

Boil dates and prunes or apples in water for 3 minutes. Stir in margarine and raisins. Let cool.

Meanwhile, preheat oven to 350 degrees. Grease a baking dish. In a separate bowl combine eggs, baking soda, salt, flours, nuts, cinnamon, nutmeg, and vanilla. Add egg mixture to fruit mixture and stir to blend. Pour batter into baking dish. Bake for 25–30 minutes.

Zucchini Spice Cake

(low fat)

- ¾ cup all-purpose flour
- ¾ cup whole wheat flour
- ¾ cup brown sugar
- ¾ teaspoon baking soda
- ¼ teaspoon baking powder
- ¼ teaspoon salt
- 1 teaspoon cinnamon
- ½ teaspoon nutmeg
- ¼ teaspoon allspice
- 1 cup zucchini, unpeeled, shredded
- ½ cup buttermilk
- 2 tablespoons oil
- 1 egg
- 1½ teaspoons vanilla
- ½ cup nuts, chopped

Preheat oven to 350 degrees. Grease an 8 or 9-inch pan. Combine flours, brown sugar, baking soda, baking powder, salt, cinnamon, nutmeg, and allspice. Add zucchini, buttermilk, oil, egg, and vanilla. Mix well. Stir in nuts. Pour batter into pan and bake for 35–40 minutes.

Pineapple Bran Upside Down Cake

(low fat)

- 1 can (8 ounces) pineapple, sliced or crushed (reserve all liquid)
- ¼ cup brown sugar
- Maraschino cherries
- ¾ cup oats
- ¼ cup plus 2 tablespoons margarine
- 1 cup granulated sugar
- 2 egg whites
- 1 teaspoon vanilla
- 1 cup flour
- ½ cup oat bran
- 2 teaspoons baking powder

Drain pineapple and reserve juice. In an 8 or 9-inch baking pan combine 2 tablespoons margarine, 1 tablespoon reserved pineapple juice and brown sugar. Heat until sugar melts. Remove from heat. Arrange pineapple in pan. Place halved or whole maraschino cherries on pineapple or in center of each pineapple slice. Sprinkle oats over pineapple and juice mixture. Set aside.

Preheat oven to 350 degrees. Combine ¼ cup margarine and granulated sugar. Add water to remaining reserved pineapple juice to measure ½ cup. Add pineapple and water mixture, egg whites and vanilla to margarine and sugar mixture. Beat well. Add flour, oat bran and baking powder and mix well. Carefully pour batter over pineapple slices in pan. Spread batter evenly to edge of pan.

Bake 40–45 minutes. Cool in pan for 5 minutes. Invert onto serving plate. Continue to cool. Cake may be served with light whipped topping.

All Natural Fruit Cake
(fat & sugar free)

Even without the fat and sugar, this is still a wonderfully moist fruit cake, a family favorite.

- ½ cup unsweetened apple juice concentrate
- ½ cup unsweetened orange juice concentrate
- ¾ cup cranberries, chopped
- 1 cup pitted dates, chopped
- ½ cup dried apricots, apples, or sweet cherries, chopped
- ¼ cup yellow raisins
- 1 cup nuts, chopped
- 1 teaspoon vanilla
- 2 egg whites
- 1 cup unsweetened pineapple tidbits, drained
- 1¾ cups whole wheat flour
- ½ teaspoon cinnamon
- ¼ teaspoon nutmeg
- ¼ teaspoon allspice
- 1¼ teaspoons baking soda
- ¼ teaspoon baking powder

1. Combine apple juice, orange juice and cranberries. Let sit for 1 hour.

2. In a separate bowl combine dried fruits, nuts, vanilla, egg whites, and pineapple. Add to cranberry mixture and mix well.

3. Preheat oven to 325 degrees. Line with waxed or parchment paper or grease loaf pans, muffin tins, or bundt pan.

4. In a separate bowl combine flour, cinnamon, nutmeg, allspice, baking soda, and baking powder. Add to fruit mixture and mix well.

5. Pour batter into pans. Bake small pans for 25–30 minutes, large pans for 45 minutes. Cool cakes in pans for 20 minutes. Remove cakes from pans and let cool on wire racks.

6. Cover cakes with plastic wrap and then with aluminum foil. Store in a cool place. Cakes will be ready to eat in a few days.

Christmas Fruit Cake

(fat free)

- 1 cup whole red candied cherries
- 1 cup golden seedless raisins
- 2 cups dark seedless raisins
- ¼ cup flour
- ½ cup dried apricots, chopped
- ½ cup dried peaches, chopped
- ¼ cup candied pineapple chunks
- ¼ cup mixed candied fruit
- 1¼ cups unsweetened applesauce
- 1 cup brown sugar
- 4 tablespoons honey
- 8 egg whites
- 1 teaspoon vanilla
- 1 tablespoon bourbon, optional
- 1 tablespoon orange peel, grated
- 1 tablespoon lemon peel, grated
- 1½ cups all-purpose flour
- ½ cup whole wheat flour
- 1 teaspoon baking powder
- ½ teaspoon baking soda
- ½ teaspoon nutmeg
- ½ teaspoon cardamom
- ½ teaspoon cinnamon
- ½ cup apple juice

In a large bowl combine cherries, raisins, flour, apricots, peaches, pineapple and candied fruit. Set aside. In a separate bowl combine applesauce, sugar, honey, egg whites, vanilla, bourbon, orange and lemon peel. Beat thoroughly. In a separate bowl combine flours, baking powder and soda, nutmeg, cardamom and cinnamon.

Preheat oven to 300 degrees. Grease a 9 or 10-inch bundt or tube pan. Line bottom and sides of pan with waxed paper, extending waxed paper above the rim by 1 inch. Spray lined pan with cooking oil spray.

Add flour mixture to applesauce mixture, alternating with apple juice. Beat until just mixed. Stir in candied cherry mixture. Spoon batter into pan. Bake until toothpick inserted in center comes out clean and cake is firm to the touch, about 2 hours. Remove cake from pan. Peel off paper and wrap cake in aluminum foil. Store in refrigerator for up to 2 weeks, or store in freezer for up to 2 months.

Natural Fruit Cake

(sugar free)

- 8 cups dried fruit, including yellow and dark raisins, chopped
- 1½ cups unsweetened apple juice concentrate
- ½ cup unsweetened orange juice concentrate
- 2 tablespoons rum, brandy or sherry
- 4 eggs
- ½ cup oil
- 1 teaspoon vanilla
- 2¼ cups all-purpose flour
- ¾ cup whole wheat flour
- 1 tablespoon baking powder
- 1½ teaspoons baking soda
- 1½ teaspoons nutmeg
- 1½ teaspoons cinnamon
- 1½ teaspoons allspice
- ½ teaspoons ground cloves
- 3 to 4 cups whole nuts
- 3 cups fresh or frozen cranberries, chopped and thawed if frozen
- ½ cup apple, chopped
- ½ cup unsweetened pineapple or apple juice concentrate

In a medium saucepan combine dried fruit, apple juice, orange juice, and liquor. Cook over low heat for 20 minutes. Set aside while preparing remaining ingredients.

Preheat oven to 300 degrees. Grease small loaf pans or muffin tins. Combine eggs, oil and vanilla. In a separate bowl mix flours, baking powder, baking soda, nutmeg, cinnamon, allspice, cloves, and nuts together. Add egg mixture to dried fruit mixture and mix well. Add cranberries and apple to dried fruit mixture and mix well. Combine fruit mixture to flour mixture and mix well.

Fill loaf pan or muffin tins three-quarters full, as cake rises very little. Bake for 40 minutes. While still warm, brush tops with pineapple or apple juice mixed with liquor to taste. Let cakes sit in pans until almost cold. Remove cakes from pans and cover with wrap.

After 12 or more hours, brush additional juice on top. Let cakes sit for a couple of hours. Wrap in foil and store in a cool place.

Small Fruit Cakes

- 1 cup brown sugar
- ⅓ cup margarine
- 2 eggs
- 1 cup flour
- ¼ teaspoon baking soda
- ½ teaspoon cinnamon
- ⅛ teaspoon nutmeg
- ½ teaspoon salt
- ¼ cup buttermilk
- 1 cup raisins or dates, chopped
- 1 cup red cherries, whole or halved
- 1 cup candied pineapple
- 1 cup dried apricots, chopped
- 2 cups pecans or walnuts, whole
- Brandy

Preheat oven to 350 degrees. Line muffin tins with cupcake liners or grease small loaf pans. Cream sugar, margarine and eggs and beat well. Add flour, baking soda, cinnamon, nutmeg, salt, and buttermilk. Mix thoroughly. Stir in fruits and nuts.

For small cakes, fill paper-lined muffin tins three-quarters full. Bake for 20–25 minutes. If using small loaf pans, fill pans and bake until cake shrinks from sides of pans; baking time depends on size of pan.

Remove from oven. Remove cupcake liners while cakes are still warm. Let cakes cool, then drizzle a teaspoon or so of brandy over each cake.

Glazes, Fillings and Miscellaneous

Baking Mix
(fat free)

- 3¼ cups flour
- 2¼ cups sugar
- 1 cup unsweetened cocoa powder
- 1 tablespoon baking powder
- 1 teaspoon baking soda
- 1¼ teaspoons salt

Combine all ingredients. Store in an airtight container. Stir before using.

Sugar Free Cake Decoration

Use fresh flowers instead of sugary decorations.

Apricot, Peach or Raspberry Pastry Glaze
(fat free)

- 3 cups apricots, peaches or raspberries, strained
- 1 cup sugar
- 1 cup light corn syrup

Prepare fruit. In a medium saucepan, combine fruit with sugar and corn syrup. Cook over medium heat until sugar dissolves. Glaze cooled pastry while glaze is still warm.

Strawberry Glaze

(fat free)

- 3 cups strawberries
- ⅓ cup sugar
- 1 tablespoon lemon juice
- 1 tablespoon cornstarch
- Red food coloring, optional

Wash, hull and crush strawberries. Strain berries through a ricer and then through a fine sieve. Place berries juice in a medium saucepan. Add sugar, lemony juice, cornstarch, and food coloring. Cook, stirring, over low heat or microwave until thick and transparent. Cool. Spread over fruit to be glazed.

Apple Filling

(sugar free)

- 1 large apple, grated
- 1 cup unsweetened applesauce
- ¾ cup unsweetened apple juice concentrate
- ½ teaspoon cinnamon
- ⅛ teaspoon allspice

Combine all ingredients in a medium saucepan and cook, stirring occasionally, until thickened.

Dried Apricot Filling

- ½ cup water
- 1 cup unsweetened orange or pineapple juice concentrate
- 1½ cup dried apricots, chopped
- ¾ cup sugar
- 1 teaspoon lemon juice

In a medium saucepan combine water, fruit juice and apricots. Cook, stirring frequently, over medium heat until mixture thickens. Stir in sugar and lemon juice. Continue to cook until sugar dissolves and mixture thickens.

Dried Apricot Filling
(sugar free)

- 2 cups dried apricots, finely chopped
- ½ cup unsweetened pineapple juice concentrate
- 1 cup unsweetened apple juice concentrate
- 1 teaspoon lemon juice
- ½ cup nuts, chopped (optional)

In a medium saucepan combine all ingredients and cook, stirring occasionally, over medium heat until tender and thickened.

Date Filling
(sugar free)

- 1 cup dates, chopped
- ½ cup nuts, chopped (optional)
- ½ cup unsweetened apple juice concentrate

In a medium saucepan combine all ingredients and cook over medium heat until of spreading consistency.

Old-fashioned Date Filling

- 1½ cups dates, chopped
- ½ cup water
- ½ cup sugar
- 1 teaspoon vanilla
- ½ teaspoon lemon peel, grated
- ⅓ cup nuts, chopped

In a medium saucepan combine dates, water and sugar. Cook over medium heat, stirring frequently, until mixture thickens. Add lemon juice, lemon peel and nuts.

Raisin Filling

(sugar free)

Double this recipe for cinnamon rolls and tea rings.

- 1 cup raisins
- ½ teaspoon cornstarch
- ½ cup unsweetened apple juice concentrate
- ½ cup nuts, chopped (optional)
- ½ to 1 teaspoon cinnamon
- 1 tablespoon lemon juice

In a medium saucepan combine raisins, cornstarch, apple juice concentrate, nuts, and cinnamon. Cook over medium heat, stirring constantly, until mixture is of spreading consistency, about 3–5 minutes. Remove from heat and add lemon juice.

Notes:

Natural Jam or Jelly

All natural jam or jelly for tarts, cookies, bars, etc., do not contain commercial pectin. Pectin demands a higher percentage of sugar to fruit to make the juices gel. In fact, pectin manufacturers often suggest, for homemade products, a proportion as high as 60% sugar to 40% juice or pulp. They point out as advantages of using commercial pectin: greater yield, less loss of liquid, and speed of preparation. Only a minute or two of cooking is needed after adding the sugar.

I regard none of these as advantages, or in any sense comparable with the end product obtained by the open-kettle, cooked-down procedure. Fruits low in natural pectins are combined with those having high pectin content, like apples. In this way of making jam or jelly, fruit exceeds sugar, rather than the reverse, and you end up with much better flavor.

If honey is substituted for cane or beet sugar, there is a distinct and delicious change in flavor. In cooked-down jellies and preserves, honey may replace up to half the sugar, but jams and jellies made with honey require longer cooking. Prepare the fruit as you normally would to make jam or jelly. Use less sugar than if you were using commercial pectin.

Example: For 4 cups fruit, use 2 to 3 cups sugar. If using low pectin fruit, such as raspberry, blackberry, gooseberry, loganberry, elderberry or strawberry, you can add 1 tablespoon or 1 cut-up apple or apple juice (which are high in pectin). I find I don't need either. I just cook the fruit a little longer. Bring to a boil 4 cups fruit, frequently stirring slowly. Add 2 to 3 cups sugar. Boil on low to medium heat until thick, approximately 30 minutes, stirring often enough so jam doesn't start to stick and burn on the bottom.

Granola

- 3 cups quick-cooking oats
- 1 cup walnuts, almonds or pecans, chopped
- 1 cup wheat germ
- 1 cup sunflower seeds
- ⅓ cup oil
- ½ cup dark corn syrup
- 1 teaspoon cinnamon
- 1½ teaspoons vanilla
- 1 cup raisins

Preheat oven to 350 degrees. In a large bowl stir together oats, walnuts, wheat germ and sunflower seeds. In a small bowl mix oil, corn syrup, cinnamon and vanilla. Combine contents of small bowl with oat mixture. Spread mixture in 15½ x 10½ x 1-inch jelly roll pan. Bake, stirring often, until golden brown, about 30 minutes. Cool, stirring occasionally. Stir in raisins. Refrigerate in a tightly covered container.

Golden Granola

- 2 tablespoons oil
- ½ cup honey
- ½ cup brown sugar
- ¾ cup apple juice or juice of your choice
- 2 tablespoons vanilla
- 5 cups oatmeal
- 1 cup wheat germ
- 1 cup bran flakes
- 1 cup unsweetened coconut
- ¼ cup sesame seeds
- ½ cup sunflower seeds
- ½ to ¾ teaspoon cinnamon
- ¼ teaspoon salt

In a 1 or 2-quart saucepan (or microwave bowl), combine oil, honey, sugar, and fruit juice. Heat mixture together to dissolve the brown sugar. Remove from heat and add vanilla. Let sit while preparing remaining ingredients.

Preheat oven to 350 degrees. Combine oatmeal, wheat germ, bran flakes, coconut, sesame and sunflower seeds, cinnamon and salt. Pour juice mixture over the top of oatmeal mixture and mix well. Pour into a large baking pan. Bake, stirring often, until golden brown, about 25–30 minutes. Cool and store in bags or airtight containers.

Variation: Before the last 5 minutes of baking, mix in 2½–3 cups chopped dried fruits and/or 1½ cup chopped nuts.

Sugar Free Granola

(low fat, fat free)

- 5 cups oatmeal
- 4 cups wheat bran, wheat or 7-grain cereal
- 1½ cups wheat germ
- 1 cup sunflower seeds
- 1¼ cups apple juice concentrate
- 1 tablespoon vanilla
- 1 cup dates, chopped
- 1 cup raisins
- 1 cup dried apples, chopped
- 1 teaspoon cinnamon
- 1 cup dried apricots, chopped
- 1½ to 2 cups almonds, sliced

Preheat oven to 275 degrees. Combine oatmeal, wheat bran, cereal, wheat germ, sunflower seeds, apple juice and vanilla. Bake on baking sheet for 1 hour, stirring often. Cool.

Add dates, raisins, apples, cinnamon, apricots and almonds. Mix well. Store in an airtight container to use in cookies, cakes and breads, or to snack on.

No Bake Granola

(fat free)

- 2½ cups oatmeal
- 1½ cups wheat flakes
- 1¼ cups barley flakes
- ¾ cup wheat germ
- ½ cup oat or wheat bran
- ½ cup almonds, sliced or chopped, ½ cup sunflower seeds, or both
- 1 cup raisins or dates, chopped
- 3 tablespoons brown sugar
- ¾ cup dried apple, chopped

Combine all ingredients. Store in an airtight container. Use as a topping for cookies and cakes, or as a breakfast cereal topped with milk and honey, yogurt or fresh fruit.

Index

Page

Cookies (cont.)

Cookies (cont.)

Desserts (cont.)

Desserts (cont.)

Glazes, Fillings and Miscellaneous (cont.)

Homemade Biscuits, Scones & Shortcakes 14

Ingredients 1

Ingredients (cont.)

Muffins (cont.)

Muffins (cont.)

Quick Breads

Quick Breads (cont.)

Yeast Breads (cont.)

Yeast Breads (cont.)